A SHORT HISTORY OF ENGLISH POETRY

JAMES REEVES

A Short History of
ENGLISH POETRY
1340 – 1940

American Edition

E. P. DUTTON & CO., INC.
NEW YORK

ACKNOWLEDGMENTS AND INDIVIDUAL COPYRIGHT DATES:

From "Pastorale" from *The Collected Poems of Hart Crane.* Copyright © R-1961 by Liveright Publishing Corp. Reprinted by permission
of Liveright, Publishers; N.Y.

Poetry of A. E. Housman from *Complete Poems* by A. E. Housman.
Copyright 1922 by Holt, Rinehart and Winston, Inc. Copyright renewed
1950 by Barclays Bank, Ltd. Reprinted by permission of Holt, Rinehart
and Winston, Inc. and The Society of Authors as the Literary Representative of the Estate of the late A. E. Housman, and Messrs. Jonathan
Cape, Ltd., English publishers of A. E. Housman's *Collected Poems.*

From "Whispers of Immortality" from *Collected Poems* of T. S.
Eliot, copyright, 1936, by Harcourt, Brace & World, Inc., Faber & Faber
Ltd. and Mrs T. S. Eliot.

"The Wreck of the Deutschland," "Felix Randal" and other extracts
from *The Poems of Gerard Manley Hopkins.* Reprinted by permission
of Oxford University Press, London.

From "The Recovery" by Edmund Blunden. Reprinted by permission
of the author and Rupert Hart-Davis, Limited.

From "Meditation No. 74" in *The Poems of Edward Taylor* edited
by Donald E. Stanford. Reprinted by permission of Yale University
Press.

The lines from "Miniver Cheevy" are from *The Town Down the
River* (1910) by Edwin Arlington Robinson. Reprinted by permission
of Charles Scribner's Sons.

Cordial thanks are due to Mr Roger Sharrock and to Mr Martin Seymour-Smith for general help and advice.

Thanks are due also to Professor J. R. R. Tolkien for permission to quote from his version of *Sir Gawain and the Green Knight*.

TO
ANTHONY BEAL

Contents

Preface

THIS book gives the outlines of six centuries of English poetry in brief historical perspective. It is intended, not for specialists, but for general readers and students who want to get such a perspective at a sitting. If it encourages them to read poets hitherto unfamiliar, or helps them to understand the process of birth, growth, decay and re-birth underlying the history of poetry, it will have proved its usefulness.

When I was a student of modern languages, I was much influenced – infected, perhaps I should say – by a small volume by Lytton Strachey called *Landmarks in French Literature*. I do not know whether it is still read, and I have not looked at it for many years. A re-reading might prove it to be superficial in judgement and summary in method. But it had the great quality of enthusiasm. It sent me to the original works of the masters. Strachey had a passion for everything French, and he could write without a trace of the irony, the cynicism for which in other fields he was noted. It would be worth while, I thought, if someone could write a book which would send students to the library shelves for Chaucer, Spenser, Blake, as I had pursued Ronsard and Baudelaire.

I am no Strachey; and the excellences of English poetry are, it seems to me, more varied and less definable than those of French literature. That wonderful *clarté* which informs all French writing is replaced, this side of the Channel, by a mistiness, an allusiveness, a concealment of virtues which it is hard to uncover. It is impossible for one whose main concern in life has been English poetry to be undiscriminating in his enthusiasm. Any hope I had when I began this book that a study of former critics might reveal a general consensus of judgement which I might sum up and pass on was soon discovered to be false. The remarkable divergence of views – which might be epitomised by saying that there is no English *Académie* – means that every critical historian of English literature is on his own. I fervently hope, however, that these pages will convey a sufficient sense of enthusiasm to infect some readers with the desire to make their own journeys of exploration.

This is not the first attempt of its kind; but history needs to be continually re-written. We ourselves are involved in the flux of time, and the past, as we turn to look back on it, is continually changing. The way we live now, and the ways in which we feel and write and read affect our judgement of the literature of the past. To write historically is to be immediately aware of the distinction between fact and truth. The facts of English poetry are recorded, more or less indisputably, in a variety of places, but the truth about it can be presented in many ways, and will never seem the same to any two people, or even to the same person at different times. The historian must sometimes feel like a draughtsman delineating a landscape from the back of a moving vehicle. This is a difficulty inherent in writing historically about something which is still active and living.

An even greater difficulty arises when a writer discovers a contradiction in his terms of reference. There is a sense in which, as Aristotle recognised, history and poetry are opposed. The history of poetry is everything about it which is unimportant. A poem now seems important to us exactly in proportion as it transcends the historical process. To the historian time is the dimension in which he works; to the poet it is the 'bloody tyrant' whom his work must overthrow. In practice this means that the historian must continually divide his attention between what is historically significant and what is poetically valuable. One returns with approval to the notion of 'landmarks': ideally, no doubt, a history should be as objective as a map; but a map is sometimes more useful if, apart from being factually reliable, it also makes use of those symbols which, in French tourist maps, denote *points de vue* or *panoramas remarquables*. In tracing the outlines of English poetry, therefore, I have made frequent pauses to dwell on those 'remarkable panoramas' which make the journey worth while.

Another check to the historian's objectivity is produced by his need to indicate, at least by implication, some coherent view of the nature of poetry. It is easy if, like Saintsbury, in many respects an exemplary historian, you regard it as three parts prosody. This certainly makes better sense than ignoring the continuous existence of a prosodic problem. There *is* an important sense in which the history of poetry is the development of prosody. But poetry is *not* prosody, and the non-specialist in particular is entitled to have it treated as something more.

One fact which emerges from the history of poetry is indeed the absolute necessity for a continual renewal of technical resources; again and again one sees how a situation in which poetry has become sterile, and sensibility atrophied, is changed by a return to a diction and a rhythm more in conformity with common speech. But the diction of poetry at a given period is always intimately associated with the relations of poets to society at that period. There are occasions when a poet can only revitalise his diction by detaching himself from society; ultimately this detachment is rewarded by a revitalisation of the general sensibility. The quality of Victorian sensibility, for instance, had its sources in the linguistic experiments of the first Romantics, pioneers in feeling and in diction. The first rebellious urge towards such a revitalising process comes from a dissatisfaction with current modes of feeling and expression. The dissatisfaction of Wordsworth and Coleridge with neo-Augustan diction is paralleled by Hopkins' feeling about the diction of Tennyson.

The poet's relations with society are therefore an important part of the history of poetry; for this reason, I have tried, by giving some biographical details, to offer a general notion of poets as men, not simply writers. The bio-critical approach seems to me a fruitful one because I take the view that poets and poetry exist in a continuum from which only the wholly successful poem can escape and enjoy an independent, extra-historical existence. Most poetry is to a greater or less extent mixed up with biographical matter which, to some critical schools, is irrelevant, but which is none the less inseparable.

Poets from classical times to the present day have acknowledged a power existing outside time which partakes of the nature of a divinity and which they have most often personified as 'the Muse'; this they have done, not because of a fancy or a theory, but in response to the inner prompting which impels them to poetic utterance. However this fact may be rationalised, it cannot be evaded. But the poet who discovers his allegiance to this power finds also, usually to his cost, that he owes a temporal allegiance to some other power – a feudal overlord, a religious hierarchy, a king, a landed aristocracy, a commercial middle class. One important strand in the history of poetry, then, as it appears to me, is the struggle of the poet at successive periods to emancipate himself from a temporal allegiance in favour of the only allegiance he truly acknowledges; and the efforts of each succeeding temporal power to secure the allegiance of the poets. No sooner had the Romantics delivered themselves from the rule of the aristocracy than the succeeding commercial plutocracy secured the conformity of the poets in the persons of Tennyson and Browning, and to a less degree the other Victorians. The Pre-Raphaelites might decry Victorian materialism, but they did not seriously threaten it. Morris made a quixotic and not altogether futile attempt to reform it. The only poet of the time who appeared seriously to threaten Victorian values was Swinburne, whose attack evaporated in *vox et praeterea nihil*. Hopkins alone took the decisive step of cutting himself off altogether from the conventional Victorian world, and was able to recreate poetry in obscurity and isolation. The latest chapter is that in which poetry has extricated itself from the control of a suburban petty bourgeoisie; neither they nor the rising proletariat has seriously bothered about it since. But it will go on, so long as there are individuals to speak at the dictation of the Muse and nobody else. Poetry is bound to oppose itself to collectivism from whatever quarter. With the success of any collectivist dictatorship, the poet is always the first to be silenced.

Such are some of the ideas to which a study of the history of poetry leads, but I have not obtruded them in this account, which is mainly directed, as I have said, towards encouraging the first-hand study of the poets. I have illuminated it with fairly frequent quotations, some of which may be unfamiliar to all except specialists. These pages are not likely to attract their attention; but any specialist who happens to inspect them is entitled to one apology. I have with the greatest reluctance, but I hope with discretion, modernised the spelling and punctuation of all quotations earlier than the end of the eighteenth century, because the reader's effort to accommodate himself to six centuries of variation might prove an unnecessary distraction.

A SHORT HISTORY OF ENGLISH POETRY

CHAPTER ONE

The Fourteenth Century: Chaucer

THE history of English poetry, as understood by the non-specialist reader, begins in the latter half of the fourteenth century, with Chaucer. Although poetry in England had had a continuous history for over eight centuries before his time, there are several reasons why we should begin here. We find in Chaucer's poems for the first time, at least in embryo, all, or nearly all, those qualities which are to be found in English poetry in later times: passion, humanity, wit, learning, eloquence, melody. Chaucer, we feel, was a whole man, civilised in every respect, ardently interested in life on all its planes, material and spiritual. But we should remember that he represents the end, more than the beginning of an age, the consummation of a number of old traditions rather than the headspring of a new one. It has been said that almost everything Chaucer did in poetry had to be re-learned a hundred and fifty years after his death.

A further reason for beginning the study of English poetry at about the middle of the fourteenth century is that English then became the official language of England. Ever since the Conquest, Norman-French had been the language of the ruling classes and was used for official purposes. A gradual fusion of the native Teutonic elements with the Norman-French of the invaders had produced, by about 1350, a language that is recognisably English, and by the end of the century this had won supremacy throughout the country.

There is another, more practical reason why we should start with Chaucer. He was the first to write in a language which is in the main reasonably intelligible to a modern reader without special training. Specialists, in their zeal for medieval literature, tend to minimise the difficulties of language encountered in other fourteenth-century writers. Even Chaucer, however, is not easy, when compared with a writer of, say, the early sixteenth century. He uses many obsolete words and constructions; his pronunciation is always in doubt. Nevertheless, there are many passages of some length in his poems which can be fairly well understood with little if any recourse to a glossary. This is true of scarcely any other poet of his time or before him. To turn from other fourteenth-century poets to Chaucer is to be aware of a 'modernity' both in language and in outlook which never fails to surprise and delight. We are thus faced at the outset with a paradox which will recur constantly: the great figures in English literature are often, if not invariably, those who stand outside its history. English poetry from *Beowulf*, the Anglo-Saxon epic poem of the sixth century, to the Tudor forerunners of Shakespeare would present a tidier, more continuous and more intelligible appearance if Chaucer had not existed. History deals with minor figures; the major ones are timeless. In relating the history of poetry, therefore, a balance must be kept between undue concentration on minor poets and the temptation to linger on those who are great enough to transcend history. Before dwelling more fully on Chaucer we must say something about three of his lesser, though still considerable, contemporaries.

One of the most popular poems of the period was *The Vision of Piers the Plowman*, written by WILLIAM LANGLAND (?1332–?1400). Fifty or sixty manuscripts have been preserved, and considering the hazardous nature of manuscript survival during the middle ages, this implies a very wide distribution. The poem was not printed, however, until 1550. It was forgotten during the seventeenth and eighteenth centuries, and was not revived until the early nineteenth century. Despite the efforts of scholars and teachers, it has never been in modern times a popular poem, probably on account of its language. The modern reader can scarcely tackle it except in translation. Even so, very few read it in its entirety. Most are content to know selected passages.

Of the author of *Piers Plowman*, to give the usual abbreviated title, nothing is known for certain. Modern research has reconstructed a poor country scholar from Shropshire, possibly the illegitimate son of a gentleman, who was educated for the priesthood, but did not achieve any distinction in the Church. He went up to London, where he lived in poverty with a wife and daughter, making his living by saying prayers for rich patrons.

All this is highly speculative and is deduced from the evidence of the poem itself. The writing and re-writing of this great poem was the real work of his life.

The Vision of Piers the Plowman was first drafted about 1362 and revised, with considerable additions, about 1377, and again about 1393. Most editors regard the second, or 'B', text as the best. It consists of 2400 lines.

At the beginning the writer, falls asleep and wakes to find himself in the midst of a 'field full of folk' – that is, the world of men as Langland knew it. From this opening vision emerges a kaleidoscopic series of visions of society as it was and as it might be. The picture he gives, coloured as it is by the sadness of an age ravaged by successive outbreaks of the plague, is a gloomy one. In the great and sombre picture of the Seven Deadly Sins we see men struggling with evil, their hopes of redemption through a Christian commonwealth thwarted by the avarice and corruption of the higher clergy. Piers is a half-real, half-allegorical figure who is presented first as a simple countryman striving to live honestly by the toil of his hands; then as a preacher of the gospel of charity; and finally as Christ himself, crucified for man's salvation. The poem contains passages of fierce moral invective against the rich, the oppressors of the poor; authentic sketches of what was evidently London life; tedious theological digressions; and a passionately imagined vision of true religion as exemplified in the life of Christ, contrasted with the false religion of a powerful and worldly Church. To the modern reader the poem is confused and confusing, alternating as it does between the plane of a vivid physical actuality and an allegorical vagueness which was far more acceptable to the medieval mind than to ours. Abstract and personified figures move about among real flesh-and-blood characters; dry theological speculation succeeds passages of passionate moral denunciation. If we go to Chaucer for a picture of humanity, we may go also to Langland for a picture of medieval England. We are aware of the largeness and the apparent incoherence of Langland's vision; we are aware that *Piers Plowman* is a highly ambitious attempt to comprehend the whole of life in its scope; yet despite the largeness of Langland's vision, we feel that he does not universalise it, as Chaucer does. Nevertheless, if we are prepared to struggle with a difficult medium or, alternatively, have recourse to a good modern rendering, there is much that is unique and profoundly impressive.

The chief obstacles to general acceptance are the strangeness of the vocabulary and the monotony of the verse. *Piers Plowman* is written throughout in the old alliterative metre which was inherited from the Anglo-Saxon poets. Here is a brief example, taken from a modern rendering:

> Then I began to move into a marvellous dream
> That I wandered in a wilderness, would I could say where;
> As I beheld into the East, high in the sunlight,
> I saw a tower on a hill-top, of true workmanship,
> A deepening dale beneath, and a dungeon within it,
> With deep ditches and dark, and dreadful to see.
> A fair field full of folk found I there between them,
> Of all manner of men, the meaner and the richer,
> Working and wandering, as the world asks of them.[1]

This line was the staple of poetry in England until after the Norman Conquest, and it came in for revival on a considerable scale in the latter half of the fourteenth century. The line consisted of four stressed syllables, two in each half, with a pause between, and an irregular number of unstressed syllables. There were no end-rhymes, the effect of rhyme being obtained from the use of a number of stressed syllables each beginning with the same letter. No two successive lines need use the same repeated letter. There were usually two of such words in the first half of the line, and one (sometimes two) in the second half. Not only did this scheme make for monotony, it did to some extent also dictate the choice of words. To us, therefore, and no doubt to Chaucer, who did not use it, alliterative verse appears both over-artificial and restrictive. This is, however, to judge it from the standpoint of the later developments in English verse which superseded it. Certainly, if we compare the movement of

> In a somer seson · whan soft was the sonne,

which is the opening line of *Piers Plowman* in the original spelling, with

> He was as fresh as is the month of May[2]

---

[1] *Visions from Piers Plowman*, translated by Nevill Coghill. Phœnix House, 1949.

[2] *Prologue* to *The Canterbury Tales*, line 92.

we can see why the latter established itself as the norm of English verse-movement from the sixteenth century onwards. There could be no going back, except as a piece of experimental archaism, to the old alliterative line. Yet the latter, seen for what it is, and not in contrast to what supplanted it, has great merit. There is a certain charm about its very monotony; in any case, in the hands of a skilful versifier like Langland, it could undergo modifications of some subtlety and variety; moreover, the habit of alliteration is ingrained in all English-speaking peoples, as is witnessed by the popularity of proverbial expressions such as 'hearth and home', 'wind and weather' and 'time and tide'. The fact remains, however, that the alliterative measure, which had been the basis of English versification for centuries, was superseded, despite occasional partial revivals, once and for all by the genius of Chaucer. Langland's poem was the last great monument to this form. After all, the alliterative effect was never finally lost; it was incorporated, without being the basis of a regular mechanical pattern, in all subsequent English poetry. We have only to read the first five lines of *Kubla Khan*, written four centuries after *Piers Plowman*, to know the virtue of alliteration treated as a poet's servant, not his master.

Outside the writings of Langland and Chaucer, the most interesting and the most wholly successful poem of the fourteenth century is the anonymous Arthurian romance, *Sir Gawain and the Green Knight*. This is an alliterative poem in some 2500 lines, existing in a single manuscript and not printed until 1839. Nothing whatever is known about the author, who may or may not have composed certain other alliterative poems which survive from the same period. It is almost accidental that the Sir Gawain poem has survived at all, and we are bound to speculate on what other anonymous masterpieces may have perished. *Sir Gawain and the Green Knight* is a tale of great charm and ingenuity, as well as a myth or allegory which may have had even remoter origins in some lost Celtic legend. Sir Gawain, Arthur's nephew, is the pattern of chivalry, virtue and piety. He accepts a challenge issued at Arthur's court during the Christmas festivities by a mysterious, superhuman figure coloured green all over and riding a green horse. This green knight, with his enormous axe and his holly club, is clearly an embodiment of the vegetation-spirit, the god of the New Year, the 'green man' of pre-Christian times. Gawain beheads the green knight, who rides away carrying his head by the hair. The head enjoins Gawain to meet him at a green chapel on New Year's Day a year hence and receive the answering blow. This incident recalls the ballad of *John Barleycorn*, the corn spirit who is beheaded but cannot be destroyed, rising again annually with the return of spring. The poem thus represents a combat between Christianity and the old pagan religion.

The following Christmas Gawain, in search of the green chapel, is entertained by a lord and his lady in their castle near the North Wales coast. The lady tempts Gawain's chastity, but Gawain resists, and she gives him her girdle as a protection against the Green Knight, whom he is to encounter on New Year's Day. In accepting this Gawain is guilty of cowardice and of deceiving his adversary. The Green Knight turns out to be the lord of the castle; the green chapel is a grass barrow, such as was used as a burying place before churches were built. Gawain calls this a 'chapel of mischance' and regards the Knight as an embodiment of the Devil. In their combat Gawain is grazed and loses blood; but he is not killed. The Knight exonerates Gawain for acting from the motive of self-preservation, but Gawain feels that he has betrayed his ideals, and returns to Arthur's court wearing the girdle as a mark of his weakness. The forces of nature, as represented by the Green Knight, are seen not as evil but as necessary and beneficent. His castle is a place of mirth and feasting; his hunting exploits, described in great detail, suggest a ritual sacrifice of beasts for the nourishment and strengthening of man. Arthur's court, too, is a place of joyous, purposeful and civilised living founded on Christian ideals. But the story is not a sermon. The writer does not take sides. The vigour and warmth of his narrative and descriptive writing is expended equally on the Christian and the pagan scenes. The import of the myth is that there must be a balance between asceticism and full living, between idealism and human nature; virtue is nothing unless it is put to the test; nature is indestructible and is not to be resisted without cost.

Such significances, however, need not obtrude upon the narrative, or upon the enjoyment of the splendour and force of the writing. There is an immense gusto about the whole poem, which is miraculously free from the tedious digressions which characterise most fourteenth-century writing. The chief persons in the story are tellingly characterised; the brilliant descriptions of nature are not mere background, but insist on the central importance of the natural scene as distinct from the life of a court.

The poem is written in alliterative lines grouped in stanzas of varying lengths and linked by brief rhyming passages which serve to vary what would otherwise tend to monotony. Considerable technical artistry is displayed in the use of this difficult form. Unfortunately, however, in its original language *Sir Gawain and the Green Knight* is incomprehensible to anyone without specialised knowledge of middle English. It is probably slightly earlier in date than anything by Chaucer, or than the earliest draft of *Piers Plowman*. Moreover, it is written in the dialect of the West Midlands, which, even to those who can read Chaucer with ease, is strange and unfamiliar. But it is a wonderful poem, and little of it is lost in a skilful modern rendering. Here is a stanza describing part of Gawain's long and painful journey before he reaches the castle.

> By a mount in the morning merrily he was riding
> into a forest that was deep and fearsomely wild;
> high hills at each hand, and hoar wood under them
> of aged oaks and huge by the hundred together;
> the hazel and hawthorn were huddled and tangled
> with rough ragged moss around them trailing,
> while many birds bleakly on the bare twigs sat
> and piteously piped there for pain of the cold.
> The good man on Gringolet goes now beneath them
> through many marshes and mires, a man all alone,
> troubled lest a truant at that time he should prove
> from the service of the sweet Lord, who on that selfsame night
> of a maid became man our mourning to conquer.
> And therefore sighing he said: 'I beseech thee, O Lord,
> and Mary, who is the mildest of mothers most dear,
> for some harbour where with honour I might hear the Mass
> and thy Matins tomorrow. This meekly I ask,
> and thereto promptly I pray with Pater and Ave
>   and Creed'.
>   In prayer he now did ride,
>   Lamenting his misdeed;
>   He blest him oft and cried,
>   'The cross of Christ me speed!' [1]

[1] Translation by J. R. R. Tolkien.

A poet who should be mentioned in passing is JOHN GOWER (?1325–1408), the author of the *Confessio Amantis* ('The Lover's Confession'), a poem in rhymed octosyllabic couplets some 30,000 lines long. The verse is smooth and mellifluous, tending to dullness. The poem contains some memorable passages, but few readers are able to tackle it in its entirety. In the original version, written about 1383, Gower pays tribute to Chaucer, for whom he had a profound and sincere admiration. He had previously written in both French and Latin, and did not attempt English verse until late in life. This is significant of the changing intellectual climate of the time.

Now all the poems mentioned so far are characteristic of the fine flowering of English poetry in the latter half of the fourteenth century. We go to them in order to know what that period was like. *Piers Plowman*, *Sir Gawain and the Green Knight* and the *Confessio Amantis* tell us of the medieval mind – its love of allegory, its concern with religion and courtly love – as well as of the social conditions prevailing during a crisis in the nation's history. Delightful as the Gawain story is, it is a very strange affair: it is not of our world. When we turn to Chaucer, however, we are continually amazed at his modernity. He is a copious source of information about fourteenth-century life, but it is not for that that he has been read by educated people for nearly six centuries. He reveals, not the medieval mind, but the human mind; the great portrait gallery of his Canterbury pilgrims is for all time. Even though he describes them minutely in the dress of their period, they emerge from the picture-frame and take their places among the living men and women of today or any other time. Chaucer left his great work unfinished, as he left so much else. But at his death English poetry was firmly established in Europe as a major literary institution. He is in every sense the greatest English poet until the arrival of Shakespeare two centuries later. If he has not in later ages had the wide popularity of some other poets, that is because of the language difficulty. He is easier than Langland or the author of *Sir Gawain and the Green Knight*, but the modern reader is nevertheless continually held up by difficulties of vocabulary and grammar. It is worth learning middle-English for the sake of Chaucer; failing this, it is better to read him in translation than to remain in ignorance of a poet who in some respects is second only to Shakespeare.

GEOFFREY CHAUCER (?1340–?1400) was a Londoner, the son of well-to-do parents of no particular distinction. He became page to a noble master and later entered the service of King Edward III. When he was nineteen he spent a year in France as a result of being taken prisoner on one of the king's military expeditions. There he became deeply interested in French poetry, and especially the universally admired and widely imitated *Roman de la Rose*. He adapted and translated a good deal of this thirteenth-century allegory of love for English readers. He retained for many years his love of French poetry, and from it he learned to adapt the octosyllabic couplet for the diversion of polite English audiences. In 1372 he went as the king's envoy to northern Italy, where he returned more than once, discovering the wonders of the Renaissance, and in particular the poetry of Petrarch (1304–1374) and Boccaccio (?1313–1375). Here was a source of legend and lyric hitherto unknown in England. The impact made upon him by these poets is one of the decisive factors in the history of English poetry. From them he adopted as the basis of his verse the rhymed iambic pentameter – the line consisting of five feet, each having one light and one stressed syllable. This basic line, infinitely varied by different poets in successive periods, has remained the norm of English verse from that time onwards.

> Now welcom somer, with thy sonnë softe,
> That hast this wintrës weders over-shake,
> And driven awey the longë nightës blake!

That – the opening lines of an early lyric – may be recognised, once we have accepted the syllabic value of the final 'e', as the basic measure used by Shakespeare, Milton, Wordsworth, Tennyson, Yeats. *Now welcom somer* is from *The Parliament of Fowls*, a long discursive poem which shows increasing originality and a lessening of French influence. Chaucer was a ceaseless experimenter, and by the age of forty he had achieved little, if anything, which could ensure him an important place in literature. He was a scholar of immense learning, proficient in the classical languages and in French and Italian; he read the early Church fathers, as well as modern writers on the various sciences. He had a passion for learning, and an insatiable desire to make known to his readers at the English court the fruits of his

learning. He loved books as the instruments of acquiring knowledge; they were the repositories of all wisdom, ancient and
modern. As he says in the Prologue to *The Legend of Good Women*:

> And if that oldë bokës were away
> Y-loren [*lost*] were of rèmembraunce the keye.

Then in 1382 he completed his first masterpiece, *Troilus and
Criseyde*, a poem in five books partly adapted from Boccaccio but
with considerable original additions. It is an astonishing
achievement, and nothing that remains of Chaucer's previous
work, excellent as much of it is, can explain the depth, the
maturity and the scope of what has been called the first modern
novel. It recounts at great length and with pathos, humour and
psychological realism the story of the betrayal of Troilus by
Cressida during the siege of Troy. One stanza must serve to show
the quality of the writing in *Troilus and Criseyde*. The stanza-form
is known as *rime royal* and consists of seven iambic pentameters
with three end-rhymes. Pandarus, Cressida's uncle and the
counsellor of Troilus in his ill-starred romance, is waiting with
Troilus for the return of Cressida, which he knows will never
come.[1]

> Pandarus answered, 'It may be well enough',
> And held with him of all that ever he said;
> But in his heart he thought, and softly lough, [*laughed*]
> And to himself full soberly he said,
> 'From hazel wood, where jolly robin played,
> Shall come all that that thou abidest here:
> Yea, farewell all the snow of fernë [*distant*] year'.

Chaucer was criticised for his creation of the character of the
faithless Cressida, and it is said that his next poem, *The Legend of
Good Women*, was written to pacify an influential patron whom he
had displeased. *The Legend* is written in rhymed pairs of iambic
pentameters, a metre here used for the first time in English. It is
not of course the 'heroic couplet' of the late seventeenth and
eighteenth centuries, but it is its forerunner. Chaucer used the
metre again in *The Canterbury Tales*, notably in the Prologue. The
Prologue to *The Legend* is a delightful invocation to the Muse of

[1] This and the remaining quotations from Chaucer are given in modernised
spelling, but not otherwise adapted.

poetry, and contains a fresh and alluring vision of the meeting of the God of Love and the May Queen in a daisy field. Inserted in this Prologue is a *ballade* of which the following is the first stanza. The strain of lofty and mellifluous passion derives from the tradition of courtly love, but looks forward in tone and music to Marlowe and the Elizabethans.

> Hide, Absalom, thy gilded tresses clear;
> Esther, lay thou thy meekness all a-down;
> Hide, Jonathan, all thy friendly manner;
> Penelope, and Marcia Cato,
> Make of your wifehood no comparison;
> Hide ye your beauties, Yseult and Elaine:
> My lady cometh, that all this may disdain.

Until he was forty-five or so Chaucer had lived in growing comfort in London on the proceeds of various posts to which he was appointed by favour of his lifelong patron, John of Gaunt. Then for several years he lost most of his appointments, and this left him free to begin a design on a much larger scale than anything he had written hitherto. It was not till he was nearing his fiftieth year that Chaucer began to make the great collection of stories which came to be known as *The Canterbury Tales*. The idea of a pilgrimage on which each of some thirty travellers was supposed to relate four stories was brilliant and original. That he only attempted twenty-four of the stories before his death in, or about, 1400 only reflects on his optimism in projecting anything so vast. Not only are the tales themselves of the greatest possible interest, the framework of the book is a masterly conception; it introduces us to a cross-section of fourteenth-century English society, described with consummate skill in the Prologue. The passages which link the tales and describe the interplay between the various pilgrims offer a human comedy of great wit and insight. Some of the stories had certainly been written much earlier than the period of the main design. As a sequence they offer a conspectus of Chaucer's art and outlook over a long period. They represent the romantic allegory, satire, the *fabliau* or popular tale of oral tradition, the fable or animal story, the sermon or morality, and the literary burlesque. By suiting each tale to the character of its narrator Chaucer gave unity to what would otherwise have seemed an oddly assorted anthology of different styles. Thus the Knight is appropriately given the chivalric tale of *Palamon and Arcite*, and the Nun's Priest is given an animal fable containing theological speculation and an obvious moral purpose. By the time he assembled *The Canterbury Tales* Chaucer had outgrown all foreign influences and spoke out clearly and with abundant energy as a great comic and narrative observer of society. Characteristically he presents himself as a retiring, whimsical figure, somewhat at the mercy of the boisterous and domineering host of the Tabard Inn. The psychological subtlety, the verse dialogue, the comedy and irony of the book as a whole show Chaucer's mature art at its best and most vital.

To discuss the tales individually would require a disproportionate amount of space. Instead, it would be more appropriate to try to sum up the general import of Chaucer's work. We have to consider two complementary figures: Chaucer the 'novelist', as he might be called – that is, the creator of comic fiction – and Chaucer the poet. The latter found himself heir to a French tradition of courtly love and allegory which derived from the poems of the troubadours and *trouvères* of the eleventh to the thirteenth centuries. The conventions of this tradition demanded that the poet dedicate himself to the service of the Muse, a representative of the Goddess of Love, in whose honour he must place the woman or women of his choice upon a pedestal of idealised perfection. That this convention involved much artificiality, much visionary and unreal passion, cannot be denied.

> Your eyen two will slay me suddenly;
> I may the beauty of them not sustain,
> So woundeth it throughout my heartë keen.

At the same time it corresponds to certain basic instincts of youth – the desire to serve an ideal, the unwillingness to face reality, the striving after an earthly paradise. It would be quite wrong to doubt the sincerity of a poet in this youthful strain. After all, it was experienced by Keats, by Clare, and by countless other poets long after the middle ages. The phase of courtly love and the idealisation of woman might be said to be an invariable factor in European poetry. It represents the spiritualisation of the secular side of man's nature, as Christianity represents the spiritualisation of the religious side.

But to the maturing Chaucer, as to other poets, came the inevitable realisation that idealism involves illusion. There is the world to be reckoned with. Chaucer evidently came to be fascinated by the opposition between the chivalric ideal and the reality of woman's nature. To Troilus, rooted as he is in the courtly ideal, Cressida's betrayal is incomprehensible. To Pandarus, the worldling and realist, Cressida's betrayal is inevitable: it is, on her part, sheer necessity, dictated by the instinct for self-preservation which, as perpetuator of the race, woman is bound to follow. Alone among aliens, Cressida must have a protector; Troilus must be replaced. What Cressida betrays is Troilus' self-invented idea of her. Throughout Chaucer's life, amidst all his interest in philosophy, science and literature, his central preoccupation was with the nature of woman. He moves from the poetic, ideal view to the human, realistic view: the early heroines, Emilia and the patient Griselda, give way to the Wife of Bath, that full-blooded creation of Chaucer's mature knowledge. In one of Chaucer's last tales, the Merchant's, a young, meek and comely maid is married to an old man, whom she speedily cuckolds while he is temporarily blind. The old man, January, is a foolish, good-natured man who deserves what he gets for marrying a young girl, May. May instinctively deceives him and lies about her deception to keep up appearances. It is lively, ribald comedy in which, one might say, the romantic element has been altogether suppressed. May is Cressida under a comic, not a tragic, guise. May and the Wife of Bath, whose Prologue is a merciless self-revelation of woman at her most elemental, seem to represent Chaucer's considered judgement on the sex. But now there is no trace of condemnation: Chaucer is entirely on the side of women. His portraits of the Wife of Bath and of May are at once ruthless and sympathetic. Illusion and disillusion alike are dissolved into a new conception of woman. In achieving this, Chaucer accepted the world as it is, and in doing so he accepted life. Possibly the slowness of his development as a poet was due in part to an unwillingness to accept life as he saw it. He was at once a scholar, a poet, a 'clerk' (in youth perhaps as unworldly and retiring as his own 'Clerk of Oxford'), and a man of the world, a courtier favoured by powerful patrons. The attractions of both characters fascinated him. But however much we applaud the rich comedy of his mature art, we must recognise that some of his

most appealing lyric poetry springs from the other side of his
nature, the side that despised the world and the competitive
struggle for advancement.

> What thou art sent, receive in buxomness,
> The wrestling for this world asketh a fall.
> Here is no home, here is but wilderness.
> Forth, pilgrim, forth! forth, beast, out of thy stall!
> Know thy country, look up, thank God of all,
> Hold the high way and let thy ghost thee lead,
> And truth shall thee deliver, it is no dread.

CHAPTER TWO

The Fifteenth Century

AFTER the death of Chaucer 'official' poetry – that of the scholars and courtiers–went through a long period of sterility. It was as if the creative impulse of the latter half of the fourteenth century had exhausted itself. Long-windedness and a tendency to moralise crushed inspiration. This is not to say, however, that there was no genuine poetry in the fifteenth century. Apart from the work of an important group of Scottish writers, we have to consider a body of anonymous poetry which had begun to accumulate as early as the latter half of the thirteenth century and certainly had its origins in much earlier times. This consists, on the one hand, of popular poems preserved among the common people and known to us as ballads and folk songs, and on the other, of secular and religious lyrics, mainly the work of clerics and courtiers whose names have long been forgotten. About this body of anonymous writing two things should be kept in mind: first, that two strains run through it, the popular and the learned. The poems – or more properly, songs – of the people differed in inspiration and in kind from those of the learned and the polite. There is much interconnection between the two, which can rarely be wholly separated. The ballads, of whose origin there is still very considerable doubt, probably derived to some extent from the songs sung in earlier times in the halls of the nobles by the minstrels kept for their entertainment. On the other hand, the lyrics of priests and courtiers certainly borrowed much from the traditional songs of the people. These latter, surviving as they do mainly in corrupt and fragmentary form, are connected with the seasonal rites and observances which constituted the nature-worship of pre-Christian days. It should be remembered that the ancient pagan religion, with its seasonal songs and dances, died hard in Europe, if it may be said to have died at all. Christianity existed for centuries side by side and in competition with the pagan religion. It was from the beginning the policy of the Roman Church, as laid down by Pope Gregory the Great, to avoid open conflict and forcible suppression; wherever possible, the Church was to adapt and absorb the native pagan practices. Thus in poetry there was a union between pagan and Christian imagery. To mention a single striking example: the following fragment survives in a manuscript, probably of the fifteenth century.

> Holly and Ivy made a great party
> Who should have the mastery
>   In lands where they go.
>
> Then spake Holly, 'I am free and jolly;
> I will have the mastery
>   In lands where we go.'
>
> Then spake Ivy, 'I am loud and proud;
> And I will have the mastery
>   In lands where we go.'
>
> Then spake Holly, and set him down on his knee,
> 'I pray thee, gentle Ivy, say me no villainy
>   In lands where we go.'

Now this is evidently part of a singing game or dance connected with the winter festivities, and is devoid of Christian elements. It implies a mock contest between the male Holly, which was hard and aggressive, and the female Ivy, defenceless and clinging. References to these two evergreens in this symbolic sense are common in popular verse of an early date. In the famous carol, *The Holly and the Ivy*, evidently devised by a zealous and imaginative priest or monk, the pagan theme has been adapted for Christian use, and the imagery of the Nativity has been grafted on to the old stock. In other instances the language of secular love songs has been adapted to the worship of Christ and the Virgin Mary.

> To-morrow shall be my dancing day:
>   I would my true love did so chance
> To see the legend of my play,
>   To call my true love to my dance:
>   Sing O my love, O my love, my love, my love;
>   This have I done for my true love.

Then was I born of a virgin pure,
  Of her I took fleshly substance;
Thus was I knit to man's nature
  To call my true love to my dance:
    Sing O my love, O my love, my love, my love;
    This have I done for my true love.

The other important point to be borne in mind when considering pre-Tudor literature is the hazardous nature of the survival of texts. Before the invention of printing towards the end of the fifteenth century,[1] literature was still essentially an oral art. Despite the widespread use of manuscript texts in prose and verse, the number of those who *read* for themselves, as compared with those who listened to others reading or singing from memory, must have been small. Literature was a social pursuit. Manuscripts were the treasured possessions of religious and noble houses, whose occupants gathered to hear them read by educated men, mainly clerical. The records of songs and ballads of the oral tradition are therefore scant: unless a song was handed down orally and committed to print during or after Tudor times, its survival is dependent, first on the chance of its having been written down in manuscript by some cleric whose fancy was caught by it, and secondly on the preservation of the manuscript from fire or other hazards during the ensuing centuries. For instance, an early sixteenth-century manuscript in the British Museum contains a musical setting of the well-known quatrain, *Western wind, when will thou blow*. This is the earliest known written version of these words. They were undoubtedly part of a folk ballad. A version of *The Grey Cock* recovered in Dorset in 1905 contains the stanza:

The wind it did blow, and the cocks they did crow,
  As I tripped over the plain,
So I wished myself back in my true love's arms
  And she in her bed again.

In short, the further back we go into history, the more difficult it is to be certain that what survives of the poetry of any period is really representative. It is inevitable, in view of the nature of manuscript preservation, that what remains of medieval poetry should bear a markedly religious character. About the secular

[1] The first printed book to appear in England was issued by Caxton in 1477.

songs and lyrics of the times before the invention of printing it is very difficult to say anything with complete certainty.

It is usual to distinguish two main groups: the ballads and folk songs, of 'popular' origin and oral transmission, and the secular and religious lyrics of a more recognisably literary origin. The ballads, of which the greatest single collection is that made by the American scholar, Francis James Child, between 1883 and 1898, probably originated among the minstrels who sang to entertain the chiefs and their followers, and later the nobles in their castles; with the decay of the feudal system and the invention of printing the minstrels and entertainers who had previously been in the service of rich and influential masters, were forced to earn a living by going on the roads. Thus their songs were disseminated among ordinary people at fairs and markets and other communal gatherings. These songs or ballads were on mythical and legendary subjects, or on themes of historical or local significance. Many of them came from a common European stock, as is proved by the wide provenance or dispersal of counterparts in many languages other than English – Scandinavian, Germanic, Romance and Slavic. Ballads such as *Edward* and *Lord Randal*, which appear at first sight so characteristically English, or at any rate British, have been traced to countries as far apart as Norway and Italy. The characteristics of these ballads are well known; their intensity of feeling, economy and directness of expression, and the dramatic quality of their style and construction have won them the admiration of scholars and ordinary readers for centuries. In view, however, of the prevalence of the idea that they belong only to the remote past and that the tradition somehow expired before the Industrial Revolution, it must be pointed out that many ballads exist in unbroken oral tradition right to the present century. Wherever English is spoken among long-established, non-industrialised communities, whether in Britain or in North America, some at least of the most ancient ballads survive. Versions of *Lord Randal*, *The Unquiet Grave*, *Lamkin*, *Lady Maisry*, *Lord Bateman* and many others have been recovered in rural districts by collectors throughout the first half of the twentieth century from singers who have no acquaintance with printed texts.

Child based his edition of the ballads on the printed texts made by collectors from oral sources from the sixteenth century onwards, and especially the Scottish antiquarians of the eight-eenth century. He was either not interested in, or unaware of, the continued popularity of many of his ballads in living form among singers in Britain and America. But he compared and arranged with systematic, scholarly patience and judgement over 300 examples from the more haphazard anthologies of his pre-decessors, and supplied modern readers with as full and authentic versions as could be recovered of the great treasures of anonymous ballad literature. A thorough knowledge of some at least of these ballads is indispensable to the understanding and appreciation of English poetry. Here for the first time the non-specialist reader finds great poetry which he can understand and appreciate with direct immediacy, unaided by notes and a glossary. It is true that the Scots tongue, in which some of the versions we now possess were recovered, presents certain difficulties. But in such fine examples as *Sir Patrick Spens*, *True Thomas*, *Clerk Saunders* and *The Daemon Lover* problems of language are scarcely apparent, and afford only a momentary check to the flow and sweep of the narrative. The world of these ballads is a grim, twilit one where fact and fantasy, ritual and magic, combine to give an unforgettable impression of splendour, beauty and pathos.

A fine example of a ballad which is not in the Child canon is the moving and pathetic *The Trees they Grow High*, sometimes called *Still Growing*, which may have originated as early as the fifteenth century. Printed versions prior to its recovery by late nineteenth-century collectors are poor and confused. But many good versions were taken down from old country singers in several widely separated districts of England and Ireland between 1880 and 1915. Here is a short version sung by a Hampshire labourer in 1906. The language has changed with the times, but the story is medieval. It will serve to show the persistence of the oral tradition in English poetry, which lives independently of, and side by side with, printed literature.

> The trees they grows high and the leaves they grows green.
> The days is gone and past, my love, that you and I have seen.
> It's a cold winter's night, my love, while it's I must lay alone
> While my bonny lad is young, but is growing.
>
> O, it's father, O father, you do to me much wrong.
> You marry me a boy, and you knows I am too young.

O daughter, O daughter, that will never be so,
For we'll send him to the college for another year or two.

Now as she was a-walking by her father's garden wall
She seen four and twenty gentlemen a-playing of the ball.
O, she cries, where is my love, where I wonder he can be?
For he's a bonny, bonny lad but is growing.

At the age of sixteen he was a married man,
At the age of eighteen, O she brought to him a son;
At the age of twenty-one, O his grave was dug so deep.
Pretty lad, it put an end to his growing.

When we turn to the lyrics of the later middle ages preserved in manuscript, we find an essentially fragmentary poetry in which secular and religious, popular and literary elements are curiously mixed. The best of these lyrics combine a tantalising incompleteness with a haunting beauty of phrase and melody.

He bare him up, he bare him down,
He bare him into an orchard brown.

In that orchard there was a hall,
That was hangèd with purple and pall.

And in that hall there was a bed,
It was hangèd with gold so red.

And in that bed there lieth a knight,
His wounds bleeding day and night.

By that bedside kneeleth a may [*maid*]
And she weepeth both night and day.

And by that bedside there standeth a stone,
Corpus Christi written thereon.

What are we to make of this? The theme is religious, even mystical. But the form is that of a singing game or dance. The English lyric is grounded in the dance, that pagan accompaniment to the seasonal rites and games which the Church strove to incorporate in its worship. We have seen how the pagan dance-songs were transformed into carols; evidently the secular love of woman was also adapted to the worship of the Virgin Mary.

> Suddenly afraid,
>> Half waking, half sleeping,
> And greatly dismayed,
>> A woman sat weeping,
> With favour in her face far passing my reason
> And of her sore weeping this was the encheson, [*cause*]
> Her son in her lap laid, she said, slain by treason,
> If weeping might ripe be, it seemed then in season.
>> Jesus, so she sobbed,
>> So her son was bobbed [*mocked*]
>> And of his life robbed;
> Saying these words as I say thee,
> Who cannot weep, come learn of me.

Despite the fragmentary nature of the lyrics surviving in manuscript, they represent great diversity of theme and treatment. Any representative selection of medieval poems would have to include those that lament the passing of life and strength, those that celebrate love and the coming of spring, those that idealise and those that make fun of women, those which enjoin mirth and those which preach sobriety and repentance, as well as those which sing of the Nativity or the Crucifixion. Although these lyrics are often naïve and unsophisticated in expression, they are far from primitive. It is perhaps their greatest attraction that they combine simplicity and freshness of utterance with great refinement of feeling. Their peculiar combination of delicacy, humour, pathos and seriousness is difficult to find in the poetry of any other period; later attempts at the same thing degenerate too often into archness, sentimentality or mere prettiness.

One of the most admirable longer lyrics, *The Nut-Brown Maid*, is in the form of a dialogue between a squire and his mistress. The squire attempts to test the maid's love by pretending that he has committed a crime for which he has been outlawed and must immediately fly to the woods. After a prolonged argument, in which she protests that her love will endure any hardship, she finally insists on going with him to the greenwood and sharing his banishment. He replies:

> If that ye went, ye should repent;
>> For in the forest now
> I have purveyed me of a maid
>> Whom I love more than you:

Another more fair than ever ye were,
    I dare it well avow;
And of you both each should be wroth
    With other, as I trow:
It were mine ease to live in peace;
    So will I, if I can:
Wherefore I to the wood will go,
    Alone, a banished man.

To this the maid answers:

Though in the wood I understood
    Ye had a paramour,
All this may nought remove my thought,
    But that I will be your:
And she shall find me soft and kind
    And courteis every hour;
Glad to fulfil all that she will
    Command me, to my power:
For had ye, lo, an hundred mo,
    Yet would I be that one.
For in my mind, of all mankind
    I love but you alone.

There seems to have been among poets of the later middle ages
an attempt to combine the strongly erotic element in the
popular tradition with religious mysticism. However strange a
modern reader may find the tone and temper of such a poem as
Quia Amore Langueo, no view of the medieval spirit would be
complete without taking it into account. This is perhaps the best
of the erotic-mystical poems, and there is no denying the
emotional force of its language and the almost trance-like compulsion of the rhythm.

My fair love and my spouse bright!
I saved her from beating, and she hath me beat;
I clothed her in grace and heavenly light;
This bloody shirt she hath on me set;
For longing of love yet would I not let;
Sweete strokes are these: lo!
I have loved her ever as I her het [*promised*]
    Quia amore langueo. . . .

Fair love, let us go play:
Apples ben ripe in my gardayne.
I shall thee clothe in a new array,

Thy meet shall be milk, honey and wine.
Fair love, let us go dine:
Thy sustenance is in my crippe, lo! [*scrip*]
Tarry thou not, my fair spouse mine,
    Quia amore langueo.

Part of the attraction of medieval poetry comes from its universality, and from the way in which, three centuries before the great Romantic revolution, it seems so often to foreshadow the moods of romanticism. Yet while we feel able to enter into the romanticism of Keats or Shelley, we find a barrier of strangeness between ourselves and the medieval sensibility. It is also, then, for its strangeness that we value medieval poetry. When we read, for instance, the extraordinary lyric whose first line is 'The maidens came', we know that we are experiencing something of unusual beauty and magical evocation; but what exactly it is about, no one has yet satisfactorily explained. Even allowing for its probably fragmentary character, we are as certain of its profound significance as we are of its impenetrable mystery.

> The maidens came
> When I was in my mother's bower;
> I had all that I would.
> The bailey beareth the bell away;
> The lily, the rose, the rose I lay.
> The silver is white, red is the gold;
> The robes they lay in fold.
> The bailey beareth the bell away;
> The lily, the rose, the rose I lay.
> And through the glass window shines the sun.
> How should I love, and I so young?
> The bailey beareth the bell away;
> The lily, the lily, the rose I lay.

The supposed speaker appears to be a young girl prematurely married. The line about the 'bailey' means either that the 'bailiff' – some official – bears off the prize, presumably herself, or as I think more probable, 'the castle (her home) is supreme' in her estimation – that is, all she wants. There appears to be some connection between 'lily' and 'rose', symbols of purity and passion on the one hand, and 'silver' and 'gold' on the other. Is the girl being married to restore the family fortunes? On the other hand, it is certain that 'through the glass window shines the sun' is a reference to the taking of virginity, or possibly to the virgin birth: the sun is symbolic of male sexuality; the glass remains unbroken when pierced. There is a striking parallel in a Troubadour song to the Virgin Mary by Peire de Corbiac, of which one stanza runs, as translated from the Provençal:

> Lady, virgin pure and fair before the birth was and afterwards the same, Jesus Christ our Saviour received human flesh in thee, just as without causing flaw, the fair ray enters through the window-pane when the sun shines.[1]

It is possible, then, that 'The maidens came' is part of a poem about the Annunciation and Conception; on the other hand, it may be a purely secular lyric, the reference to virginity being simply to the extreme youth of the bride. Whatever its meaning, the poem, like so much else in medieval literature and art, is full of symbolic suggestion; here, if ever, we are surely entitled to respond to poetic suggestion without understanding the precise import of the lines.

The reference to Peire de Corbiac reminds us that English lyrical poetry is rooted in Troubadour poetry. Indeed, so profound is the influence of the Troubadours on the literature of western Europe that a brief account of this important movement must here be given.

At the break-up of the Roman Empire the *joculatores* wandered about Europe in their capacity as professional entertainers. Many of them wrote songs, both words and melodies, performing them with or without instrumental accompaniment wherever they could get a hearing. They found ready imitators in the countries where they travelled, and gradually a tradition was established. The *jongleurs*, as they were called in France, entered the service of the feudal landowners and came under their protection. In the castles of the Provençal petty nobility especially these minstrels found encouragement; and under the name of Troubadours, or 'inventors', they developed a highly artificial style of composition. The first known Troubadour was writing at about the close of the eleventh century. The names of about five hundred poets are known. Their aim was to achieve formal elaboration of stanza and melody. They are said to have invented nearly a thousand stanza forms. The subject of their

[1] H. J. Chaytor: *The Troubadours* (Cambridge 1912).

songs was pre-eminently love, though they also wrote political, social and moral satires.

There is doubt as to the sources from which they drew their inspiration. It has been suggested that they were influenced by Arabic poetry, but it seems more likely that their songs were founded on the popular dance-songs of southern France performed at the spring festivals. Whether or not its origins were popular, Troubadour love poetry is aristocratic in character and artificial in sentiment. It expresses the poet's sense of allegiance to the wife of his feudal overlord; to her he professes boundless and eternal love, not with a view to marriage – she was already married, and the unmarried woman has no place in Troubadour poetry – but in order to secure her favour. The lover was expected to protest that his rejection would result in death or suicide, but there is no recorded instance of this having actually happened. Whether the relation of poet and châtelaine was purely formal, or whether it involved an open or clandestine intrigue is uncertain; no doubt circumstances varied.

The Troubadours were of all classes – kings and nobles, monks and priests, scholars and sons of poor men. Some were women. Bernart de Ventadour was the son of a stoker. Poor Troubadours were patronised by rich ones; the aristocratic employed *jongleurs* to circulate their poems at other courts.

Although *amour courtois* was the principal theme of Troubadour poetry, and that which later had the greatest influence, there was also a vein of devotional verse. Some of the Troubadours ended their lives in monasteries and turned to piety in repentance for the worldliness of their early lives. Among the best known of these were Bertran de Born and Folquet of Marseilles. The Church in southern France, as elsewhere, became increasingly critical of the profligacy and corruption of Rome, and the papal power found itself faced with hostile or heretical movements in its provinces. The Albigensian heresy in southern France was a poor man's heresy, a movement towards piety and simplicity among the local clergy in protest against the profligacy of the higher orders. It received sympathy and support from the nobility. By the end of the twelfth century it had developed into an anti-Roman rebellion which the Pope could not ignore. In 1208 he organised a crusade against the Albigensians, and during the subsequent years resistance to Rome was stamped out with considerable severity and violence. The Inquisition was established to deal with heresy and heretics throughout the Holy Roman Empire.

Troubadour poetry took on an increasingly religious complexion; the cult of the Virgin Mary tended to supersede that of the feudal patroness. Much of the imagery of the secular love poem was adapted to the theme of mariolatry. But the conditions under which Troubadour poetry had flourished no longer existed. Provençal feudal society was broken up, and the poets were dispersed to wander about Europe, finding protection wherever they could. The importance of this dispersal for the future of English poetry is immense. We have seen how, in the fourteenth century, Chaucer naturalised the idiom of courtly love through his translations from the French and Italian. The same idiom is to be found in both the secular and religious lyrics of the fifteenth century and the love poetry of the Renaissance.

The fifteenth century saw, if not the beginnings of Scottish poetry, at any rate its establishment as a distinctive manifestation of the national spirit. Tradition credits Thomas of Erceldoune, the thirteenth-century 'Rhymer', with being the father of Scots poetry. He is the subject of the ballad of *True Thomas*, and of many other legends. But historians regard John Barbour, a late fourteenth-century Archdeacon of Aberdeen, as the real founder of the national school. The late development of Scots literature is ascribed to the turbulent political situation north of the Border and to the delayed establishment of Scotland as a separate kingdom. The bardic phase in Scotland continued into the fifteenth century, when such nationalistic lays as Blind Harry's epic poem on William Wallace were being composed. It was during this century also that the Renaissance came to Scotland through certain poets who felt and transmitted the influence of Chaucer. JAMES I, King of Scotland (1394–1437), was very probably the author of a long poem written in imitation of Chaucer and entitled *The Kingis Quair* (The King's Quire, or Book). This is an allegorical meditation in the tradition of the *Roman de la Rose* and full of Chaucerian echoes. It is not a work of sustained and original inspiration, and the language is in places difficult. It is, however, a landmark in Scots literature. It has a certain natural freshness and simplicity, and an attractive and sober seriousness. The versification is smooth and regular; *The*

Kingis Quair is written in the metre of *Troilus and Criseyde*, the *rime royal* so named on its account.

Among Chaucer's successors in Scotland a more powerful and original writer was the Dunfermline schoolmaster, ROBERT HENRYSON (?1430–?1506), about whose life next to nothing is known for certain. His minor poems and his original variations on themes from Æsop's fables show him to have been a moralist and a sympathetic observer of peasant life. His most memorable work is the long and sombre *Testament of Cresseid*. He pictures himself sitting beside the fire reading Chaucer's great poem, and this induces him to muse upon the ultimate fate of the heroine. He writes a sequel which tells of Cressida's desertion by the Greek philanderer, Diomede, and of her subsequent punishment for her betrayal of Troilus. She is smitten with leprosy, and is forced to beg for a livelihood at the roadside. Here she encounters Troilus, and neither recognises the other. In this climax to the poem there is an irony and pity as moving as anything in pre-Tudor poetry outside Chaucer.

Mention must be made briefly of the scholar and churchman GAVIN DOUGLAS (?1474–1522), who, though not a poet of the first rank, has earned a place in the history of Scottish poetry by his translation of Virgil's *Æneid*. The introduction of Latin poetry into Britain was an essential feature of the English Renaissance; but it is doubtful whether Douglas is to be regarded as a forerunner of the great translators of the sixteenth century or simply as a late follower of Chaucer.

By far the greatest Scots poet of this time, and perhaps of all times, however, was WILLIAM DUNBAR (?1465–?1530). Born of noble parentage, he graduated at St Andrews University, took holy orders, travelled on the European continent, and went to the court of James IV in search of a pension and preferment. He got the pension at about the age of forty; the preferment he may or may not have achieved. He disappears from the records soon after the disaster of Flodden in 1513.

The historical Dunbar is highly conjectural. Dunbar the man and the poet emerges much more clearly from his writings. He was plain-spoken, outspoken, quarrelsome, something of a lone wolf, wryly critical of James's not too brilliant reconstruction of a Renaissance court, vigorously ironical at the expense of merchants, friars, professional rivals, and the surgeons and charlatans whom James took more interest in than poets. He was on the side of the Queen – the gay and frivolous Margaret Tudor – against the King; on the side of the poets against quacks; on the side of life against the pains of sickness and the terrors of death; he was on the side of Dunbar against the world.

He stands, as it were, almost alone, on a bridge of which one end rises from the grim splendours of medieval Christianity, and the other is lost in an incalculable future. He looks backward, not forward – backward to the one-man Renaissance achieved by Chaucer, not forward to that later Renaissance of which he has no inkling. Yet, difficulties of language apart, his poems are surprisingly modern – that is, of no time. They are, for the most part, short, occasional and personal. They show great technical fluency, and above all astonishing versatility. They include lyric, satire and broad comic narrative; their tone and language vary from the racy, colloquial bawdry of *Ane Brash of Wowing* to the gilded artificiality of *The Thrissill and the Rois*, written to commemorate the marriage of James IV and Margaret Tudor. Dunbar is by turns amused, angry, tender, sarcastic, scurrilous, devout. He alternates between cocky self-assurance and humble self-abasement. In his *To the Merchantis of Edinburgh* his attack on the commercial class is pungent and forthright.

> May nane pas throw your principall gaittis,
> For stink of haddochis and of scaitis;
> For cryis of carlingis and debaittis;
> For fensum flyttingis of defame:
> Think ye nocht schame,
> Befoir strangeris of all estaittis
> That sic dishonour hurt your name!

[None may pass through your principal gates for the stink of haddocks and skates, for the cries and arguments of fish-wives and their foul slanging matches. Are you not ashamed that your good name should be thus dishonoured before strangers of all classes?]

Elsewhere he composes his personal variations on the great Christian commonplaces, so deeply pondered by medieval clerks. In *Of Manis Mortalitie* he considers the theme of 'Dust thou art, and unto dust shalt thou return'.

> *Memento, homo, quod cinis es!*
> Think, man, thow art bot erd and ass;
> Lang heir to dwell na thing thow press,

> For as thow come, so sall thow pass;
>   Lyk as ane schaddow in ane glass
> Hyne glydis all thy tyme that heir is;
>   Think, thocht thy bodye ware of brass,
> *Quod tu in cinerem reverteris.*

> Worthye Hector and Hercules,
>   Forcye Achill, and strong Sampsoune,
> Alexander of grit nobilnes,
>   Meik David, and fair Absolone,
>   Hes playit thair pairtis, and all are gone,
> At will of him that all thing steiris:
>   Think, man, exceptioun thair is none;
> *Sed tu in cinerem reverteris.* . . .

> Thy lustye bewtë and thy youth,
>   Sall feid as dois the somer flouris,
> Syne sall the swallow with his mouth
>   The dragone death, that all devouris;
>   No castell sal the keip, nor touris,
> But he sall feche the with thy feiris;
>   Thairfore remembeir at all houris,
> *Quod tu in cinerem reverteris.*

[*Memento, homo, quod cinis es!* – Think, man, thou art but earth and ashes. It is useless to strive after long life, for as thou camest, so shalt thou pass. Like a shadow in a glass, all thy time upon earth glides away. Remember that, even though thy body were made of brass, unto dust thou shalt return.

Worthy Hector and Hercules, lusty Achilles and strong Samson, Alexander of great nobility, meek David and fair Absalom have played their parts and all are gone, at the bidding of him who directs all things. Think, man, there is no exception, but unto dust thou shalt return. . . .

Thy lusty beauty and thy youth shall fade as do the summer flowers. In the end the dragon death, who devours all things, shall swallow thee with his mouth. No castle nor towers shall protect thee, but he will fetch thee away with thy companions. Therefore remember at all times that unto dust thou shalt return.]

Of all the impressions left by Dunbar's work, the most permanent is this sense of the solemnity and gloom of man's mortality. The most famous and the most splendid of his poems is undoubtedly his great *Lament for the Makaris quhen he wes seik* (Elegy on the poets in time of sickness). Some critics have regretted the inclusion of the catalogue of dead poets as over-lengthy. Yet surely it is this particularising of the cruel ravages of death the all-powerful that gives the poem its immediacy and pathos. Life eternal may be assured us by the Resurrection, but a poet is impelled to lament, on behalf of all mankind, the ending of life on this earth.

> He hes Blind Hary and Sandy Traill
> Slane with his schour of mortall haill,
> Qhilk Patrik Johnestoun myght nocht fle;
> *Timor Mortis conturbat me.* . . .
>
> He hes tane Rowll o Aberdene,
> And gentill Rowll of Corstorphyne;
> Two bettir fallowis did no man sie;
> *Timor Mortis conturbat me.* . . .
>
> And he hes now tane, last of aw,
> Gud gentill Stobo et Quintene Schaw,
> Of quhome all wichtis hes pitie: [*wights*]
> *Timor Mortis conturbat me.* . . .
>
> Sen he hes all my brether tane,
> He will nocht lat me leif allane,
> On forss I mon his nixt prey be;
> *Timor Mortis conturbat me.* . . .

It is lines like these that touch our sympathies at their most universal, making us forget that Dunbar was a man of the Middle Ages, a priest and a Christian. He was one of the first poets to be printed in Scotland, and his work is perhaps the first unmistakable manifestation of the Scots temper with all its vitality and its contradictions.

> What an antithetical mind! – tenderness, roughness – delicacy, coarseness – sentiment, sensuality – soaring and grovelling, dirt and deity – all mixed up in that one compound of inspired clay.

This is Byron's verdict on another Scottish poet, Burns. Yet another Scotsman,[1] in quoting it, adds the comment: 'A true observe, and one that could well be applied to the Scots genius as a whole.'

[1] Sydney Goodser Smith: Introduction to *The Merry Muses of Caledonia* (Edinburgh 1959).

CHAPTER THREE

The Early Tudors

THE century which followed the death of Chaucer is
generally agreed to have been the most sterile in the history
of English literature. It was, as we have seen, to some extent
redeemed by an indeterminate number of anonymous writers
who were responsible for a fine, though small, heritage of lyrics,
secular and religious; and, towards the end of the period, by a
flowering of intense poetic growth in Scotland. Yet a third factor
must be mentioned, if only in passing – that of the anonymous
religious drama in verse which had its origins in the earlier
Middle Ages and came to fruition in the miracle and morality
plays of the fourteenth and fifteenth centuries. It is impossible
to elaborate here upon the characteristics of the drama, though
the following facts should be remembered when considering its
later, illustrious history. It was popular in origin, religious in
character, and poetic in style. The verse of which it was composed exploited the qualities of rhyme and alliteration common
in all the popular verse of the period. Something of the dullness
which afflicted poetry settled also upon the drama. This was the
age of long-winded exhortation and moralising. With certain
notable exceptions, most of the moralities of the fifteenth century
dealt at great length, and with little purely dramatic skill, with
subjects more suitable for sermons and pious homilies.

It is sometimes forgotten that the first writer of any note as a
poet and scholar to experiment with dramatic form was Skelton.
He wrote a number of moralities, of which only one, *Magnificence*, has survived. This has its full share of dullness, though to
contemporary audiences the daring attack upon Wolsey's
ascendancy over the affairs of England and especially his influence over Henry VIII must have had considerable interest.
It is not, however, on account of *Magnificence* that its author is
chiefly remembered.

JOHN SKELTON (?1460–1529), possibly a native of Norfolk,

was a classical scholar of great learning and repute. He became tutor to the young Prince Henry, later Henry VIII. As a poet, he obtained honours at both Oxford and Cambridge which qualified him to be called 'Laureate', though not in the later sense of this title. He took holy orders and left London to become rector of Diss, a thriving market town on the borders of Norfolk and Suffolk. He was evidently a man of marked individuality, even eccentricity, and gained a reputation as something of a clown. He caused a scandal by marrying, which was forbidden to priests of the Roman Church. A legend has survived which, though entirely unproved, is characteristic. In order to put a stop to gossip about his marriage and consequent parenthood, he exhibited his baby, it was said, in the pulpit before the whole congregation, of which his wife was a member. He then asked the people to look at it and judge whether it was in any way mis-shapen or at all inferior to their own children.

Skelton looked with anger at the increasing power of the upstart Wolsey, whose influence over the young king he de-plored. He attacked the Cardinal in a series of vigorous and out-spoken satires, notably *Colin Clout*, and *Why Come ye not to Court*? These were circulated widely, and lampoons against Wolsey were got by heart and sung in public by ballad-singers. In attacking the king's favourite at the height of his power, Skelton was acting with both patriotism and sincere religious feeling, and his courage drew down upon him Wolsey's enmity; so that in 1523 Skelton was obliged to take sanctuary at Westminster. Towards the end of his life he made his peace with Wolsey and emerged from sanctuary to enjoy fame and security under the protection of noble patrons.

As a writer Skelton has always annoyed or embarrassed academic historians and those who profess a concern for the 'correctness' of English verse. The eighteenth century regarded him as 'beastly' and little better than a barbarian. Later times considered him a buffoon, and his best poetry near-doggerel. Despite a considerable growth in his reputation during the present century, especially among poets, the official academic view is still grudging in its praise. The fact is that he does not fit easily into the history of poetry. He is an awkward figure to 'place'; so that conventional criticism, unable either to account for Skelton's poetic origins, or to discover any continuous in-

fluence flowing from his work, has tended to treat him as a mere
eccentric, well outside what it has decreed to be the 'main
stream' of literature.

The fact is, Skelton inherited a moribund tradition of poetry
which looked back to its great master, Chaucer, and was unable
to perceive the way marked out for it towards the great Elizabethan Renaissance. Moreover, the language itself was in a state
of flux, and the pronunciation a matter of considerable variation
and uncertainty. He composed a good deal of more or less
'aureate' and correct verse in the dying tradition, but soon discovered that it was no fit medium for true poetry. He could only
discard it and attempt something radically different. How
exactly he hit upon the brilliant rhythmical innovation which
has been named 'Skeltonics', it is hard to say. He may have been
influenced by the somewhat degenerate style of the popular
drama; more likely, he realised the possibilities of naturalising
rhymed Latin verse and prose, the monkish Latin of the later
Middle Ages. Here is an example from one of his most delightful
poems, *The Book of Philip Sparrow*, a long, rambling, sparklingly
loquacious elegy on the death of a pet belonging to the Norfolk
girl, Jane Scroop.

> When I remember again
> How my Philip was slain,
> Never half the pain
> Was between you twain,
> Pyramus and Thisbe,
> As then befell to me:
> I wept and I wailed,
> The tearës down hailed,
> But nothing it availed
> To call Philip again,
> Whom Gib our cat hath slain. . . .
> It had a velvet cap,
> And would sit upon my lap,
> And seek after small wormës,
> And sometime whitebread-crumbës;
> And, many times and oft,
> Between my brestës soft
> It wouldë lie and rest;
> It was proper and prest! [*pretty and neat*]
> Sometime he would gasp
> When he saw a wasp;

A fly, or a gnat,
He would fly at that;
And prettily he would pant
When he saw an ant!
Lord, how he would pry
After a butterfly!
Lord, how he would hop
After the gressop! [*grasshopper*]
And when I said, 'Phip, Phip!'
Then he would leap and skip,
And take me by the lip.
Alas, it will me slo [*slay*]
That Philip is gone me fro!

So the lament goes on, pouring out its breathless sorrow for the dead bird and its full-mouthed, learned execrations against the whole race of cats. No critic, however disapproving, has been able to deny the abundant vitality, the freshness and pungency of Skelton at his best. All agree that what was lacking in early Tudor poetry was vitality; yet when a poet appears whose vitality is overflowing, they can only speak of his 'doggerel'. It is often forgotten that his poems include serious devotional pieces, for example the moving and terrible *Woefully Arrayed*; and that he was a satirist of genuine reforming zeal. It is surely wide of the mark to dismiss as a mere buffoon the author of *The Manner of the World Nowadays*:

Such boasters and braggers,
So new fashioned daggers,
And so many beggars,
  Saw I never:
So many proper knives,
So well apparelled wives
And so ill of their lives,
  Saw I never.

So many cuckold-makers,
So many crakers, [*boasters*]
And so many peace-breakers,
  Saw I never:
So much vain clothing
With cutting and jagging,
And so much bragging,
  Saw I never. . . .

> Among them that are rich,
> Where friendship is to seche, [*seek*]
> Such fair glosing speech, [*flattering*]
>   Saw I never:
> So many poor
> Coming to the door,
> And so small succour,
>   Saw I never.

The critics, one is inclined to think, cannot forgive Skelton for not having ushered in the Renaissance, as the courtly Wyatt and Surrey did a generation later. Despite Skelton's frequent use of Latin, it is the great merit of his verse that it employs the idiom and the rhythm of native English speech. Moreover, Skelton did not employ 'doggerel' *faute de mieux*. He used it deliberately. In *Colin Clout* he writes with a certain mock-apologetic irony of his verse:

> For though my rhyme be ragged,
> Tattered and jagged,
> Rudely rain-beaten,
> Rusty and moth-eaten,
> If ye take well therewith,
> It hath in it some pith.

But he used this verse because it expressed his personality, his angular, combative, rebellious temper, his relish for the saltiness of native speech, his disdain for the 'official' line in poetry. No doubt, as one writer has said, we should think more highly of Skelton if no poetry had been written since his time – that is, if we could read him with the mind of an intelligent contemporary. But this is exactly what we should try to do, instead of under-rating him because poetry subsequently developed along different lines. It is probable, however, that Skelton's immediate influence was greater than has been allowed. For undoubtedly his lively example killed the old, sterile tradition stone dead, and made way for the lyric impulse which spoke through Wyatt. In any case, he remains the only English poet between Chaucer and Wyatt who can be read in large quantities for pure pleasure. He has something in common with his contemporary Dunbar; but whereas Dunbar expresses in his own fashion the doubt and gloom of the later Middle Ages, Skelton seems more to express a bubbling delight in life itself. In spirit, if not in form, he is a man of the Renaissance.

In one respect, however, he has more in common with Dunbar than with his Renaissance successors. The latter were aristocratic and ignored much of life. Skelton, though he was associated with noble families, refused to confine himself to aristocratic subjects. True, in *The Garland of Laurel* he adopted the medieval convention of allegory, though it is rather for the charming and spirited impressions of certain well-born ladies that we read it.

> Merry Margaret,
> As midsummer flower,
> Gentle as falcon
> Or hawk of the tower:
> With solace and gladness,
> Much mirth and no madness,
> All good and no badness;
> So joyously,
> So maidenly,
> So womanly
> Her demeaning
> In everything,
> Far, far passing
> That I can indite
> Or suffice to write
> Of Merry Margaret,
> As midsummer flower,
> Gentle as falcon
> Or hawk of the tower.

Yet in some ways the medieval man was more nearly a whole man than the Renaissance courtier. Chaucer touches life at more points than does Spenser. Skelton has been termed 'coarse' and 'beastly', and no doubt this is on account of his full-blooded, richly malodorous legend of bad women, *The Tunning of Elinor Rumming*. This account of a booze-up at the home of a Leatherhead ale-wife is as vivid a piece of social realism as any tavern scene by a Flemish painter. It is in the tradition which begins with Langland and Chaucer, re-emerges in Gay, Fielding and Burns, and is still to be recognised in the pages of James Joyce. But almost alone among the portrayers of low life, Skelton is neither a libertine nor a puritan. He neither preaches against drunkenness nor relishes it for its own sake. *The Tunning* has been called Hogarthian, but Skelton has none of Hogarth's fierce moral passion – not, at any rate, in this context: the scarifying of vice in high places is another matter. The quality most apparent in *The Tunning*, as elsewhere in Skelton, can only be termed humanity, especially as it is called forth by the contemplation of woman – woman at her most degraded and woman at her most enchanting. It is evidence of the breadth of Skelton's humanity that he can appreciate both Elinor Rumming –

> For her visage
> It would assuage
> A man's courage. . . .
> Her youth is far past!
> Footed like a plane,
> Leggèd like a crane,
> And yet she will jet
> Like a jolivet.

— and Mistress Isabel Pennell:

> Star of the morrow grey,
> The blossom on the spray,
> The freshest flower of May;
> Maidenly demure,
> Of womanhood the lure.
> Wherefore I make you sure
> It were an heavenly health,
> It were an endless wealth,
> A life for God himself,
> To hear this nightingale
> Among the birdës small
> Warbling in the vale.

In considering the next two poets of importance, Wyatt and Surrey, it is worth while remarking that we are here faced with the question of historical status and intrinsic merit. How important is historical status? Expressed in a sentence, the historical importance of Wyatt arises from his having introduced the sonnet, of Surrey from his having introduced blank verse. When we think of the blank verse of Shakespeare, Milton and Wordsworth, to name no others, we are entitled to regard as of prime importance the man who first wrote in that form in English. If for no other reason, then, Surrey is entitled to his place in the history of poetry. We shall return to him later. Again, when we think of the sonnets of Shakespeare, Keats and Hopkins, to name

no others, we are bound to accord an important place to the poet
who first wrote an English sonnet. But neither Wyatt's sonnets
nor Surrey's blank verse are of much intrinsic worth, and nobody
reads either today except for the purpose of historical study.
Moreover, it is inconceivable that blank verse and the sonnet
would not have been introduced into England sooner or later.
We are obliged to conclude that, to the general reader, purely
historical considerations are not very important. As has been said
before, the great poets are those who stand outside history; it is
essential to remember this. For historical considerations so often
become confused with, or are mistaken for, æsthetic ones.
Literary history often seems to imply that a poet is good because
he is important. The view underlying the present study is rather
that a poet is important because he is good. Wyatt was important, not because he was the first to do what others were to do
much better after him, but because he did supremely well what
nobody had done before or was to do later. That he was the first
to write lyrics of a particular kind is an added merit, but it is not
important; what is important is that his best lyrics are unique.
They have something of the quality which makes us read them
for their own sake, without wishing to compare them with other
poems.

THOMAS WYATT (1503–1542) was the son of a Kentish
squire and was educated at Cambridge. He entered the service of
Henry VIII, by whom he was knighted in 1537. He was imprisoned twice in the Tower and released. It was usual with
Henry's courtiers to be imprisoned when temporarily out of
favour. When in favour, Wyatt was employed on ambassadorial
missions, and it was on one of these that he caught a fever and died
prematurely at Sherborne. It is one of the traditions about
Wyatt that he had been a lover of Anne Boleyn before her
marriage to Henry. While this is not proved, it is by no means
improbable. The circumstance may be referred to in the lyric
beginning *Who so list to hunt*. That this has been discovered to be a
translation from the Italian does not discount the personal
interpretation. It is natural that a poet, in adapting foreign
originals, should choose those which express his own situation.

From this poem it is evident that he was a man of passionate
and intellectual temper, not naturally melancholy but to some
extent made so by circumstances. His affinities are with Donne

more than with any other poet. He was one who had known happiness and good fortune, but was deprived of both during much of his short life.

The fourteen-line poem in rhymed iambic pentameters which alone is now called a sonnet (though the term was originally used for poems in quite different forms) was adapted from the Italian models of Francis Petrarch (1304–1374). The Petrarchan form, consisting of an eight-line stanza (the octet) followed by a six-line stanza (the sestet) was abandoned by the Elizabethans in favour of a simpler form, but taken up again by Milton and other later poets. English poets have always found it difficult to express an idea in the exact compass of the sonnet, which by the very reason of its technical difficulty has fascinated them at most periods from the time of Wyatt onwards.

During the course of early travels on the Continent, Wyatt had acquired a profound love and admiration for lyric poetry; and many of his poems are translations or adaptations, not only of sonnets from Petrarch and other Italians, but also of short poems in other metres. Wyatt was a ceaseless experimenter with stanza forms, of which he adapted or invented over seventy. None of his poems was published during his lifetime, but most were included in an anthology which appeared some fifteen years after his death. Tottel, the editor of this collection, wrote of Wyatt thus:

> That to have well written in verse, yea and in small parcels, deserveth great praise, the works of divers Latines, Italians, and other, do prove sufficiently. That our tongue is able in that kind to do as praiseworthily as ye rest, the honourable style of the noble earl of Surrey, and the weightiness of the deep-witted sir Thomas Wyat the elders verse, with several graces in sundry good English writers, do show abundantly.

These words convey in essence what was essentially new in Wyatt – the writing of short poems in English expressive of personal, individualised feeling. He attempted three longish satirical passages in imitation of Horace, and these still read pleasantly. He also adapted the penitential psalms. But it is his original lyrics of private emotion that have achieved him his real status.

Poetry before Wyatt is not of course devoid of personal feeling; but where this occurs, it is incidental. With Chaucer or the anonymous medieval lyrists and the writers of ballads, we may assume that they were men abundantly capable of private emotions, but we do not feel that they made these the subject of their verse. Before the Renaissance, all poetry was grounded in certain conventions – that of epic narrative, for instance, of allegory or of courtly love. It is true that many of Wyatt's love poems, especially those he translated, were grounded in the convention of *amour courtois*, but in his truly characteristic lyrics we do for the first time meet a poet who explores his own psychic condition for its intrinsic interest, as a completely new field of poetic experience.

> Once, as me thought, fortune me kissed
>   And bade me ask what I thought best;
> And I should have it as me list,
>   Therewith to set my heart in rest.
>
> I askèd nought but my dear heart
>   To have for ever more mine own:
> Then at an end were all my smart,
>   Then should I need no more to moan. . . .
>
> My most desire my hand may reach,
>   My will is alway at my hand;
> Me need not long for to beseech
>   Her that hath power me to command.
>
> What earthly thing more can I crave?
>   What would I wish more at my will?
> No thing on earth more would I have,
>   Save that I have, to have it still. . . .

This shifting of the centre of interest from a convention to the poet's actual states of mind is bound up with the new interest in man which characterises the Renaissance. We take it so much for granted that an individual man's or woman's state of mind at any given moment is a legitimate subject for poetry, that we are inclined to forget that it was not always so. It is not easy to realise that when Wyatt made a poem out of an actual situation which had been of crucial emotional significance to him, he was doing something without precedent in English. He was a pioneer in the exploitation of autobiographical material.

There was never nothing more me pained,
    Nor nothing more me moved,
As when my sweetheart her complained
    That ever she me loved.
        Alas the while!

With piteous look she said and sighed:
    'Alas, what aileth me
To love and set my wealth so light
    On him that loveth not me?'
        Alas the while! . . . .

She wept and wrung her hands withall,
    The tears fell in my neck;
She turned her face and let it fall;
    Scarcely therewith could speak.
        Alas the while! . . . .

Certain qualities in Wyatt which are in some ways to his credit have often been regarded by critics as shortcomings. First, it has been remarked that his verse is bare and without vivid imagery. We rightly value some poetry for its concrete physical imagery, because this gives it immediacy and actuality. But there is also a poetry of austere intellectual beauty which, as it were, scorns imagic graces. There is room for both kinds of poetry. Neither concrete nor abstract strength, in itself, makes a poem good or bad; naturally we delight in *The Ancient Mariner* the more because we can see or hear almost every line: it is a triumph of concrete expression. But in some of Shakespeare's sonnets, for instance, we are ready to dispense with imagery for the sake of intellectual passion. It is the same with Wyatt. We accept his intellectualism because it is nearly always touched or informed with feeling. It may be added that, though Wyatt undoubtedly wrote in order to be read, many, perhaps most, of his poems were intended also to be sung to the lute. Undoubtedly the best words for music are those which are sparing in concrete imagery: it is as if the melody supplies the colour, and the mind of the hearer needs to be braced by intellectual argument if the performance is to be more than a merely sensuous experience.

More important than imagery in expressing the emotional side of Wyatt's thought is the rhythm. Few criticisms of poetry have been more mistaken and more unperceptive than that which used to condemn Wyatt for lack of smoothness. Some historians of poetry are essentially prosodists, and see the history of a verse form as a progress from rough to smooth. Spenser has been justly admired for his smoothness, and earlier poets have been valued according to the contribution they made towards the Spenserian achievement. But to the poet's ear it is just as important, at certain periods, to avoid smoothness as to aim at it. We have seen how Skelton escaped from the soporific regularity of established practice by deliberately aiming at roughness. Later, Donne was to stand in the same relation with the Spenserian school, and later still Hopkins with the school of Tennyson. Hardy, again, would be completely misunderstood if we took his rhythmical angularities for mere gaucherie. Judged by the canon of metrical regularity, Wyatt's verse is often strange and difficult to speak. Undoubtedly pronunciation at that time was in a state of flux; no doubt also some of the apparent irregularities may be explained on the ground that the poems were written for music. But occasional rhythmical awkwardness is probably the price Wyatt paid for keeping the movement of his verse free, and so able to carry whatever precise emotional stress was required. For flexibility of rhythm and for psychological realism there had been nothing like Wyatt's lyrics before.

> Madam, withouten many words
>   Once I am sure ye will or no;
> And if ye will, then leave your bordes, [*jests*]
>   And use your wit and show it so.
>
> And with a beck ye shall me call,
>   And if of one that burneth alway
> Ye have any pity at all,
>   Answer me fair with Yea or Nay.
>
> If it be Yea, I shall be fain;
>   If it be Nay, friends as before;
> Ye shall another man obtain,
>   And I mine own and yours no more.

But in the appreciation of such a poem as this, there is no need to make historical allowances. Wyatt's best lyrics are as true today as they were four centuries ago. Anthologists have continually reprinted such pieces as *They flee from me*, *Awake my lute* and *Forget not yet the tried intent*; and the excellence of these has thrown into obscurity others almost, if not quite, as good. The following may perhaps be a translation, but as yet no original has been discovered.

> Nature, that gave the bee so feat a grace
> To find honey of so wondrous fashion,
> Hath taught the spider out of the same place
> To fetch poison, by strange alteration.
> Though this be strange, it is a stranger case
> With one kiss by secret operation
> Both these at once in those your lips to find,
> In change whereof I leave my heart behind.

Henry Howard, Earl of SURREY (1517–1547), usually known simply by his title of Surrey, was a disciple and admirer of Wyatt. Born of almost the noblest and most ancient blood of England, he became involved in the intrigue and suspicions which poisoned the atmosphere of the court in the latter years of Henry VIII's reign, and on a trumped-up charge of high treason was beheaded by the King's order only nine days before the King's own death. Surrey's premature death robbed England of its most promising poet. Ten years later appeared Richard Tottel's miscellany of *Songes and Sonettes*, which, if not the first anthology of English poetry, was one of the most influential. It contained not only the poems of Wyatt but thirty-six pieces by Surrey.

In his *Arte of English Poesie* (1589) George Puttenham gives what was probably the standard Elizabethan view of the two poets.

In the latter end of the same king's reign sprang up a new company of courtly makers, of whom Sir Thomas Wyatt the elder and Henry Earl of Surrey were the two chieftains, who having travelled into Italy and there tasted the sweet and stately measures and style of the Italian poesy as novices newly crept out of the schools of Dante, Ariosto and Petrarch, they greatly polished our rude and homely manner of vulgar poesy, from that it had been before, and for that cause may justly be said the first reformers of our English metre and style . . .

Henry Earl of Surrey and Sir Thomas Wyatt, between whom I find very little difference, I repute them (as before) for the two chief lanterns of light to all others that have since employed their pens upon English poesy, their conceits were lofty, their styles stately, their conveyance cleanly, their terms proper, their metre sweet and well proportioned, in all imitating very naturally and studiously their master, Francis Petrarch.

Later critics tended to regard Surrey as superior to Wyatt because of the greater smoothness of his verse; certainly there is much to be said in his favour.

His verse is smooth and melodious. He dropped the Petrarchan form of the sonnet and introduced that which was to become the normal form for later poets of the sixteenth century, notably Shakespeare. When in prison awaiting execution, he translated part of Virgil's *Æneid* into English blank verse, the first of its kind ever written. This seems to us a natural and proper medium to choose for rendering unrhymed Latin hexameters, but Surrey's innovation proved to be revolutionary. Neither his blank verse, however, nor his sonnets are of great intrinsic worth, agreeable though some of them are. Here is the first of his sonnets, given by Tottel under the title of *Description of Spring, wherin eche thing renewes, save onelie the lover.*

The spelling is here modernised.

> The softë season, that bud and bloom forth brings,
> With green hath clad the hill and eke the vale:
> The nightingale with feathers new she sings;
> The turtle to her make [*mate*] hath told her tale.
> Summer is come, for every spray now springs:
> The hart hath hung his old head on the pale;
> The buck in brake his winter coat he flings;
> The fishes fleet with new repairèd scale.
> The adder all her slough away she slings;
> The swift swallow pursueth the fliës small;
> The busy bee her honey now she mings; [*mixes*]
> Winter is worn that was the flowers' bale.
> And thus I see among these pleasant things
> Each care decays, and yet my sorrow springs.

If this appears superficially archaic, it is worth pointing out that the same thought is expressed, though with much greater sophistication, in Tennyson's *In Memoriam* (CXV) three centuries later.

On strictly æsthetic considerations there is nothing in Surrey which can arouse the same admiration as the best lyrics of Wyatt. Surrey had an excellent ear, and his influence as a pioneer was probably even greater; but because of his historical importance he has been over-valued, and both in poetic sensibility and in imaginative power and sheer inventiveness he is not to be compared with the older poet. Nevertheless, for being one of the headsprings of English poetry and for having, well before his time, foreshadowed the main line of its development, he deserves our credit and respect.

CHAPTER FOUR

The Earlier Elizabethans

THE reign of Elizabeth I is rightly regarded as one of the golden ages of English poetry, but the first twenty years were almost as barren of great achievements as any preceding period. All the great poetry of the reign was written during its latter twenty-five years. Shakespeare's finest work was accomplished in the succeeding reign. The full tide of the Renaissance, which had swept over France from Italy some fifty years earlier, was slow in reaching England. The most significant work produced in the early part of Elizabeth's reign was in the form of translations from other languages, especially Latin. The violent and rhetorical tragedies of Seneca were put into English, and had an immense influence on the development of the drama. The most important translation of any of the Latin poets was Arthur Golding's version of the *Metamorphoses* of Ovid, which appeared in 1565–1567. As a poet, and even as a translator, Golding cannot be called either great or good. He adopted a jog-trot metre known as 'fourteeners', an iambic line of fourteen syllables, chosen no doubt because it contained about the same number of syllables as a Latin hexameter. It is a monotonous and soporific metre, which frequently descends to bathos. As a medium for narrative, however, fourteeners have their points and Golding's renderings of the imperishable myths of the Greek and Roman gods enjoyed long popularity and were extremely influential. A brief passage from the story of Pyramus and Thisbe will be sufficient to illustrate Golding's qualities.

> The wall that parted house from house had riven therein a cranny
> Which shrunk at making of the wall. This fault not marked of any
> Of many hundred years before – what doth not love espy? –
> These lovers first of all found out, and made a way whereby
> To talk together secretly, and through the same did go
> Their loving whisperings very light and safely to and fro.

The most interesting poet writing between Wyatt and Sidney was the now unjustly neglected GEORGE GASCOIGNE (?1525–1577).[1] He was a versatile and serious poet, with satires and translations to his credit, as well as original lyrics. He was a pioneer, anticipating in his best things the mature manner of the later Elizabethan lyrists. He could throw off all the stiffness of metre and awkwardness of word-order of some of his predecessors, and achieve a rhythmical flexibility and grace which make the lines sing themselves.

> Sing lullaby, as women do,
>   Wherewith they bring their babes to rest;
> And lullaby can I sing too,
>   As womanly as can the best.
> With lullaby they still the child;
> And if I be not much beguiled,
> Full many a wanton babe have I,
> Which must be still'd with lullaby.
>
> First lullaby my youthful years,
>   It is now time to go to bed:
> For crookèd age and hoary hairs
>   Have won the haven within my head.
> With lullaby, then, youth be still;
> With lullaby content thy will;
> Since courage quails and comes behind,
> Go sleep, and so beguile thy mind!

It is, as has been noted, a common error of literary history to see all poetry except the greatest as a preparation for the greatest. The historian writes with a knowledge of what was to come, and cannot always keep this knowledge out of his judgement of earlier poets. We should, I think, try to judge them, not in relation to what was to come, but in relation to their predecessors. Imagine that a poet now living is the author of certain minor but interesting work which receives some recognition and even popularity. In due time he dies, and a younger and more gifted writer, profiting by his knowledge of the whole of poetry before him, becomes great and reaches heights of achievement far beyond the earlier poet's. After his death his greatness is universally recognised, and in time literary historians come along and assess the earlier, minor poet according to how far he

[1] Birth date highly conjectural: some authorities give it as late as 1539.

foreshadows the later, major poet. So judgement is falsified, and the minor poet is assessed by standards which do not apply. It is tempting, but quite futile, to regard all pre-Shakespearean poets as leading up to Shakespeare. It is human to err, but this error, it seems to me, is fatal to the just appreciation of poetry. Poets are themselves, and their poems are the expression of their nature and talents. We should try to appreciate their work for its intrinsic merits, to judge it as if we knew nothing of what was to come. To judge the minor poet by his influence or lack of influence on the great poets of a later time, of whose existence he was unaware, is pointless. It is like supposing that Everest is in North Wales and assessing the beauty of Snowdon as if it were one of the Himalayan foothills.

The difficulty of writing about the poetry of the sixteenth century is that everyone knows that its crown was Shakespeare, one of the later Elizabethans. No one can write fairly of a poet if he regards him simply as a forerunner. We should aim at thinking of the earlier Elizabethans not as 'leading up to' Shakespeare, but as having an independent life of their own. We should judge their work by its intrinsic worth in the light of what had preceded it.

If we can forget Shakespeare, the lesser Elizabethans become much more interesting – or rather, we can judge of their interest without the distorting influence of foreknowledge. Historians sometimes write of the sudden flowering of English poetry which took place about 1579 as if the poets of that moment were trying consciously to prepare for the coming of one much greater than themselves. No poet could possibly see himself in this light. To do so is to perpetrate a kind of historical fiction. Both Sidney and Spenser have sometimes been misrepresented because they have been treated too much as forerunners. Every poet is, and is not, a forerunner: every poet's work represents both an end and a beginning.

SIR PHILIP SIDNEY (1554–1586) was two years younger than Spenser, but his poetic development took place earlier. He was of noble birth and was educated at Shrewsbury School and Christ Church, Oxford. In the course of foreign travel he met many of the savants and celebrities of the day. He fell in love with Penelope Devereux, daughter of the first Earl of Essex, to whom he proposed marriage. But she was married against her will to

Lord Rich. Sidney became an M.P. and was knighted in 1583. In 1585 he was appointed Governor of Flushing, and the following year was involved in fighting in the Netherlands and died of wounds received at Zutphen.

In his *Apology for Poetry*, one of the first prose treatises on the subject, he writes of poetry as 'my unelected vocation', and proceeds to defend it against its various detractors. He asserts its essentially moral nature, and claims that it is the highest activity of the human mind because it teaches virtue through delight. He regards poetry as the archetype of all intellectual pursuits, and the only one which is truly creative. He goes on to assert the superiority of English over all other languages for the purposes of poetry. In a famous passage[1] he refers to the emotional effect produced on him by hearing the traditional ballads. This is one of the earliest references by an aristocratic poet to the ballads, and it is important because it underlines the need of sophisticated taste to be rooted in a just appreciation of the popular idiom. He was not only vindicating poetry itself, but also expressing the new-born spirit of patriotism which followed the triumph of Protestantism and the secure establishment of Elizabeth on the throne of England. This new spirit permeated the life of the nation and infused every aspect of men's activities — artistic, religious, scientific and practical.

The ideas which Sidney expressed in the *Apology*, on the whole with eloquence, and certainly with enthusiasm and conviction, were no doubt the fruit of his association with the Leicester House circle. This was a sort of Elizabethan Bloomsbury, of which Sidney himself was the centre, and the best known of the other members were his sister, the Countess of Pembroke, Spenser, Sir Fulke Greville (afterwards Lord Brooke), Gabriel Harvey and Sir Edward Dyer. This circle adopted the conscious aim of reforming and reviving English poetry; it was a central tenet of their doctrines that poetry existed to maintain and inculcate virtue through pleasure. Fortunately, not much of this got into Sidney's poems, which nevertheless express a loftiness and generosity of outlook which is typical of Sidney as we know him. His prose romance, *Arcadia*, contains some excellent lyrics, but

[1] 'Certainly I must confess mine own barbarousness, I never heard the old song of Percy and Douglas, that I found not my heart moved more than with a trumpet.'

his chief claim as a poet rests on his series of sonnets entitled *Astrophel and Stella*. Sidney is Astrophel; Penelope Lady Rich is Stella. There are over a hundred sonnets, which are of the Shakespearean type, of three quatrains and a concluding couplet. Sidney does not, however, confine himself strictly to iambic pentameters; he sometimes writes in alexandrines – lines having six stresses, as in French verse, not five. The very first sonnet in the sequence is written in alexandrines. It ends with the famous line

> Fool! said my Muse to me, look in thy heart and write.

In other words, in *Astrophel and Stella* Sidney consciously gives up foreign models and relies for inspiration on his own feelings. He was not the first to do this, but he may have been the first to adopt it deliberately as a poetic credo.

The sonnet sequence remained fashionable throughout the Elizabethan period, and apart from Shakespeare's, Sidney's was one of the best, if not the best; it was also the first. The quality of the individual sonnets is uneven. At their poorest they are exercises in the conventions of courtly love: the lover, if not already killed by the power of his mistress's eyes, will shortly die from the effects of her scorn; or the mistress is implicated in an imaginary contest between the gods of classical mythology. But Sidney is too good a poet to perpetrate much in this vein. He achieves a lofty and passionate utterance coupled with freedom and ease of verse movement. His sonnet on sleep, for instance, contains a hint of most of the lyric qualities which appear so profusely in later poets, whether of the Elizabethan or the Romantic age. Its especial merit lies in its power to suggest, by its rhythm and diction, the mood of serious and earnest meditation.

> Come, Sleep; O Sleep! the certain knot of peace,
> The baiting-place[1] of wit, the balm of woe,
> The poor man's wealth, the prisoner's release,
> Th'indifferent judge between the high and low;
> With shield of proof shield me from out the press
> Of those fierce darts Despair at me doth throw:
> O make in me those civil wars to cease;
> I will good tribute pay, if thou do so.

[1] Place for refreshment.

Take thou of me smooth pillows, sweetest bed,
A chamber deaf to noise and blind of light,
A rosy garland and a weary head;
And if these things, as being thine by right,
   Move not thy heavy grace, thou shalt in me,
   Livelier than elsewhere, Stella's image see.

A quality to be noted in Sidney, as in most of the Elizabethans, but not in the Romantics, is that of wit – the use of verbal artifice to draw attention to the writer's meaning, the conscious playing with the rhetorical or antithetical aspects of language. In the common run of minor Elizabethan poets this is the quality that remains even when all other merits are absent. At its worst it is mere cleverness and exceedingly tedious in the mass. But used without extravagance, as by Sidney, wit always gives to poetry a certain distinction, of which the reader is aware when he experiences emotion restrained by intellect. Coldness is the vice of the witty poet, but Sidney's wit is as a rule no more than an adornment to the expression of a warm humanity. He believed that poetry should not be didactic, and yet should be informed by an ethical intention. If his poetry teaches anything, it is refinement of feeling and sweetness of spirit. A brief epitaph from *Arcadia* illustrates the combination of wit and deep feeling.

His being was in her alone:
And he not being, she was none.

They joyed one joy, one grief they grieved;
One love they loved, one life they lived.
The hand was one, one was the sword
That did his death, her death, afford.

As all the rest, so now the stone
That tombs the two is justly one.

Sidney's tragic and noble death on the battlefield at the age of thirty-two enrols him in the melancholy ranks of young poets who died before their promise was fulfilled – Surrey, Chatterton, Keats, Owen and the rest.

The mention of wit in writing of Sidney suggests that, before going on to discuss Spenser, it would be well to mention an influential prose work, *Euphues*, by John Lyly. This appeared in two parts in 1579–80, a date which is crucial also in the history of poetry. *Euphues* was the first deliberate attempt to write ornate, artificial and variegated prose in English; as a prose romance it is today scarcely readable in bulk, since its very virtuosity acts as a deterrent when prolonged for many pages. As a *tour de force*, however, it is remarkable, and in small doses palatable as a tonic and stimulant. The reader cannot help marvelling at its fresh exuberance, its sheer playing with the rhetorical and poetic qualities of language. It is the work of a man who, having been brought up to regard Greek and Latin as the height of excellence, suddenly discovers English and revels in its potentialities. He is like a child with a new toy. The writing sparkles with assonance and alliteration, pun and antithesis.

Euphuism was as much a social as a literary phenomenon. Young men up from the country, whose parents were of the parvenu class created by Henry VIII's spoliation of the monasteries, acquired a veneer of Italianate polish in order to shine in court circles and make a career for themselves. Among their accomplishments might be the capacity to show off conversationally by a display of euphuistic wit. Such characters were satirised on the stage, and a typical late example of the euphuistic courtier is Shakespeare's Osric. Such caricature, however, shows only the abuse of euphuism. Its real value lay in the mastery over language which it helped the younger writers to achieve; it helped to give language, especially as the vehicle of stage comedy, a flexibility, lightness and musical grace which it had not had before. The main effect of euphuism was undoubtedly felt in the theatres, but it was influential also in the development of the language for poetic purposes.

Stage comedy flourishes wherever a nation's language is active – that is, wherever there is a consciousness of linguistic display as a social accomplishment. For many years English stage comedy – except as written by Irishmen, who have a natural instinct for theatrical speech – has displayed a certain deadness. Only those dramatists who could exploit the patois of the so-called smart set have been able to write passable comedy during the last few decades. The theatre in America is much more alive, because the English language is still in a highly active state on the other side of the Atlantic.[1] The importance of euphuism in the period of its

[1] The value of euphuism in revitalising a moribund theatrical tradition is well illustrated by the successful comedies of Christopher Fry. It is not certain, however, that this success represents more than a literary *impasse*.

origin is that it helped to keep the language in an active and fluid state. There was a general awareness of the rhetorical and poetic potentialities of language, and this has much to do with the vitality and energy of poetry during the last two decades of the sixteenth century. Spenser was not pre-eminently a witty poet; he avoided stylistic extravagance and never indulged in mere verbal exhibitionism; but the atmosphere of the time must have had its effect on the vocabulary and rhetoric of his poems.

EDMUND SPENSER (1552–1599) was born of poor parents in London, where he was to die, once more in poverty, less than fifty years later. He was educated at Merchant Taylors' School under the beneficent influence of its headmaster, Richard Mulcaster, and at Pembroke Hall, Cambridge. While at Cambridge he published some minor poems, and formed a friendship with Gabriel Harvey. Later he was introduced to Sidney's Leicester House circle. A movement led by Harvey in favour of imitating and naturalising the classics, both in theme and style, had an unfortunate influence, not only on Spenser but on others. Spenser's earliest published work, *The Shepherd's Calendar*, was written in a vein of neo-classical pastoralism and an archaic vocabulary quite unsuited to his, or anyone else's, talents. Few read it now for pleasure, though it shows Spenser as a conscientious and promising versifier. It was a dead end.

During the Leicester House period Spenser seems to have begun the great poem which was to occupy him, with many and frequent interruptions, for the next fifteen years. *The Fairy Queen* was in every sense his life work. It occupied him through all the trials and disappointments of his career, and it served to ensure his reputation, above all changes of fashion, until the present day.

In 1580 he went to Ireland as secretary to the Lord Deputy, Lord Grey de Wilton. He acquired Kilcolman Castle in County Cork, where he proceeded with his *magnum opus* whenever official duties would allow. It seems likely that he regarded Ireland with that mixture of affection and exasperated despair felt by other members of the English ruling class when obliged to spend most of their lives there. Ireland sent Swift mad, and perhaps it broke Spenser's heart. He thought of himself as an exile, yet in some sense he regarded it as his home. During an insurrection in 1598 his castle was burnt down, and he returned to London, to die in destitution the following year. He was buried in Poets' Corner in Westminster Abbey, near the tomb of Chaucer.

His marriage to Elizabeth Boyle in 1594 was the occasion of his sonnets, the *Amoretti*, and also the *Epithalamion*. The *Amoretti* are unduly neglected. They are not all worth reading, but some are above the common run of Elizabethan sonnets. The *Epithalamion* and the later marriage poem, *Prothalamion*, are among his best work. He wrote also a mass of minor poetry, none of which receives much attention except from professional scholars, and most of which would perhaps have been altogether forgotten were it not for *The Fairy Queen*. Among the minor poems most deserving of rescue are the *Four Hymns* in honour of Love and Beauty. These are said to have been written early in Spenser's career; if so, they well illustrate the comparative absence of what is usually called 'development' in his style. The mature Spenser is rightly regarded as mellifluous: this is the only quality for which readers in all ages have esteemed him. But he was far from mellifluous in much of his verse: it was a question of subject matter. When he had to deal with something alien to his genius – satire, controversy, bare narrative – he could be bare and harsh in style. It is true that the form of his greatest work was narrative; yet Spenser is esteemed above all as a lyric poet. The *Four Hymns* suggest his mature manner, and the lyric passages in them are very good indeed.

> Thou that hast never loved canst not believe
> Least part of th'evils which poor lovers grieve:
> The gnawing envy, the heart-fretting fear,
> The vain surmises, the distrustful shows,
> The false reports that flying tales do bear,
> The doubts, the dangers, the delays, the woes,
> The feignèd friends, the unassurèd foes,
> With thousands more than any tongue can tell
> Do make a lover's life a wretch's hell.

When we come to *The Fairy Queen*, we have to consider the biggest non-dramatic poem in English between *The Canterbury Tales* and *Paradise Lost*. The first three books were published in 1589, with an explanatory letter to Sir Walter Ralegh, who had succeeded Leicester as Spenser's patron. The remaining three books appeared in 1596. Spenser had projected twelve books but, apart from the *Two Cantos of Mutability*, the remainder was never written. Spenser's intention as expressed in the letter to Ralegh was to illustrate twelve moral virtues, one in each book. 'The general end, therefore, of all the book,' he says, 'is to fashion a gentleman or noble person in virtuous and gentle disposition.' But since, as a subscriber to the doctrines of Sidney and his circle, he believed that poetry must instruct through delight, virtue was inculcated by means of stories of the court of the Fairy Queen. The Queen was Gloriana, an allegorical representation of Queen Elizabeth, who appears also in the guise of other heroines. The central narrative is that of Arthur, whose contemporary counterpart was Leicester, and his search for ideal perfection in the person of the Queen herself. Arthur represents Magnificence, the crown of all the virtues; others are Temperance, Chastity and Holiness. Gloriana also represents Protestantism, and in this she is opposed by the false Duessa, daughter of Deceit and Shame, who represents Roman Catholicism. The allegorical significances of the poem are thus to be looked for on several planes – the religious, the ethical and the political. But even if the reader were interested in the poem as controversial writing, he would find it difficult to disentangle all the threads. It is safe to say that no one who now reads it cares much about its meaning in the larger sense, whatever may have been the contemporary attitude; the modern reader is beguiled by the narrative, and above all by the vivid and exuberant verse. If he cannot see the wood for the trees, he must admit that there never were more sparkling and verdant trees. Beneath them sport the knights and lovers of medieval allegory and Italian romance, with its ogres, enchantresses, dwarfs and damsels. *The Fairy Queen* was modelled ostensibly on the *Orlando Furioso* of the early sixteenth-century Italian poet, Ariosto, and the world it depicts is one of pure make-believe. It is for this that readers have found inexhaustible delight in the poem for more than three centuries. It is to be doubted whether if Spenser had carried out his plan in full, the poem would have been any more popular. We may respect his moral purpose; we may recognise that it is more consistent with present-day critical notions about the purpose of poetry that a poet should discuss allegorically the important issues of his day than that he should transport his readers to a romantic never-never land. At the same time, it must be owned that there was, behind the poem, a more profoundly poetic purpose, which was at odds with the declared purpose; and that the two were mutually destructive.

I have called *The Fairy Queen* a 'big' poem in preference to a 'great' or a 'good' poem. This is to sit on a critical fence. We may call it a great fragment, or perhaps a series of great fragments; we may say that it contains innumerable passages of good verse. But it is certainly 'big' in the sense that in any consideration of English poetry it can never be overlooked, if only because of its size and the proportions on which it was conceived. Its size or scale is something which makes itself felt, even though the scheme was only half finished. It is not unlike the ruins of some medieval castle where the size is apparent, not only from the remains of the total plan, but also in the scale of the undestroyed portions. It is universally admired, yet few read it as a whole. This is the paradox of *The Fairy Queen*. I must confess that I have never heard a poet, a critic or any other reader say anything against *The Fairy Queen*, or claim to have read it all.

The fact is that English readers, whatever they are brought up to say, do not like long poems; if they are confronted with one, they read it, not as a whole or for the whole, but for the more pleasing and memorable passages. The question arises, indeed, whether there *is* such a thing as a long poem. Poetry, according to my conception of the English genius, resides in comparatively short passages – passages long enough to be memorised, or at any rate apprehended as a whole. The long poem dates back to the ages of oral communication, when the power of memory on the part of both speaker and hearer was much greater than with us. Ever since the decline of oral poetry in England, which began with the invention of printing, we have tended to demand a greater and greater degree of verbal concentration. We cannot give our attention to a long poem; and we do not look to poetry for narrative or for abstract disquisition: we have the various prose forms for such things – the novel and the tract.

Spenser, as has been said, was a backward-looking poet. He had little in common with such a man as Donne, who was a poet of the new age. He looked back to the medieval allegory, the romance of chivalry, the Platonic idea of virtue and the good life. His conscious aim was a return to a golden age that had never existed, except in the minds of poets, of whom Plato was head. This is one of the major themes of poetry. One of the recurrent activating forces behind poetry is the contrast between the ideal and the actual, the sense of a tragic discrepancy between society as it is and society as, judged by the poet's intuition, it was meant to be. This conflict between the actual and the poetic takes infinitely varied forms: some poets, such as Swift, react violently; others, such as Keats, despairingly. Coleridge, usually regarded as a visionary, was one of the most practical of men, and attempted to translate into terms of reality his vision of the ideal society. When his 'Pantisocracy' failed, he was adrift.

It is clear that Spenser was not sure all the time what his life-work was really about. It grew and changed with him. Judged as an achieved artefact, consciously planned, *The Fairy Queen* is a failure; the conscious aim was predestined to fail. That failure was inherent in the scheme is probably the reason why it was never completed. But the achievement of a harmonious style, the realisation of a vivid actuality through a brilliant re-creation of the particular, remained a realisable poetic aim which was frequently and abundantly achieved. For poetry resides in the particular and the concrete. What after all was the ideal perfection, the 'glory', which was the object of Arthur's quest? A poet is a particular man, not an abstract thinker. The ideal is only to be realised, if at all, in the real. What Arthur sought, in his quest for the half-human, half-divine woman he had seen in a vision – a vision at least partly actual – was the ideal human relationship. This quest, which was undoubtedly also Spenser's own, was distorted by political and social realities, by human imperfections, by the incursion of vice into the commonwealth of virtue, by the appearance of ugliness and discord where there should be only beauty and harmony.

It is because it bears witness to these ideas, and is the record of Spenser's struggle, that *The Fairy Queen* may be called, if it is to be called, a great poem. It is not a great poem because it is long. The 'long poem' snobbery still exists in critical utterance. A poet who writes only short poems is never willingly accorded full honours by the critical faculty. Herrick is an exquisite trifler; Burns a lyrist; dozens of others are 'minors' because they wrote no long poems. On the other hand, how many reputations have been inflated because their owners attempted long poems? Byron, Browning, Pope and Bridges – to mention only four. Whether or not Spenser consciously sought for reputation by attempting a long poem is not certain. In view of the reverence in which Homer and Virgil were held, and the esteem accorded to Ariosto, it may have seemed a worthy ambition in 1570 to compose an epic. One is tempted to say that Spenser was too good to succeed. The epic was never finished, but the poetry remains. While admiring many exquisite passages in *The Fairy Queen*, therefore, I offer no excuses for preferring a shorter work which is poetry all through.

The achievement of the ideal human relationship, and the consummation of that relationship in marriage, is celebrated in Spenser's best poem, the *Epithalamion*. Its lofty and impassioned splendour can be felt, not only in the separate stanzas, but in the work as a whole. It is a prolonged paean of triumph in the achievement of a hallowed and harmonious love, in which the physical and the spiritual, the Christian and the pagan elements are fused and balanced. The florid imagery and intricate verse-form are ideally adapted to sustain the mood of chaste voluptuousness. One might say that, at its best, the Renaissance achieved a synthesis between the natural religion of paganism, which had never been altogether suppressed, and the spiritual religion of the Platonic and Christian tradition. The *Epithalamion* is the perfect expression of the Renaissance in English poetry.

> Now all is done: bring home the bride again;
> Bring home the triumph of our victory:
> Bring home with you the glory of her gain;
> With joyance bring her and with jollity.
> Never had man more joyful day than this,
> Whom heaven would heap with bliss,
> Make feast therefore now all this livelong day;
> This day for ever to me holy is.
> Pour out the wine without restraint or stay,
> Pour not by cups, but by the belly full,
> Pour out to all that wull,
> And sprinkle all the posts and walls with wine,
> That they may sweat, and drunken be withall.
> Crown ye God Bacchus with a coronall,
> And Hymen also crown with wreathes of vine;
> And let the Graces dance unto the rest,
> For they can do it best:
> The whiles the maidens do their carol sing,
> To which the woods shall answer, and their echo ring.

The reputation of Spenser has always been high and his influence immense. Milton borrowed freely from him: to read the one poet and then the other is to be aware of frequent verbal borrowings. Either directly, or through Milton, Spenser influenced many of the poets of the eighteenth and nineteenth centuries – for instance, Thomson, Wordsworth, Keats and Tennyson. He was at no time out of fashion. It should be borne in mind, however, that he was esteemed, not on account of his avowed purpose, as expressed in the letter to Ralegh, but as the high priest of mellifluous fantasy. The view expressed by Hazlitt about 1818 is a fair statement of how posterity viewed Spenser.

The language of Spenser is full, and copious, to overflowing: . . . . he was, probably, seduced into a certain license of expression by the difficulty of filling up the moulds of his complicated rhymed stanza from the limited resources of his native language. This stanza, with alternate and repeatedly recurring rhymes, is borrowed from the Italian. It was peculiarly fitted to their language, which abounds in similar vowel terminations, and is as little adapted to ours, from the stubborn, unaccommodating resistance which the consonant endings of the northern languages make to this sort of endless sing-song. – Not that I would, on that account, part with the stanza of Spenser. We are, perhaps, indebted to this very necessity of finding out new forms of expression, and to the occasional faults to which it led, for a poetical language rich and varied and magnificent beyond all former, and almost all later example. His versification is, at once, the most smooth and the most sounding in the language. It is a labyrinth of sweet sounds, 'in many a winding bout of linkèd sweetness long drawn out' – that would cloy by their very sweetness, but that the ear is constantly relieved and enchanted by their continued variety of modulation – dwelling on the pauses of the action, or flowing on in a fuller tide of harmony with the movement of the sentiment. It has not the bold dramatic transitions of Shakspeare's blank verse, nor the high-raised tone of Milton's; but it is the perfection of melting harmony, dissolving the soul in pleasure, or holding it captive in the chains of suspense. Spenser was the poet of our waking dreams; and he has invented not only a language, but a music of his own for them. The undulations are infinite, like those of the waves of the sea: but the effect is still the same, lulling the senses into a deep oblivion of the jarring noises of the world, from which we have no wish to be ever recalled.

In other words, it doesn't matter what *The Fairy Queen* is about: it is a glorious verbal symphony. It is, perhaps, dissatisfaction with this view that is the cause why modern readers hesitate to award Spenser the highest honours. We no longer look upon poetry as an anodyne. We are not satisfied to regard *The Fairy Queen* as a voluptuous labyrinth. Yet we cannot take its ethical pretensions quite seriously. We have to content ourselves, therefore, with viewing it as a masterpiece of uncertain status, and a copious source of inspiration to other poets for three centuries.

CHAPTER FIVE

The Later Elizabethans

NOTHING is more remarkable in the whole history of English literature than the sudden flowering that took place during the last twenty years of Elizabeth's reign. It may be compared to the outburst of Romanticism between 1790 and 1820; but in the latter period what is remarkable is the work of a mere half-dozen men of genius, the minor verse of the age being of small interest. This is not so with the later Elizabethan period. Not less notable than the splendour of the best poetry is the excellence of the average. Men whose talents might have been of small account at any other time composed at least a few lyrics of lasting worth; and men who did in fact compose a mass of very ordinary verse might, in moments of inspiration, break into something of outstanding quality. There is no accounting for the appearance at this time of the greatest poetic genius of all time; but it can at least be said that if genius is in any way to be attributed to the spirit of the age, Shakespeare emerged at the moment when he might most confidently be expected. All our judgements of the Elizabethan poets are made under the shadow of Shakespeare, but if he had never lived, that age would still be of surpassing interest.

It is true that modern taste has tended to prefer the decadence of the period to its prime. The exuberant lyrical and dramatic impulses which were responsible for the poetry of the eighties and nineties inevitably declined with the death of Elizabeth, who had been for more than a generation almost the secular patron saint of England; both the poetry and the prose of the reign of James I show a certain weariness and disillusion. Our present age, torn by war and by social and psychological problems which still seem insoluble, has turned to the poetry of tension and disillusion rather than to that of harmony and joyful self-confidence; but the literary historian must recognise the positive and peculiar merits of that poetry also. Only one poet of the golden age – John

Donne, who must be reserved for the next chapter – has received the attention he merits in the present century. Most of the others have been unjustly neglected because their work is out of sympathy with our preoccupations.

The spirit of the later Elizabethan age is a combination of sheer joy, national self-confidence, and a new zeal for discovery. The tide of nationalism ran high: England seemed to have extricated herself finally from foreign domination, and the decisive defeat of Spain in 1588 confirmed this; the navigators had opened up new worlds for British merchant seamen; the release of men's minds from medieval scholasticism, and the influence of the Continental Renaissance, gave the poets and dramatists un-explored tracts of experience in the hearts and passions of men; the whole social and political structure was surmounted by the enigmatic and dazzling figure of the Queen, who was venerated by the poets as the Virgin Muse, and by the nation at large as the spiritual and temporal head of a vigorous, self-assertive and prosperous nation. This is not to say that the Elizabethan age had no intellectual, social and political problems; but during the eighties and nineties the atmosphere was buoyant and optimistic.

Apart from the spirit of the age, three other factors were influential in promoting the development of poetry. In part these must be regarded as being due to those intangible influences we call 'fashion'. The first was the fashion for stage plays which came in with the growing wealth and importance of London. We cannot here consider the history of drama, but we must acknow-ledge that during this period, as at no other time, the history of poetry is inescapably involved with the drama. No real dividing line can be drawn between dramatic and non-dramatic poetry. There were, it is true, lyrists and sonneteers who had no dealings with the stage, and playwrights whose work was exclusively dramatic; but the mere fact that Shakespeare was supreme in both dramatic and non-dramatic writing, and that a host of other playwrights made significant contributions to lyric poetry, means that there is no real distinction to be insisted upon.

The two other factors which have some bearing on the astonishing poetic flowering of the eighties are the growth of the printing industry, especially in the City of London, and the emergence of a national school of musical composition. Poetry was in fashion; the writing of sonnets and love-lyrics became an acknowledged pastime of courtiers; and the demand from city printers for modish anthologies and sonnet sequences to please the taste of the times was insatiable. Much, perhaps most, of the verse so produced was little better than the minor verse of any other period; but at least there was no lack of a market for the best as well as the mediocre.

The English school of lutanists and madrigalists, of whom Byrd, Morley, and Dowland were at this time supreme, also created a continuous demand for lyric verses. It is not known how many of the lutanists composed their own words. But it must be assumed that hundreds of the lyrics printed in the song-books were the work of anonymous poets of considerable inventive talent and frequent high inspiration. It will probably never be known, for instance, whether Captain Tobias Hume, a lutanist and soldier of fortune, was the author of the words, as well as the melody, of *Fain would I change that note*. Both are near perfection, and perfectly matched.

> Fain would I change that note
> To which fond love hath charmed me
> Long, long to sing by rote,
> Fancying that that harmed me:
> Yet when this thought doth come,
> Love is the perfect sum
> Of all delight,
> I have no other choice
> Either for pen or voice
> To sing or write.
>
> O love, they wrong thee much
> That say thy sweet is bitter,
> When thy ripe fruit is such
> As nothing can be sweeter.
> Fair house of joy and bliss,
> Where truest pleasure is,
> I do adore thee;
> I know thee what thou art,
> I serve thee with my heart,
> And fall before thee.

Perhaps, however, the prior impetus was given to lyric poetry, not by chamber music, but by the stage. The earlier dramatists – Lyly, Lodge, Greene and Nashe,[1] known as the University

---

[1] John Lyly (?1554–1606), Thomas Lodge (?1558–1625), Robert Greene (?1560–1592), Thomas Nashe (1567–1601).

Wits – were among the first to explore, for purposes of stage entertainment, the infinite varieties of verse pattern for which the Elizabethan lyric is remarkable. The great majority of the lyrics deal with love in all its moods – rapturous, despairing, triumphant, frivolous, tormented, playful, disillusioned. What is remarkable about the Elizabethan love lyric, however, is not its psychological depth or subtlety, but its formal variety and charm. It is a commonplace that the average Elizabethan must have had a marvellous ear; but it is probable that, despite the popularity of the printed word, the importance of the theatre and of music meant that poetry was still largely an oral art. To read aloud any dozen pages from an anthology of Elizabethan lyrics is to be aware of a rhythmical subtlety and delicacy never achieved before or since. It is to make even the rhythms of the French Pléiade, a group of poets who had considerable influence on the Elizabethans, seem mechanical by comparison. At its most healthy and vigorous, English poetry has never been far removed from the rhythms of everyday speech, and these prose rhythms always have a vitalising and quickening influence. Whenever poetry has fallen into a rhythmical habit exclusively *poetic*, as with the later Augustans, it has been attacked by a certain deadness, and the only way to renewed vitality has been through a return to the sound and movement of common speech: this is the essence of the rediscovery of the popular ballad rhythms by the early poets of the Romantic movement as an escape from the *impasse* of neo-Augustan practice. The same might be said of the interest in free verse shown in the early twentieth century by the Imagists in reaction against neo-Victorian prosodic flatness. Shakespeare, who surpassed his contemporaries in every form he handled, was supreme also in his prose. Splendid as is his dramatic verse, whether early or late, nowhere does he show the vitality of his rhythmic sense better than in his prose. One might instance the comic dialogue of Benedick and Beatrice, the Falstaff scenes, or some of the passages of mixed prose and verse in the later tragedies; but a few lines of exquisite pathos from *I Henry IV* will serve to illustrate the point.

FIRST CARRIER: Heigh-ho! an it be not four by the day, I'll be hanged: Charles' wain is over the new chimney, and yet our horse not packed. What, ostler!

OSTLER : [*Within*] Anon, anon.

FIRST CARRIER : I prithee, Tom, beat Cut's saddle, put a few
flocks in the point; poor jade, is wrung in the withers out of all
cess.

SECOND CARRIER : Peas and beans are as dank here as a dog,
and that is the next way to give poor jades the bots: this house is
turned upside down since Robin Ostler died.

FIRST CARRIER : Poor fellow, never joyed since the price of oats
rose; it was the death of him.

To some readers the pastoralism of the earlier Elizabethan
lyrists may seem unduly artificial, but it is a pastoralism which
had not hardened into convention. It leaves ample room for
variety and surprise. We can believe in the shepherds and
shepherdesses of Lodge and Lyly as we cannot believe in those of
the pastoral poets of the time of Queen Anne. This is perhaps
because we think of the England of Elizabeth as almost exclusively rural – after all, even London was a country town –
while that of the Augustans was increasingly urban: the Phoebes
and Sylvias of 1580 were still country girls, while those of later
times were dressed in the silks and laces of urban sophistication.
At all events, the charm and ingenuity of the stanza form in
Lodge's *Rosalind* are sufficient to give to the lyrics a naturalness
and grace which more than offset the artificiality of the pastoral
convention.

> Phoebe sat,
> Sweet she sat,
>   Sweet sat Phoebe when I saw her,
> White her brow,
> Coy her eye;
>   Brow and eye how much you please me!
> Words I spent,
> Sighs I sent;
>   Sighs and words could never draw her.
> O my love,
> Thou art lost,
>   Since no sight could ever ease thee.

The lyrics of this period are frequently distinguished by the
rhythmic subtlety which combines a hesitant with a flowing
movement. A lyric from Peele's *David and Bethsabe*, which has
escaped the anthologists more than some which are no better,
illustrates this rhythmic inventiveness to perfection.

Hot sun, cool fire, tempered with sweet air,
Black shade, fair nurse, shadow my white hair;
Shine, sun; burn, fire; breathe, air, and ease me;
Black shade, fair nurse, shroud me and please me:
Shadow, my sweet nurse, keep me from burning,
Make not my glad cause cause of mourning.
    Let not my beauty's fire
    Inflame unstaid desire,
    Nor pierce any bright eye
    That wandereth lightly.

Another distinguishing mark of the Elizabethan lyric is its delight in external nature. For all its concern with the moods and fancies of lovers, and the varying perfections of the mistress' outward form, we feel that its setting is a harmonious and charming natural scene, realised in concrete and sometimes homely terms. It is not the wild nature of some of the Romantic poets, nor does it insist on naturalistic detail; it is none the less real and pervasive, though generalised and humanised by comparison. Nature is celebrated not for itself, but as a setting for human activity. Professor C. S. Lewis speaks of the 'note of almost idiotic happiness' in Nashe's famous *Spring the sweet spring* – a note which I think can sometimes be detected also in Blake. And the happiness is the happiness of innocence, a sense of harmony between man and nature, of sheer joy in country pleasures. Such a note cannot be faked; its spontaneity is self-evident.

Among the longer non-dramatic poems written by playwrights, the best-known are Shakespeare's *Venus and Adonis* and the *Hero and Leander* of Marlowe and Chapman. CHRISTOPHER MARLOWE (1564–1593) is famous chiefly for his plays, which are the work of a young man, sensual, passionate, and ambitious. Little is known for certain of the sudden and violent death which put an end to a dramatic career of unusual promise. At its best Marlowe's dramatic verse has a lofty and overflowing eloquence unrivalled even by Shakespeare. It abounds in daring metaphor and hyperbole. Marlowe raised dramatic blank verse to altogether new heights. *Hero and Leander*, written in rhymed pairs of iambic pentameters, tells the story of the tragic drowning of a young man of Abydos while swimming the Hellespont to woo the beautiful priestess of Aphrodite at Sestos. This subject gives Marlowe scope for his tragic sense, his passionate intensity, and above all, his almost obsessive interest in rich and sensuous detail. No poet has ever crowded his lines with more gorgeous and highly-coloured imagery. These qualities may be discovered almost anywhere in the part of *Hero and Leander* written by Marlowe. But he was not content with mere sensuous description. He was a man of restless intellectual curiosity, and at its best his verse has a speculative eloquence, a music of thought as well as of sound and imagery. Here is a speech from Part I of his tragedy of *Tamburlaine*:

> What is beauty? saith my sufferings then.
> If all the pens that ever poets held
> Had fed the feeling of their masters' thoughts,
> And every sweetness that inspired their hearts,
> Their minds, and muses on admirèd themes:
> If all the heavenly quintessence they still
> From their immortal flowers of Poesy,
> Wherein as in a mirror we perceive
> The highest reaches of the human wit,
> If these had made one poem's period
> And all combined in beauty's worthiness,
> Yet should there hover in their restless heads
> One thought, one grace, one wonder at the least,
> Which into words no virtue can digest.

GEORGE CHAPMAN (?1559–?1634) was a dramatist very highly esteemed in his day and somewhat underestimated since. Apart from his plays, he was responsible for a translation of Homer and for the last four of the six parts ('sestiads') of *Hero and Leander*. Chapman's work has not the splendour of Marlowe's, but it is in every way a worthy continuation, and shows considerable narrative skill.

Among the more rewarding of lesser known Elizabethan poets is SIR WALTER RALEGH (1552–1618), sometimes slighted by literary historians as an 'amateur': that is, he was careless of the fate of his work, he left many of his poems unfinished, and he did not dedicate his major energies to the Muse. In one respect he was typically Elizabethan: one feels that he may have been called to write poetry by virtue of the prevailing fashion. In another age he might have been no poet. At the same time his work, which is mainly lyrical and reflective, carries the stamp of an individual sensibility and deserves its share of recognition. His satirical attack on the age, entitled *The Lie*, has a certain trenchant economy of phrase; and several others of his reflective lyrics are worthy to be remembered. But his long, semi-autobiographical meditation on unrequited love, *The Ocean's Love to Cynthia* has a sardonic intensity of feeling and a tone of almost desperate bitterness which distinguish it from most of the lyrical verse of the time.

> But in my mind so is her love enclosèd,
> And is thereof not only the best part,
> But into it the essence is disposèd:
> O love! (the more my woe) to it thou art
>
> Even as the moisture in each plant that grows;
> Even as the sun unto the frozen ground;
> Even as the sweetness to the incarnate rose;
> Even as the centre in each perfect round. . . .
>
> Thou art the soul of that unhappy mind
> Which, being by nature made an idle thought,
> Began even then to take immortal kind,
> When first her virtues in thy spirits wrought.

A notable characteristic of the poetry of this period is its power to assimilate the most varied kinds of experience. The song-writers express an unreflecting joy in love and the natural world; Marlowe explores the possibilities of a classical legend; Ralegh's poems are the subjective expression of a personal malaise; elsewhere we find a more objective treatment of philosophical themes. The two long poems of SIR JOHN DAVIES (1569–1626) are perhaps the best of this kind. Their subjects do not sound promising. *Orchestra* (1596) is a long and discursive dissertation on dancing, and *Nosce Teipsum* (1599) is a reasoned assertion of the immortality of the soul. These poems were formerly regarded as merely 'fantastic'; but recently it has been recognised that their themes are integrally related to the most important aspects of Elizabethan thought. Davies was a grave and serious moralist, capable of sustaining a long argument gracefully and without flatness. Dancing, the subject of his most attractive poem, is basic to the Elizabethan concept of cosmic harmony on which rests their notion of an ordered and hierarchic society. Of the beauty and sweetness of the language in which Davies deals with this apparently intractable material, one quatrain will suffice for an example. Davies was a lawyer and a man of learning, but he carried his learning lightly.

> What mean the mermaids when they dance and sing
> But certain death unto the mariner?
> What tidings do the dancing dolphins bring
> But that some dangerous storm approacheth near?

Of the host of sonneteers who, inspired by Sidney's *Astrophel and Stella*, published sequences in the nineties, two of the most notable are Daniel and Drayton. SAMUEL DANIEL (?1563–1619) was a West Country man who found for himself a patron in Sidney's circle, and achieved a respectable rôle among Court poets. At a time when the lives of many literary men were turbulent, Daniel's was placid, and his quietism is reflected in his verse. He tried his hand at most literary forms, including the drama, to which he was ill suited, and historical narrative verse, which earned him the reputation of a somewhat leaden-footed spirit in an age of daring inventors. But he had those merits for which poets are usually less esteemed than they should be: though unadventurous, he was scholarly and diligent. The sonnets in his *Delia* are less uneven in quality than those of most of his contemporaries. They have a dignity of feeling and a natural flow and music which remind us of the more contemplative of Shakespeare's sonnets.

> When men shall find thy flower, thy glory, pass,
> And thou with careful brow, sitting alone,
> Receivèd hast this message from thy glass,
> That tells the truth and says that *All is gone*;
> Fresh shalt thou see in me the wounds thou mad'st,
> Though spent thy flame, in me the heat remaining:
> I that have loved thee thus before thou fad'st –
> My faith shall wax, when thou art in thy waning.
> The world shall find this miracle in me,
> That fire can burn when all the matter's spent:
> Then what my faith hath been thyself shall see,
> And that thou wast unkind thou may'st repent. –
>   Thou may'st repent that thou hast scorned my tears,
>   When Winter snows upon thy sable hairs.

The attraction of the sonnet form to the Elizabethans lay no doubt partly in its difficulty: the mere technical ingenuity needed to write a sonnet acted as a check on the excesses of undisciplined emotion, and the frequency with which minor poets not otherwise very distinguished managed to bring off at least a few fine sonnets is a sign of the poetic vigour of the time.

Judged by his immense output and by the esteem in which he was held by his contemporaries, MICHAEL DRAYTON (1563–1631) was something more than a minor poet. Like Shakespeare, he was a Warwickshire man and, like other poets of no fortune, succeeded in obtaining the support of a noble patron. He was, he tells us, attracted to poetry at a tender age.

> In my small self I greatly marvelled then,
> Amongst all other, what strange kind of men
> These poets were; and pleasèd with the name,
> To my mild tutor merrily I came,
> (For I was then a proper goodly page,
> Much like a pygmy, scarce ten years of age)
> Clasping my slender arms about his thigh.
> O my dear master! cannot you (quoth I)
> Make me a poet? Do it if you can,
> And you shall see I'll quickly be a man.

He responded to the demand for historical writings which arose in the nineties not with stage plays, as in Shakespeare's case, but with long chronicle poems, and a few shorter ones, such as *Agincourt*, which is among the best battle poems in the language. Everyone has heard of, but no one reads, the enormous topographical survey of Britain, *Polyolbion*, written in smooth and soporific alexandrines. In short extracts it reads pleasantly enough, but like nearly everything Drayton wrote, it lacks fire. On the other hand, his best lyrics have the serene grace and clarity which have earned them a permanent place in the lyric heritage. Among these are the superb sonnet, *Since there's no help, come let us kiss and part*, the lines *To the Virginian Voyage*, the exquisite *Sirena* stanzas, and some of the songs in *Muses' Elizium*.

> Clear had the day been from the dawn,
> All chequered was the sky,
> Thin clouds like scarfs of cobweb lawn
> Veiled Heaven's most glorious eye.
> The wind had no more strength than this
> That leisurely it blew,
> To make one leaf the next to kiss
> That closely by it grew.

The rhythmic sweetness of this and the truth to nature of its imagery exemplify the kind of surprise which is always to be found by the reader of Elizabethan verse. We are apt to regard impressionism and naturalism as things which came into poetry at a much later date – say with Collins in the 1740's – but it is one of the delights of Elizabethan poetry that almost everything which it looks forward to in later times is there to be found at least in embryo. Drayton was a dedicated poet who, when very young, consciously desired to be blessed by the Muse. Few have worked harder for this honour and, although no one would call him great, posterity has acknowledged that the Muse was generous to him. He may never arouse the fiercest passions of literary critics, but his place is secure in the affections of generations of ordinary readers.

WILLIAM SHAKESPEARE (1564–1616) is supposed by tradition to have been born on 23 April, and is known to have been baptised on 26 April 1564. He was the son of John Shakespeare, a not very prosperous merchant of Stratford-on-Avon. He was educated at the Grammar School and attended no university. He married at eighteen a yeoman's daughter named Anne Hathaway, by whom he had three children – Susanna, Judith and Hamnet. When exactly he went up to London and became an actor is not known, but we have the date of his first poem, *Venus and Adonis*, 1593. *The Rape of Lucrece* followed in 1594. He became connected with various theatrical ventures, and was prosperous enough by 1597 to buy a substantial house, New Place, at Stratford. How much of his time was spent in London and how much at Stratford, and the success or failure of his marriage, are matters of pure speculation, about which nothing is known for certain. He died at Stratford on 23 April 1616. Apart from his will, the printed texts of his plays and poems, and a few references to him by contemporary writers, this is virtually all the known evidence about him. The immense interest attaching to the author of the plays and sonnets has made it inevitable that a forest of legend has grown up around him.

With Shakespeare as a dramatist this book is not concerned, except to comment generally on the importance of his influence on all subsequent poetry. It is probable that his reputation during life was high; it is certain that it rose consistently during the seventeenth century and that by the beginning of the eighteenth it achieved the supreme eminence from which it has never been dislodged. His plays have attracted the critical attention of poets from Dryden onwards; and even before Dryden, the poems of Milton show the direct influence of Shakespeare. The same is true to a greater or less degree of all English poets since Milton. In short, English poetry has been so moulded by the conviction of Shakespeare's absolute supremacy that the extent of his influence is incalculable.

Of his non-dramatic work only the Sonnets show him as the genius we know him to be. *Venus and Adonis* has always been admired but never popular. It was contemporary with *Hero and Leander*, but is less a narrative poem than an extended descriptive lyric or dramatic episode. It is admired chiefly for the brilliant pictures it gives of animal life. Its subject, the immoderate wooing of the young Adonis by the sexually rapacious Venus, is not, and was not intended to be, a pleasant theme; but as a piece of erotic realism the poem has power and vitality. It was dedicated to Shakespeare's patron, the Earl of Southampton.

The Rape of Lucrece, a companion poem contrasting with *Venus and Adonis*, is concerned with the theme of male debauchery. It has never been greatly admired, although it shows something of the technical virtuosity of the earlier poem. The poetic qualities in *Lucrece* are, however, somewhat obscured by tedious digressions and tiresome conceits.

In the songs which were incorporated in many of the plays, Shakespeare exceeded all his contemporaries in technical subtlety and emotional range. Beautiful as are the hauntingly suggestive *Full fathom five* and *Come away, come away Death, Fear no more the heat o' the sun* and *Take, O take those lips away,* read simply as anthology pieces, they can be infinitely more moving as musical episodes in a dramatic context. Shakespeare's plays contain many references to the power of music, and by his dramatic use of song he shows himself to have handled that power like a master.

Of all Shakespeare's lyrical writing, however. it is his sonnets that place him most securely among the greatest love poets in any language. Indeed, had he written nothing but the sonnets, he would still have to be accorded a very high position. Two thousand lines of good, often superb, poetry give ample proof of Shakespeare's scope and quality. Moreover, they are not the work of a young man, comparatively early though they are dated in the canon. Shakespeare developed late, and the available evidence suggests that they belong to his middle years. The earliest edition of the one hundred and fifty-four sonnets is the Quarto of 1609, issued by Thomas Thorpe. The mysterious dedication (by Thorpe, not Shakespeare) to 'Mr W. H.' has engendered a library of speculation, none of which has any foundation in fact. The whole question of the biographical background has indeed been the subject of long and exhaustive research, but no indisputable evidence has come to light. Scholars have found out very little more than what can be inferred from the sonnets themselves. The general situation is stated in Sonnet 144, which begins:

> Two loves I have of comfort and despair,
> Which like two spirits do suggest me still:[1]
> The better angel is a man right fair,
> The worser spirit a woman colour'd ill.
> To win me soon to hell, my female evil
> Tempteth my better angel from my side,
> And would corrupt my saint to be a devil,
> Wooing his purity with her foul pride.

Speculation about the identity of the noble young man and the dark lady, or of the other *personæ* of the sonnets, especially the rival poet, is fruitless, and perhaps pointless. It is enough that the relationship between Shakespeare and these others engaged his deepest feelings, and moved him to as passionately personal an utterance as had ever appeared in English poetry. There are reasons for thinking that the order of the sonnets has been confused, and attempts have been made to rearrange them to make a consecutive 'story'; yet none is very convincing. The fact is that we must forego a connected story and be satisfied with separate sonnets or groups of sonnets. The first group, in which the young man is urged to beget children in order to defy the destructive power of Time, forms a fairly coherent sequence.

> But wherefore do not you a mightier way
> Make war upon this bloody tyrant, Time? (16)

and

> Shall I compare thee to a summer's day? (18)

and

> Devouring Time, blunt thou the lion's paws (19)

[1] *Suggest me still*: influence me continually.

magnificent as they are, are variations on common Elizabethan
themes, and are comparatively formal in tone, raised by their
qualities of imagery and rhetoric far above the common level.
Many of the later sonnets, however, transcend accepted themes
and reveal the ideas, moods and feelings of an intensely individual man. No aspect of the sonnets is more remarkable than
their marvellous variety, and in this we can detect the creator of
the almost infinite range of characters to be found in the plays.
Tired with all these, for restful death I cry (66) is a profound, but
essentially simple, statement of the necessity for love; *Let me not to
the marriage of true minds* (116) and *The expense of spirit in a waste of
shame* (129) are opposed expressions, both equally valid, of the
extremes of idealism and revulsion in the mind of a lover. By
their imagery, their reasoning and their rhythmic vitality they
strike us, again and again, as the product of a man of equally
keen senses and intellect, with an emotional range and a
command of language exceeding anything found elsewhere
except in the dramatic writings of the same poet.

CHAPTER SIX

The Seventeenth Century

I. Donne and the Metaphysicals

A S we emerge from the golden age of Elizabethan poetry, we can distinguish two main streams, not indeed clearly separated at all points, but mingling and merging in a way which makes precise definition difficult. On the one hand there is the Spenserian tradition, with its emphasis on smooth versification and vivid, sparkling imagery. On the other hand there is a new tradition of 'fantastic' verse, based on far-fetched images or 'conceits', as they were called, and on innovation in form and rhythm. The heirs of the Spenserian tradition were John Fletcher, Thomas Campion, Ben Jonson, Herrick, the Cavalier poets and many other minor figures; and ultimately Milton himself. They were the authors of many imperishable lyrics; and although the freshness, the spontaneity and the innocence of the earlier Elizabethans had given place to a more reflective mood and a more studied artificiality of form and diction, there is in the conscious artistry of these Jacobean and Caroline lyrists a sweetness of tone and mellowness of feeling which suggest a serene autumn with a long and fruitful summer behind it.

Most of the heirs of Spenser were, with the exception of Milton, what we should call traditionalists: in the great struggle between Parliament and the monarchy which split the nation, and in the religious differences by which it was torn, they tended towards the Royalist and High Church causes. They tended to identify themselves with the established, soon to become the old, order; they looked to the past, and whether or not they felt themselves to be adherents of a losing cause, their poetry was in a sense outmoded, as their social position was doomed.

The school of 'fantastic', or as they were later called, in the phrase borrowed from Dryden by Dr Johnson, 'Metaphysical' poets, were much more in tune with the temper of the new age: they drew for their imagery not on the Petrarchan and pastoral tradition that had reached, or nearly reached, the point of exhaustion; they drew on the new knowledge, scientific and contemporary, which had come to them with the spread of humarism from the Continent. To attempt to draw a close parallel between the poetic and the social and political revolutions of the early seventeenth century would, however, be to grossly over-simplify. To say, for instance, that Donne was a contemporary poet – indeed, a poet before his time – in the sense in which Jonson was not, is simply to state that he was a leader in the poetic revolution; it is not to imply that he was, from a religious or political standpoint, a revolutionary. Moreover, there is plenty of 'fantasticating', plenty of reference to the new scientific humanism, in Jonson's dramas. Again, Herbert, Crashaw and Vaughan, Donne's immediate heirs, were traditionalists in religion, they were not reformers, as Milton was. We realise, in short, that to over-simplify the history of literature is to ignore the capacity of individuals for defying classification and for refusing to remain consistently within the categories invented by historians. Nevertheless, it remains broadly true that at the beginning of the seventeenth century the school of Spenser represented a departing order, while that of Donne looked forward to the future.

What was the nature of the poetic revolution heralded by Donne? Donne is sometimes written of as if he shot like a comet across the literary sky, unannounced and unpredicted. One-man revolutions in fact probably never occur. The fantastic style of writing was very much 'in the air' during the last decade of the sixteenth century, and it offered something new in contrast to Spenserian smoothness and regularity. A remarkable French poem, the *Semaine* of the Huguenot Du Bartas was translated by Joshua Sylvester among others, and achieved wide popularity in England, though it was ridiculed in France as offending against all the rules of poetic decorum. Its linguistic innovations and its outlandish imagery appealed to the English, as they disgusted the French. English readers have always, during the most active and formative periods of their literature, been ready to receive foreign influences and to listen to whatever is outlandish, unconventional and eccentric. Literary curiosities have often had an influence disproportionate to their intrinsic merits. Certainly Du Bartas' long and discursive poem on the Creation of the World is a literary curiosity, but in its day it had a considerable vogue among younger poets. Not only in its style, but in its subject matter, it was an innovation: there was something peculiarly attractive to English readers in this early example of a Protestant, religious epic narrative.

To what extent JOHN DONNE (?1571–1631) was directly influenced by Du Bartas and other 'fantastic' writers, and to what extent his own influence was felt directly by later English poets, it is not easy to determine. It is improbable that any of his poems were printed during his lifetime, and most did not appear until two years after his death. But copies of them were circulated between their composition in the 1590's and the year of their publication, and were very highly regarded, even – with reservations – by the exponents of Spenserian smoothness. Not less remarkable than the apparent suddenness of Donne's appearance on the scene is the rapidity of his disappearance after the Restoration, and his eclipse during the two centuries which followed; during the second quarter of the twentieth century he has once more achieved a status almost unrivalled among the poets of the past. The present generation has placed Donne, in some respects, among the very greatest of English poets, and a literary revolution which could once again displace him seems inconceivable. A poet who has been the subject of such extreme fluctuations of taste must have remarkable qualities of attraction and repulsion.

In an age of militant Protestantism Donne received the education of a Roman Catholic, and the danger and suspicion in which Catholics lived during the years of his infancy may have had some effect in making him restless, violent, passionate and melancholic in temperament. He went to both Oxford and Cambridge, where he became an avid student of the new doctrines which permeated learned circles. He was as well versed in traditional Catholic theology as he was an eager devourer of new ideas. He next became an 'Inns of Court man', the foppish, quarrelsome, passionate 'Jack Donne' of his early love poems: one is inevitably reminded of Shakespeare's contemporary creation, the Romeo of the early scenes before he became infatuated with Juliet – witty, the boon companion of wits, as ready with the pen as with the sword. He was one of the crew of daring and rakish young men who sailed with Essex on his expedition against the Spanish to Cadiz in 1596. In 1597 he became Secretary to the Keeper of the Great Seal, Sir Thomas Egerton, and ruined his prospects of promotion by his rash and clandestine marriage to Egerton's niece, Anne More. For this he was imprisoned in the Fleet, but released shortly afterwards when a reconciliation took place with his wife's family. So far as is known, the love between Donne and his wife remained peculiarly intense and intimate until Anne's death in 1617. In disgracing himself by his imprudence from a worldly standpoint, Donne achieved that wholly satisfying relationship for which he had evidently been searching during his turbulent early manhood – a relationship only strengthened by the poverty and insecurity of his first years of marriage. In 1616, after considerable heart-searching, he took orders in the Anglican Church. In 1621 he became Dean of St Paul's, and later preached before the King. His sermons are impressive for their gloomy splendour; they have something of the air of a sustained epitaph upon the glories of the previous age.

The mind and temperament revealed by Donne's poems would probably in any age have been remarkable. A restless intellectual curiosity and an extreme impatience with convention are combined with a warm and passionate emotional nature. He delighted in paradox and contradiction, but there is nothing cold about his probing and analytical intelligence. In his Satires and Epigrams he delighted to shock by a display of unconventional wit; and in his verse letters to friends he discourses in familiar but paradoxical terms on topics of public and private interest. The Elegies, which contain some of his finest passages, are discursive and at times random, but at their best they have a dramatic intensity which reminds us of the mature style of Shakespeare.

> Since she must go, and I must mourn, come Night,
> Environ me with darkness, whilst I write:
> Shadow that hell unto me, which alone
> I am to suffer when my Love is gone.
> Alas the darkest Magick cannot do it,
> Thou and greate Hell to boot are shadows to it.
>
> (*Elegy XII*)

But Donne's reputation as a poet rests mainly on the fifty-five *Songs and Sonnets* begun in his early twenties and not published until after his death. This is one of the most superb series of love poems ever written. It is not a meditation about love, nor a sequence of secular hymns in praise of unattainable beauty, nor a collection of exercises in a fashionable pursuit. It is the confessions of a man actually and passionately in love, exploring with ruthless psychological realism the varying states of mind of himself and the women he addresses. It is, in substance, a protest against the whole Petrarchan tradition of courtly love; a woman is treated as a woman – emotional, sensual, tender, fickle, kind and heartless by turns – not as a demi-goddess or an Arcadian shepherdess.

> I wonder by my troth what thou and I
> Did till we loved? Were we not weaned till then?
> But sucked on country pleasures, childishly?

Thus, at the very opening of *The Good-Morrow*, the first of the *Songs and Sonnets*, Donne utters what sounds like a manifesto against the Arcadian child's play of conventional love poetry.

For the exploitation of his psychological realism Donne forged a new style not unlike the dramatic soliloquy of the Elizabethan theatre. It is harsh, angular, explosive, metrically irregular and rhythmically nervous. It deliberately outrages the proprieties of Elizabethan prosody, avoiding Spenserian smoothness and sweetness. For this Donne was censured by critics of his time; but he knew what he was doing. He was forcing the raw urgency of passionate speech to break through the restrictions of accepted poetic modes. In doing so, he was creating a style which had its own new and exciting harmony.

> For Godsake hold your tongue and let me love,
>   Or chide my palsy or my gout,
> My five grey hairs, or ruined fortune flout;
>   With wealth your state, your mind with arts improve,
>   Take you a course, get you a place,
>   Observe his honour, or his grace,
> Or the King's real or his stampèd face
>   Contemplate; what you will, approve,
>   So you will let me love.

It is this dramatic quality, the capacity to open a poem with the familiarity, the immediacy, the spontaneity of unrehearsed speech, which is Donne's most striking innovation. This immediacy is to be found occasionally in Shakespeare's Sonnets:

> Then hate me when thou wilt; if ever, now;
> Now, while the world is bent my deeds to cross,
> Join with the spite of fortune, make me bow,
> And do not drop in for an after-loss.
>
> (*Sonnet* 90)

But even Shakespeare does not sustain it so consistently as Donne.

> So, so, break off this last lamenting kiss,
> Which sucks two souls and vapours both away;
> Turn thou, ghost, that way, and let me turn this,
> And let ourselves benight our happiest day.
> We asked none leave to love, nor will we owe
> Any so cheap a death as saying, Go:
>
> Go; and if that word have not quite killed thee,
> Ease me with death, by bidding me go too.
> O, if it have, let my word work on me,
> And a just office on a murderer do;
> Except it be too late, to kill me so,
> Being double dead, going, and bidding Go.

This is the language of a man actually experiencing the pangs of separation. Its dramatic force is compressed like that of a coiled spring suddenly released at the repetition of the word 'Go'. It is worth comparing this with Drayton's *Since there's no help*, in its way equally fine and no less emotionally authentic. But whereas Drayton's is a calm, reflective temperament, Donne's is at once more intellectual and more theatrical, even to the point of hysteria. Donne does indeed mar some of his work with over-fantastic, over-rhetorical hyperbole; but mere intellectual ingenuity seldom takes the place of true feeling. Some love poets strike us as putting their reason to sleep when they make love; Donne is almost alone in remaining a rational man under the pressure of extreme emotion. Indeed, it might be said that with him desire stimulates intellect. He can be on occasion brutally coarse and cynical about women, but he never writes of them as if they were beneath the notice of a rational man. In his love poems he shows how, when the unrealities of conventional love-making are stripped away, men and women find their greatest fulfilment in one another.

It seems likely that the phase of the *Songs and Sonnets* was not a long one. The later, religious poems have found ardent admirers, and the *Holy Sonnets* have something of the emotional urgency and rhythmical excitement of the early lyrics. In them Donne struggles with God as he had once struggled with woman. The problems of sin and damnation take the place of those of erotic psychology. The hyperboles, the conceits, the theatricality, even the hysteria, are still there; but the familiarity and the spontaneity are lacking. Nevertheless, the religious poems had an even greater influence on seventeenth-century poetry than the secular.

The distinguishing mark of Metaphysical poetry, as initiated by Donne, was its use of imagery not obviously connected with the immediate subject of the poem; this imagery might be drawn from any sphere of interest, familiar and domestic on the one hand, remote or scientific on the other. These conceits might appear in the work of almost any poet during the first three quarters of the seventeenth century, so it is difficult to say precisely which poets were, or were not, Metaphysicals. It is easier to agree as to how far we consider that the 'metaphysical' element in a particular poem or poet is a merit or a defect. In Donne alone we feel it to be entirely integral to his way of thinking and writing. It is rarely a mere added extravagance, as with some of his later followers. Nevertheless, the Metaphysical habit of mind, which admitted intellect, wit, and even mere cleverness as additions to imagination and observation as part of the poetic faculty, was an essential characteristic of the seventeenth-century mind.

Of Donne's followers, as a religious poet, GEORGE HERBERT (1593–1633) is in some ways the least likely: the temper of his verse is quiet, and its mood contemplative. It is seldom dramatic, never hysterical. Yet in his diction, his rhythm and his frequent and often surprising conceits he was unmistakably a Metaphysical. He was born in Wales of a noble family and educated at Cambridge. It seems that he was intended for a political career, but worldly hopes were abandoned on the death of James I, and he took holy orders. He passed the last years of his short life as a humble Anglican priest in the parish of Bemerton in Wiltshire. His one hundred and sixty short religious poems appeared under the title of *The Temple* about the year of his death. Though we may not like the fantastic element in his poems, their homely and sometimes naïve conceits, we cannot but be moved by their sincerity, by the charity and sweetness of their tone, and by their grave and unaffected simplicity. When he composes a poem on Easter in the shape of a pair of wings, we are uncertain whether to smile at his naïveté or his ingenuity. But such extravagances are uncommon. Far more characteristic is the quiet naturalness of a poem such as *Redemption*, with its intimate and unaffected speech rhythm.

> Having been tenant long to a rich lord,
>   Not thriving, I resolved to be bold,
>   And make a suit unto him, to afford
> A new small-rented lease, and cancel th'old.
>
> In heaven at his manor I him sought;
>   They told me there that he was lately gone
>   About some land, which he had dearly bought
> Long since on earth, to take possession.
>
> I straight returned, and knowing his great birth,
>   Sought him accordingly in great resorts;
>   In cities, theatres, gardens, parks, and courts:
> At length I heard a ragged noise and mirth
>
> Of thieves and murderers: there I him espied,
> Who straight, *Your suit is granted*, said, and died.

RICHARD CRASHAW (1612–1649) was much more of the temper of Donne than of Herbert, though he was so much an admirer of the latter as to have called his volume of religious poems *Steps to the Temple* (1646).

He was born in London and educated at Charterhouse and Cambridge, where, reacting against his father's extreme Puritanism, he came under Roman Catholic influence. He went to Paris, joined the Church of Rome, and obtained a benefice in Italy, where he died. One at least of his secular poems, *Wishes to his Supposed Mistress*, is an anthology favourite, but his fame rests chiefly on his devotional lyrics, which at their best are un-surpassed. Nowhere perhaps outside the plays of Marlowe is to be found the note of sustained and rapturous ecstasy we hear in the address to Saint Teresa in *The Flaming Heart*.

O thou undaunted daughter of desires!
By all thy dower of lights and fires;
By all the eagle in thee, all the dove;
By all thy lives and deaths of love;
By thy large draughts of intellectual day,
And by thy thirsts of love more large than they;
By all thy brim-filled bowls of fierce desire;
By thy last morning's draught of liquid fire;
By the full kingdom of that final kiss
That seized thy parting soul and sealed thee his;
By all the heavens thou hast in him
(Fair sister of the Seraphim);
By all of HIM we have in THEE
Leave nothing of my SELF in me.
Let me so read thy life, that I
Unto all life of mine may die.

In Italy Crashaw came under the influence of Spanish and
Italian mystical writers; eighteenth-century critics who did
not understand the baroque convention, with its love of the
flamboyant, condemned what they considered Crashaw's extravagance and absurdity. Lifted out of their context and judged
by the standards of reason and good sense, the references to Saint
Mary Magdalene's tears in *The Weeper* are no doubt absurd. To
speak of a cherub sipping them so that his songs 'taste of this
breakfast all day long', and of angels bottling them to use as
wine, is to invite a charge of bathos; but in their context these
references have a certain naïve sincerity which is strictly in
harmony with the spirit of the poem as a whole. Those who make
fun of the sipping cherub and the bottled tears (after all, to name
a wine 'Lacrima Christi', as the Italians do, may be un-English
but it is not unpoetic) omit to quote those other beautiful lines
from the same poem:

> Does the night arise?
> Still thy tears do fall and fall.
> Does night lose her eyes?
> Still the fountain weeps for all.

Like Crashaw, HENRY VAUGHAN (1622–1695) was a disciple
of Herbert. He was born in Brecknockshire in Wales, and
remained all his life deeply attached to the scenes of his childhood. He was not a priest, but a Christian mystic dedicated to the

contemplation of life, death and eternity. His religious poems, published between 1650 and 1655 under the title of *Silex Scintillans* ('The Glittering Flint'), are less fantastic and more mystical than Herbert's. He writes, not in the rhetorical but in the familiar style, and is often able to convey the sense of surprise which comes from understatement.

> I saw Eternity the other night.

Vaughan drew upon nature for his imagery to a far greater extent than the other Metaphysicals, and it is his strength to be able, at his best, to combine a sense of the infinite with an awareness of the concrete and the immediate. In *The World of Light*, for instance, a comparatively homely image such as the following anchors his contemplation of eternity to the solid world of rural nature.

> He that hath found some fledged bird's nest may know
> At first sight if the bird be flown;
> But what fair well or grove he sings in now,
> That is to him unknown.

To Vaughan man was a restless and dissatisfied creature, moving uncertainly between the two eternities of infancy and death.

> Weighing the stedfastness and state
> Of some mean things which here below reside,
> Where birds, like watchful clocks, the noiseless date
> And intercourse of times divide,
> Where bees at night get home and hive, and flowers,
> Early as well as late,
> Rise with the sun and set in the same bowers;
>
> I would, said I, my God would give
> The staidness of these things to man! For these
> To His divine appointments ever cleave,
> And no new business breaks their peace;
> The birds nor sow nor reap, yet sup and dine,
> The flowers without clothes live,
> Yet Solomon was never dressed so fine.

His poems tend now and again to flatness and monotony, but at their best they derive a peculiar charm and dignity from

Vaughan's familiarity with nature and with the English Bible.

Religiously akin to both Herbert and Vaughan, though more important, perhaps, in the history of mysticism than in that of poetry, is THOMAS TRAHERNE (born about 1633). When his poms were discovered at the end of the nineteenth century it was at first thought, in fact, that they were unknown poems by Vaughan; they were not published until 1903. A country parson and then a chaplain, Traherne is most famous for his prose work, *Centuries of Meditations*, now recognised as central to the English mystical tradition. The lack of psychological conflict in Traherne, owing to his justly celebrated sweetness of character, makes him far less vital and absorbing a poet than Vaughan; nevertheless, his best poems compensate for this absence of stress by a quality of childlike ecstasy that equals Vaughan's in its intensity.

ANDREW MARVELL (1621–1678) has been called 'the only Puritan among the Metaphysicals'. But he was not really either a Puritan or a Metaphysical. Being a man of sense and integrity, he could not easily take sides in the struggle which divided the nation at the time of his maturity. Temperamentally he was no Puritan. As a poet, while he displays that combination of wit and passion which is the hall mark of the Metaphysicals, he was in point of style as much a Cavalier: his terse smoothness and regularity ally him rather with the school of Jonson than with that of Donne. Moreover, he was in the main a secular poet. In short, Marvell was a supremely good poet and, as such, defies classification.

Born in Yorkshire, he went to Hull Grammar School and Cambridge. After some years on the Continent he returned home and entered the service of the Roundhead commander Lord Fairfax as tutor to his daughter at Nun Appleton House. Up to this time he had had royalist sympathies, which were expressed in references to the execution of Charles I in 1649. During the Commonwealth he was associated directly with Cromwell and became Milton's assistant in the Latin secretaryship. He wrote poems in honour of Cromwell. He spent the years after the Restoration as a Member of Parliament for Hull, a violent pamphleteer, and a satirist of outspoken and independent views.

The majority of his poems were not published until 1681, three years after his death.

Marvell's best work is small in quantity and superlative in quality. Everybody admires, without reservation, a handful of lyrics – *Bermudas*, *To his Coy Mistress*, *The Definition of Love* and *The Garden*. These, and a number of others almost equally good, were written during the brief two or three years of his stay at Nun Appleton in Yorkshire. This sudden and short-lived flowering of a lyrical genius so consummate is one of the most extraordinary phenomena of English poetry. We may try to account for it by saying that the beauty and tranquillity of Marvell's situation combined with the excitement of the great crisis in national affairs to produce a state of heightened sensibility. Moreover, the middle of the seventeenth century was a period of high poetic excellence in which no single figure dominated. But Marvell's lyric achievement remains unique and unaccountable.

> How vainly men themselves amaze
> To win the palm, the oak or bays,
> And their uncessant labours see
> Crowned from some single herb or tree,
> Whose short and narrow-vergèd shade
> Does prudently their toils upbraid;
> While all the flowers and trees do close
> To weave the garlands of repose!. . . .
>
> No white nor red was ever seen
> So amorous as this lovely green.
> Fond lovers, cruel as their flame,
> Cut in these trees their mistress' name:
> Little, alas! they know or heed
> How far these beauties hers exceed!
> Fair trees! wheresoe'er your barks I wound,
> No name shall but your own be found.

In form, in diction, in the neatness and smoothness of its iambic couplets, *The Garden* might have been written by almost any seventeenth-century poet of the school of Jonson; but in its thought it is pure Marvell and could have been written by no one else. Wit without ostentation, charm without prettiness, learning without pedantry, controlled passion and rhythmical subtlety – it is the fusion of these qualities which constitutes Marvell's especial contribution to poetry. However often these poems are quoted, they have the capacity, reserved only to the very best, of remaining untarnished.

In contrast to Marvell, ABRAHAM COWLEY (1618–1667) is the type of the poet who belongs essentially, not to literature itself, but to literary history. In other words, since his poetry went out of favour within fifty years of his death few have read it for pleasure, though his influence can be traced at least as far as the later Romantic movement.

Cowley was born in London and educated at Westminster and Trinity College, Cambridge. He was a scholar and wit of extreme precocity. His first poems were published when he was fourteen. During the Commonwealth he went abroad to escape the effects of his anti-Puritan views, but after the Restoration he returned home to enjoy a period of relative tranquillity. The great popularity of his verse during his lifetime and for a generation after it is due to his being in so many respects a man of his age. Until Milton took his place, he was generally regarded as the greatest English poet since Shakespeare. When we read his poems now, we find this hard to believe; but the very qualities which gave him his exaggerated reputation are those which, when his age was past, are seen to be ephemeral.

Cowley had a varied and facile talent. His well-turned lyrics in regular stanza form look back to Jonson; his early Metaphysical poems were of their time and reflect his admiration for Crashaw; his unfinished sacred epic in four books, *Davideis*, anticipates Milton in theme, and the heroic couplet in form; his interest in science (he was the friend of scientists and helped to found the Royal Society), and his ability to write easy, graceful prose; his preference for the temperate virtues rather than passion and enthusiasm; his intellectual coldness when compared with, say, Donne and Crashaw – all these make him the ideally typical representative of the spirit of the age. The Restoration was an age of transition when, tiring of the stress and turbulence of their youth, mature men were feeling out towards moderation in religion, compromise in politics and the triumph of reason, tolerance and good sense over extravagance, violence and conflict. That age had not come by the time Cowley died, but it was on the way; looking at him in perspective, we can see Cowley as one of its heralds. Hence his extraordinarily high reputation.

His *Davideis* was not especially popular: the age was not quite ready for sacred epic, of which in any case it was a singularly poor example, nor the heroic couplet, at which Cowley did not excel. His really important contribution to poetry, and that which earned him his chief fame, was his development of the Pindaric Ode. This was a rhetorical address, of medium length, to some person or to the personification of an abstraction such as 'Liberty' or 'Solitude', in rhymed stanzas and lines of assorted lengths, in imitation of the style of the Greek poet Pindar.

> Say, for you saw us, ye immortal lights,
> How oft unwearied have we spent the nights,
> Till the Ledean stars, so famed for love,
>   Wondered at us from above!
> We spent them not in toys, in lusts, or wine;
>   But search of deep philosophy,
>   Wit, eloquence, and poetry –
> Arts which I loved, for they, my friend, were thine
>
> Ye fields of Cambridge, our dear Cambridge, say
> Have ye not seen us walking every day?
> Was there a tree about which did not know
>   The love betwixt us two?
> Henceforth, ye gentle trees, for ever fade;
>   Or your sad branches thicker join
>   And into darksome shades combine,
> Dark as the grave wherein my friend is laid!

These lines from the ode *On the Death of Mr William Hervey*, the discoverer of the circulation of the blood, show Cowley at his best, and are rather too good to be called quite characteristic. They are more personal in feeling and less rhetorical in diction than most seventeenth-century odes. But a critic who happened to be unfamiliar with them might well take them to be of a much later date than 1657; and they remind us, like a pre-echo of the nineteenth century, that the tradition initiated by Cowley reached forward through the lofty and splendid public odes of Dryden, the turgid failures of Swift, and the meditations of Gray and Collins, to the great romantic odes of Wordsworth and Coleridge, Shelley and Keats. We would have to go to much less happy examples of Cowley's art to be reminded of the hundreds of inflated and bombastic effusions which also passed as odes during the century and a half which followed his death.

CHAPTER SEVEN

The Seventeenth Century

2. Jacobean and Caroline Lyrists; Milton

BEFORE the arrival of Milton on the scene there was no major non-dramatic poet after Spenser and Donne. We have to consider a host of minor poets who reached a generally high standard of excellence in form, but had nothing very original to say. To mention everyone of the Jacobean and Caroline lyrists (often called Cavaliers) with a claim on our attention would be to merely compile a catalogue. It would be more profitable to direct attention to any standard anthology of the minor poets of the seventeenth century. For present purposes it will be best to say something of their general characteristics, and then to illustrate the work of some representative individuals.

I have described these poets as 'Spenserian', to distinguish their form and manner from the harsher and more irregular style of Donne and his followers. They believed that verse should please by its melody, rather than startle by its oddity. Nevertheless, in some respects the school of Jonson represented a reaction against Spenser, especially in the sources of their inspiration. They ceased to draw upon Italian poetry for their models, preferring the Greek and Roman classics. They wrote love poems, epigrams and satires; and these were inspired, not by Petrarch but by Horace, Martial and the Greek Anthology. Their poems reflected not so much the fresh spontaneity of nature as the ingenuity of wit and craftsmanship. With an Elizabethan lyric, we admire what is done – with a Jacobean or Caroline, we admire the way it is done. Nevertheless, the two schools represent stages in a single tradition – the English tradition of *amour courtois* which, transplanted from the soil of Provence, first took shape in the medieval love lyric. In the seventeenth century the long tradition went to seed; and in the cynicism, frivolity and sexual realism of the Restoration the tradition died. Romantic love poetry had to be re-born a century later. At the beginning of the decline the poems of Herrick, Suckling, Lovelace and the rest may strike us as passionless, but they are extremely civilised. This is partly because they were trying to preserve a way of life which, consciously or unconsciously, they felt to be vanishing – that of a propertied aristocracy centred on the Court, which held its authority by divine right.

BEN JONSON (1572–1637), the most influential writer of Jacobean times, was educated at Westminster, and for a time joined his stepfather in the bricklaying trade. His early twenties were spent with the army in Flanders. In 1597 he joined a London theatrical company and became in time a leading dramatist and a writer of Court masques. In 1616 he was made, in effect though not formally, the first Poet Laureate and granted a royal pension. He was the friend of many writers and enjoyed the patronage of the nobility. He was buried in Westminster Abbey, where the epitaph inscribed on his tomb – O RARE BEN JONSON – is a happy expression of the honour in which he was held. Although he was proud and contentious, his intellectual honesty gained him general esteem; his wit, his talents and his generous spirit made him the friend of younger poets, among them Herrick and Suckling, who came to be known as 'the sons of Ben'.

Apart from his influence on younger writers Jonson's principal importance derives from his plays; as a lyric poet he is remembered chiefly for a number of brief, exquisite pieces, some of them translated from Latin or Greek, some of them embedded in his masques and comedies. In the best of them there is a haunting delicacy of rhythm, and a formal neatness which springs, not from the mere love of neatness, but from a deliberate cultivation of the classical virtues of economy and compression.

> Follow a shadow, it still flies you;
>   Seem to fly it, it will pursue:
> So court a mistress, she denies you;
>   Let her alone, she will court you.
> Say, are not women truly then
> Styled but the shadows of us men?
>
> At morn and even, shades are longest;
>   At noon they are or short or none:

So men at weakest, they are strongest,
But grant us perfect, they're not known.
Say, are not women truly then
Styled but the shadows of us men?

Jonson was not only a poet; he was a critic·and an unofficial
arbiter of literary taste during the reigns of James I and Charles I.
He was a severe judge, but he knew how to censure without
carping, and to praise generously. He was one of the first to
proclaim the genius of Shakespeare. In the lines prefixed to the
first folio edition of 1623 he says of Shakespeare, 'He was not of an
age, but for all time'; and when he addresses him as 'soul of the
age', 'sweet swan of Avon' and 'thou star of poets', we feel that
these phrases are not the hyperboles of conventional dedication
but a sincere and judicious estimate of his dead friend's status in
world literature.

A slightly older contemporary of Jonson, THOMAS CAMPION
(1567–1620) might be classed with the Elizabethans, but he
belongs rather to the decadence of the tradition of *amour courtois*.
He went to Cambridge and then to Gray's Inn, published poems
and airs in the 1590's and Court masques in the reign of James I.
He was a classicist and wrote Latin poems. In spite of his views on
prosody, which were expressed in a treatise against rhyme, most
of the best of his one hundred and fifty short lyrics are in rhymed
stanzas, whose rhythmical variations are subtle and complex.
His delicately melancholy love poems seem to be almost passionless: it is as if all his emotions are purely verbal and musical.

Follow your saint, follow with accents sweet!
Haste you, sad notes, fall at her flying feet!
There, wrapped in cloud of sorrow, pity move,
And tell the ravisher of my soul I perish for her love:
But if she scorns my never-ceasing pain,
Then burst with sighing in her sight, and ne'er return again!

All that I sung still to her praise did tend;
Still she was first, still she my songs did end;
Yet she my love and music both doth fly,
The music that her echo is and beauty's sympathy:
Then let my notes pursue her scornful flight!
It shall suffice that they were breathed and died for her delight.

When we read this, or 'Follow thy fair sun, unhappy shadow',
or the wonderful sonnet 'When thou must home to shades of

underground', we are so charmed by their ascetic refinement of thought and form that we forget that all Campion's songs are technical experiments; but if technical experiments can be great poetry, the status of Campion is high.

Among the later Spenserians whose collective influence is important as a link between the Elizabethans and Milton were John Fletcher and William Browne of Tavistock. JOHN FLETCHER (1579–1625) was a prolific dramatist in the pastoral tradition, whose smooth and regular lyrics reveal much observation of nature and that love of the countryside which was one of the more attractive features of late Elizabethan patriotism. Here is the Satyr's song from his play *The Faithful Shepherdess*.

> See the day begins to break,
> And the light shoots like a streak
> Of subtle fire, the wind blows cold,
> Whilst the morning doth unfold;
> Now the birds begin to rouse,
> And the squirrel from the boughs
> Leaps to get him nuts and fruit;
> The early lark, that erst was mute,
> Carols to the rising day
> Many a note and many a lay.

Writing of this kind can easily degenerate into prettiness and insipidity. These were the faults of much of the verse of WILLIAM BROWNE (?1591–1645), whose *Britannia's Pastorals*, a long and discursive poem in the tradition of Drayton's *Polyolbion*, is of uneven quality but considerable descriptive and documentary interest. Among Browne's finest lyrics is his Sirens' song from *The Inner Temple Masque*.

> Steer, hither steer your wingèd pines,
>   All beaten mariners!
> Here lie love's undiscovered mines,
>   A prey to passengers;
> Perfumes far sweeter than the best
> Which make the Phoenix' urn and nest.
>   Fear not your ships,
> Nor any to oppose you save our lips,
>   But come on shore,
> Where no joy dies till love hath gotten more.
>
> For swelling waves our panting breasts,
>   Where never storms arise,

Exchange; and be awhile our guests:
   For stars, gaze on our eyes.
The compass love shall hourly sing
And as he goes about the ring
    We will not miss
To tell each point he nameth with a kiss.

Of the personal life of ROBERT HERRICK (1591–1674), the best of the 'sons of Ben', very little is known, though his poems give us an unusually intimate sense of the man, or at least of his tastes and temperament. He was born in London, the son of a city goldsmith, and this fact has often been adduced to account for the lapidary character of his poems, many of which are intricate and finely wrought miniatures. He may have been at Westminster School and was certainly at St John's College, and afterwards Trinity Hall, Cambridge. In London he sat at the feet of Ben Jonson and began to write lyrics which surpassed those of his master. Some of these were circulated in manuscript. In later life he looked back nostalgically to the literary and convivial gatherings of this period. He took holy orders, and in 1629 was presented to the living of Dean Prior on the edge of Dartmoor. Here he took upon himself the rôle of a Horatian scholar-gentleman among the savages, and retained his cheerfulness and good humour by writing exquisite love poems to a bevy of unidentified Julias, Antheas and Corinnas, as well as obscene epigrams on his bumpkin neighbours. It is possible that his *amours* were purely hypothetical; according to his own avowal, 'his life was chaste'. There is no record of his ever having married. He was an ardent Royalist, and was ejected from his living on the triumph of the Puritans in 1647. During the Commonwealth he was in Westminster and was restored to his Devonshire living in 1662.

Herrick's one book, comprising his *Noble Numbers*, or religious poems, and the secular *Hesperides*, appeared in 1648 and was a failure. The ruin of the Royalist cause and the decline in the vogue for Jonsonian lyrics are sufficient to account for this failure. Herrick was forgotten for nearly a hundred and fifty years; his revival during the Romantic period and the growing popularity of some of his pieces throughout the nineteenth and the beginning of the twentieth centuries were due, in part, to a misunderstanding of the real character of his poetry. The epithets 'delightful' and 'charming' are inseparable from the criticism of Herrick; and on the strength of a dozen or so lyrics such as *Gather ye Rosebuds*, *To Anthea who may command him anything*, *To Daffodils* and *Upon Julia's Clothes*, he has been typed as a roguish old clergyman with a nose for flowers. A reading of the *Hesperides* as a whole indicates that he is worth taking more seriously.

Hesperides – 'Songs of the West' – consists of about 1,200 poems, mostly very short, some mere epigrams and squibs of a couple of lines. Many of these could certainly be dispensed with, yet as a whole the book has a serious and coherent purpose. It opens with a dedication to Charles, Prince of Wales, and continues with a statement of the 'argument' of the book, that is, a summary of its contents.

> I sing of brooks, of blossoms, birds and bowers:
> Of April, May, of June, and July flowers.
> I sing of maypoles, hock-carts, wassails, wakes,
> Of bridegrooms, brides, and of their bridal cakes.
> I write of youth, of love, and have access
> By these to sing of cleanly-wantonness.
> I sing of dews, of rains, and piece by piece
> Of balm, of oil, of spice and ambergris.
> I sing of time's trans-shifting; and I write
> How roses first came red, and lilies white.
> I write of groves, of twilights, and I sing
> The court of Mab, and of the fairy King.
> I write of hell; I sing, and ever shall,
> Of heaven, and hope to have it after all.

Then follow some lines to his Muse, urging her to stay at home and dwell among the simple pleasures of the country. Next, after some short pieces to the reader, he indicates the proper occasions for reading poetry.

> In sober mornings do not thou rehearse
> The holy incantation of a verse;
> But when that men have both well drunk and fed,
> Let my enchantments then be sung or read.

The remainder of *Hesperides* consists of hundreds of skilfully turned lyrics celebrating the matter set forth in the prefatory lines. Herrick was a believer in the classical view of poetry, which he derived from the Latin poets, Catullus, Ovid, Horace, Martial. The poet was a receiver of divine inspiration; his function, as conceived by Herrick for himself, was to celebrate the immemorial ritual of country life, with its roots far back in pagan custom, and to pay homage to the natural head of the social order, the sovereign by divine right and representative of God on earth. The way of life for which Herrick stood was doomed; the social order of an agricultural community based on a balance between Christian and pagan elements could not survive the attacks of the Puritans allied with the new merchant class which made its wealth in the towns. The Church, as it had evolved during its one thousand years' connection with Rome, had more or less successfully absorbed the pagan seasonal rites and customs; but the Puritans were waging a successful war, under the name of anti-Popery, upon all survivals of pagan practice. As a traditionalist Herrick loved these survivals, and some of his best poems are hymns in their honour.

Corinna's Going a-Maying, one of his longest pieces, is a fusion of the classical philosophy of *carpe diem* and a love of the English May-rites, expressed in verse of Spenserian sweetness with overtones of nostalgia for a passing order.

> There's not a budding boy or girl this day
> But is got up and gone to bring in May.
>> A deal of youth, ere this, is come
>> Back, and with white-thorn laden home.
>> Some have despatched their cakes and cream,
>> Before that we have left to dream:
> And some have wept and wooed and plighted troth
> And chose their priest ere we can cast off sloth:
>> Many a green gown has been given,
>> Many a kiss, both odd and even:
>> Many a glance, too, has been sent
>> From out the eye, love's firmament:
> Many a jest told of the key's betraying
> This night, and locks picked: yet y'are not a-maying.
>
> Come, let us go, while we are in our prime
> And take the harmless folly of the time:
>> We shall grow old apace and die
>> Before we know our liberty.
>> Our life is short, and our days run
>> As fast away as does the sun.

And, as a vapour or a drop of rain,
Once lost, can ne'er be found again,
  So when or you or I are made
  A fable, song, or fleeting shade,
  All love, all liking, all delight
  Lies drowned with us in endless night.
Then, while time serves, and we are but decaying,
Come, my Corinna, come, let's go a-maying.

Of the host of minor Royalist, or Cavalier, poets the best
are THOMAS CAREW (pronounced 'Cary': ?1590–?1639),
RICHARD LOVELACE (1618–1658), and SIR JOHN SUCKLING
(1609–1642). Carew was the devotee both of Jonson and of
Donne; on the latter he wrote an enthusiastic elegy.

      But the flame
Of thy brave soul, that shot such heat and light
As burnt our earth and made our darkness bright,
Committed holy rapes upon our will,
Did through the eye the melting heart distil,
And the deep knowledge of dark truths so teach
As sense might judge what fancy could not reach,
Must be desired for ever. So the fire
That fills with spirit and heat the Delphic choir,
Which kindled first by thy Promethean breath,
Glowed here a while, lies quenched now in thy death.
The Muses' garden, with pedantic weeds
O'erspread, was purged by thee: the lazy seeds
Of servile imitation thrown away;
And fresh invention planted, thou didst pay
The debts of our penurious bankrupt age;
Licentious thefts, that make poetic rage
A mimic fury, when our souls must be
Possessed or with Anacreon's extasy
Or Pindar's, not their own.

This is excellent criticism, pointing as it does, first to Donne's
imaginative power as a Metaphysical poet, and then to his
originality.

Lovelace – wealthy, handsome, ruined in the Royalist cause,
twice imprisoned, dying in abject poverty – loved extravagant wit
and paradox, and achieved immortality with two epigrams:

    I could not love thee, dear, so much
    Loved I not honour more

and

> Stone walls do not a prison make,
> Nor iron bars a cage.

A finer poem than either of these two – to Lucasta and to Althea – is the less well-known *To Gratiana Dancing and Singing*, where the same love of extravagant metaphor is shown in such lines as

> The floor lay paved with broken hearts.

Suckling, equally the Cavalier of legend, became a leader in the King's forces, fled to France, and was said to have committed suicide in Paris. He was a dramatist, but he is remembered chiefly for his witty and sparkling lyrics. A fundamentally serious and sane attitude to love is disguised as careless frivolity. His *Ballad upon a Wedding*, too long to quote, must be read in full. It describes with relish and actuality a London wedding as seen by a countryman, and in its tender and healthy sensuality it is an implied, but never explicit, protest against the Puritan way of life, which was gradually superseding the best of what the Cavaliers stood for, especially the 'cleanly-wantonness' which delighted Herrick.

It is instructive to compare Suckling's *Ballad* with Spenser's *Epithalamion* of a mere fifty years earlier. Admittedly, the purpose of the two poems was different; at the same time they represent a change in poetic temper in accordance with the changed spirit of the times. Both are excellent poems, but while Spenser's expresses a lofty Platonic idealism, Suckling's is rooted in the humorous but earthy realism of the country attitude to love. It was in order to voice this attitude that Suckling, himself a courtier, put his account of a wedding into the mouth of a peasant. These two attitudes are in no way opposed; like the two sides of a coin, they are complementary. But whereas Spenser represents the English tradition of love-poetry at its zenith, with Suckling it is on the decline. It has felt the chill of repressive Puritanism, and it will never be the same again. After the Civil War and the Commonwealth, Restoration poets took up the theme where the Cavaliers had left it, and found that it had gone stale. Men might still enjoy themselves, but not without self-consciousness; love became sex, mirth became bawdry, chivalry became a modish and rapacious gallantry. Romantic love was dead; the tradition of *amour courtois* had run its course. Men and women might behave much as they had done before, but their mental outlook, as reflected by the poets, had undergone an absolute change. After the Restoration there was no more romantic love poetry for over a century. It is significant that the writer who, in the minds of literary historians of the eighteenth and nineteenth centuries, bestrode the seventeenth century like a colossus was the first major English poet to write no love poems. He was also the first great Puritan poet. Milton's anti-romanticism has not always been noticed, but it is of critical importance.

JOHN MILTON (1608–1674) was born in London, the descendant of an Oxfordshire family. His father, a money-scrivener,[1] was a man of artistic and musical tastes who had quarrelled with his family because of his Puritan sympathies. He encouraged his son in a discipline of plain living and high thinking, the reward of which was to be a career of supreme distinction. John went to St Paul's School and Christ's College Cambridge, where he was noticed for his almost effeminate good looks and his dislike of subjection to his superiors. On attaining his degree, he joined his father at Horton in Buckinghamshire. Here he continued to study and to prepare himself for the destiny to which he believed himself elected. It was at Horton that he wrote the best known of his early poems, the ode *On the Morning of Christ's Nativity*, *L'Allegro* and *Il Penseroso*. These, together with his masque of *Comus*, are the principal constituents of the group of early poems which he completed before his Italian tour in 1638–1640. They represent a conscious preparation for the great English epic which Milton projected during the years at Horton. For he determined, in his middle twenties, that the destiny intended for him was to create some great poetic monument which would place England on equal terms with Greece, Rome and Italy in the world's literature. It was for this that he took no regular employment, but remained quietly with his parents in the country, reading the English poets, especially Chaucer, Spenser and Shakespeare, the Greek and Roman authors, and books of theology and religious controversy.

The earliest of his poems to receive universal approbation is

[1] A profession whose functions are now absorbed into those of solicitor and banker.

the *Nativity Ode* (1629), a work of sustained rapture and fervent religious adoration, whose rhythm and verse-structure are adapted from the mellifluous style of Spenser, but already with a characteristic and unmistakably Miltonic accent.

In *L'Allegro* and *Il Penseroso* (1632) Milton describes the pleasures first of cheerfulness and secondly of melancholy. They celebrate with charm and grace the pleasures of life in the country and in academic solitude, and they represent two moods which must at times have been in conflict in the mind of the young Milton. Both contain much learning, introduced with a light touch; they have been among the best known of the longer English lyrical poems from the seventeenth century till the present day. Undoubtedly they reveal the same superb ear which had conceived the music of the Nativity Ode, but there is less originality. Milton was a man of wide reading, and his ear was responsive to all the melodies and tones of earlier poets in the Spenserian tradition. The octosyllabic couplet had been a favourite measure in the Elizabethan period, notably with Nicholas Breton, the Fletchers, and Shakespeare in *A Midsummer Night's Dream*. There are also echoes from such lesser poets as William Browne of Tavistock. *Il Penseroso* was the amplification of a dramatic lyric by John Fletcher, 'Hence, all you vain delights.' It was natural that in his apprentice work Milton should make a synthesis of various elements to be found in the favourite poems of the period, and it is the skilful artifice with which the synthesis was effected that is the most remarkable feature of the two poems.

In 1634 Milton composed *Comus*, a masque to be performed in honour of the Earl of Bridgwater at Ludlow Castle. It is a curious medley of lyrical and dramatic elements, and contains Milton's first efforts at sustained argument in blank verse. The songs are charming, and some of the descriptive passages have the freshness and musical grace we should expect. Milton had no dramatic power, and his theme is of the slightest. It is in effect a reasoned defence of chastity, reflecting Milton's Puritan outlook and the almost obsessive interest in this subject which he exhibited as a young man.

Lycidas (1637) completes the list of the longer poems of Milton's first period. It was written as a contribution to a number of elegies by Cambridge men on a young poet, Edward

King, drowned in the Irish Sea. For the pastoralism of his treatment Milton returns to Spenser, and it is clear that the
artificiality of this convention made it unsuitable for the expression of sincere grief. But there is no denying the splendour of
Milton's rhetoric, and his absolute command over the musical
and evocative qualities of the language.

> Ay me! Whilst thee the shores and sounding seas
> Wash far away, where'er thy bones are hurled,
> Whether beyond the stormy Hebrides,
> Where thou perhaps under the whelming tide
> Visit'st the bottom of the monstrous world;
> Or whether thou to our moist vows denied,
> Sleepst by the fable of Bellerus old,
> Where the great vision of the guarded mount
> Looks toward Namancos and Bayona's hold;
> Look homeward, angel, now, and melt with ruth,
> And, O ye dolphins, waft the hapless youth.

Nevertheless, *Lycidas* is a cold poem. It is no elegy on a dead
fellow poet, but the expression of Milton's own overmastering
egotism. For of all the great English poets (including even
Wordsworth, like Milton a sublime egotist), only he could have
used such an occasion as an expression of the fear that he too
might suffer the fate of King, thus by implication depriving the
world of the supreme masterpiece he was destined to create.

It is on this point of his egotism that one's response to the
young Milton must turn. Judged by ordinary standards of
human character, Milton was a prig. Few of even the most
ardent admirers of his poetry have been able to deny this. The
Puritans in whose ideas Milton was nurtured believed in the
virtues of self-discipline, self-sufficiency and self-importance.
His father encouraged him to regard himself as above the
common herd. It is probable that a natural tendency in youth to
enjoy the pleasures of normal human intercourse and the life of
instinct was severely and deliberately repressed. Puritans were
taught to consider the repression of natural instincts as in itself
virtuous. They came to look upon themselves as reserved for a
more than common destiny. Milton's priggishness is therefore
understandable, and most of his admirers consider his poetic
achievement a sufficient justification for it. For more than two
centuries he has been regarded as among the two or three

greatest, if not the greatest, of England's non-dramatic poets, and the judgement of time has forgiven him his unattractive personal character. As long as the poems remain supreme, the personality does not matter. If, however, there is reason to believe that even the greatest of his poetry is defective, then it is legitimate to regard its defects as being connected with Milton's defects as a man. Whatever the beauties of his early poems, it must be admitted that there is a certain coldness and artificiality, a sense of reserve, of unwillingness to be emotionally involved in life in a way which might threaten the supremacy of the ego. Much more attractive than the better-known poems is the early sonnet 'O Nightingale, that on yon bloomy spray', which reveals true humility. Curiously revealing, also, are some lines to Shakespeare written when Milton was only twenty. What he admired in Shakespeare was, above all, his spontaneity:

> To the shame of slow-endeavouring art
> Thy easy numbers flow.

Again, in *L'Allegro* he speaks of

> Sweetest Shakespeare, fancy's child,
> Warbl[ing] his native woodnotes wild.

The later reference, it is true, is more patronising, as if Milton no longer admitted Shakespeare's absolute supremacy. But it reflects the same regard for the earlier poet's natural and spontaneous melody. Now it is possible that Milton felt himself to be deficient in this all-important quality; possibly he identified his own efforts with 'slow-endeavouring art'. If so, then he must have come to regard a poem as a deliberate artefact, achieved by sheer will-power and technical skill. Those who hold the same view of poetry have no difficulty in regarding *Paradise Lost* as an outstanding masterpiece, and a triumph of will against enormous difficulties.

After *Lycidas* Milton went abroad, spending the greater part of two years in Italy, and in 1640 he returned to settle in London, where he took up the position of a tutor to his nephews and to other pupils. He wrote no poems except sonnets during the twenty turbulent years of the Civil War and the Commonwealth. He used the greater part of his energies pamphleteering in various causes – the legalisation of divorce, the freedom of the press, and the reform of the Church. He became Latin secretary to Oliver Cromwell. The sonnets he wrote during this phase are important because they re-establish the Petrarchan form, as against the Shakespearean, and they establish the sonnet as an appropriate form for occasional pieces of a topical and personal character. It was the Miltonic form of the sonnet which was revived by Coleridge, Wordsworth and Keats.

In 1643 Milton married his first wife, Marie Powell, the seventeen-year-old daughter of a Cavalier family in Oxfordshire. To Milton she appeared hopelessly frivolous, as the Puritan schoolmaster must have appeared to her unbearably domineering and self-important. She left him after a few weeks, but in 1645 she returned to him, repentant; she died in 1652, leaving him three daughters. In the same year Milton went blind. In 1656 he married a second wife, the 'late espousèd saint' of the sonnet, but she died two years later. At the Restoration in 1660 he expected to be molested for his pro-Cromwell activities, but he was left alone to devote himself at last to his *magnum opus*. *Paradise Lost* was written between 1656 and 1663, but was not published until 1667, after London had recovered from the Plague and the Great Fire. He published *Samson Agonistes* and *Paradise Regained* in 1671. In 1663 he married a third wife, and in 1674 he died, and was buried at St Giles, Cripplegate.

Paradise Lost was first published in ten books, and then revised and re-published in twelve. The great Protestant religious epic which Milton had designed to be the crown of his life's work made its way slowly into public favour. The age into which it was born was not especially propitious for a poem of this character, but its very impressiveness and grandeur made themselves felt, and it was not long before it was established in the canon of English poetry in a place inferior to that of no other work outside the theatre. Its merits have been questioned by reputable critics in the present century, and its place is not as secure as it was a hundred years ago. On the whole, however, Milton must be regarded as the most influential poet, apart from Shakespeare and possibly Spenser, during the whole of the eighteenth and nineteenth centuries.

The twelve books of *Paradise Lost* contain in reality two separate narratives: the first is that of the fall of Satan from his place in Heaven as an angel subordinate to God. After their unsuccessful rebellion Satan, Moloch, Beelzebub, Belial, Mammon and a vast multitude of minor angels are hurled over the walls of Heaven, to take possession of the gloomy and painful tracts of Hell. The lines describing their fall are among the grandest and most impressive in the whole poem.

> Him the Almighty Power
> Hurled headlong flaming from the ethereal sky,
> With hideous ruin and combustion, down
> To bottomless perdition, there to dwell
> In adamantine chains and penal fire,
> Who durst defy the Omnipotent to arms.
>   Nine times the space that measures day and night
> To mortal men, he, with his horrid crew,
> Lay vanquished, rolling in the fiery gulf
> Confounded, though immortal.

It does not matter that the language is artificial, and that the phrase 'adamantine chains' is borrowed from Spenser.[1] The very unnaturalness of the diction, its lofty magniloquence, and above all its sheer rhythmic impetus are admirably suited to the description of something which by its nature is purely imaginary. Milton is venturing to put into words what none had ever seen, and what had never before been described in English.

At the very outset Milton announces his intention of doing 'Things unattempted yet in prose or rime', and for this purpose he appeals to the 'Heavenly Muse' of the Old Testament writers. His ambition is no less than to 'justify the ways of God to men'; it has often been pointed out that Milton in no way achieves this end. The reader is not persuaded by the end of the poem that God is just; and many readers, including poets such as Blake and Shelley, who took Milton's supremacy for granted, have remarked on the way in which Satan is, at any rate during the first two books, the hero of the poem. Indeed, Satan's heroism is the one feature of the poem where we feel Milton to have been writing entirely from his heart; it is evident that this figure held for him a compulsive fascination which he could not altogether control. Evidently he felt himself to be temperamentally sympathetic to a character who symbolised the spirit of rebellion. At all events, it is Satan who evokes the most splendid lines in the epic.

[1] *Hymn in Honour of Love*, line 89.

The second narrative deals with the more specifically Christian aspect of the fall of man: the temptation of Adam and Eve, their expulsion from Paradise for disobedience to God's will, and Christ's intercession for mankind. This latter narrative calls for much less dramatic treatment and for far more theological speculation. Versified theology makes dull reading, and most readers agree in finding the latter part of *Paradise Lost* less interesting than the beginning. Moreover, Milton's views on the relations between husband and wife do not make his picture of the domestic life of Adam and Eve attractive. It is perhaps the sensuous delights of Paradise itself which call forth Milton's finest skill as a descriptive poet.

Paradise Regained, in four books, is concerned with the temptation of Christ in the wilderness, since to Milton it was through Christ's successful resistance that mankind won back what had been lost by Adam's failure.

The poem has little of the splendour of the longer epic, and the tempter, Satan, has sadly shrunk in stature. It shows rather Milton as a master of reasoned exposition in blank verse. This may not be the ideal medium for controversy, but none has used it more persuasively.

> They err who count it glorious to subdue
> By conquest far and wide, to overrun
> Large countries, and in field great battles win,
> Great cities by assault. What do these worthies
> But rob and spoil, burn, slaughter, and enslave
> Peaceable nations, neighbouring or remote,
> Made captive, yet deserving freedom more
> Than those their conquerors, who leave behind
> Nothing but ruin wheresoe'er they rove,
> And all the flourishing works of peace destroy;
> Then swell with pride, and must be titled Gods,
> Great Benefactors of mankind, Deliverers,
> Worshipped with temple, priest, and sacrifice?

Samson Agonistes has found greater favour. In the form of a Greek tragedy, though not intended for the stage, it tells the story of the final phase in the life of Samson. Undoubtedly Milton identified himself with the blind hero in the hands of the Philistines, and he is personally concerned with Samson's successful revenge. No doubt also, in the account of Samson's betrayal by the seductive and frivolous Dalila, Milton was thinking of his own disastrous first marriage to Marie Powell.

This final image of himself as a lonely, blind and struggling hero among the Philistines of a debauched and worldly Restoration has impressed itself upon later criticism. In the nineteenth century, for instance, Matthew Arnold praised Milton for his lofty, neo-classical style, which he regarded as a bulwark against the vulgarity, the philistinism he so much deplored. It is indeed on this question of Milton's style that recent controversy has turned. He forged for himself a highly personal idiom based partly on his previous reading of English poetry and partly on a close familiarity with the Latin tongue. That this style is bookish, studied and intensely idiosyncratic cannot be denied. But these are the very qualities which have recommended it to countless readers during the past two and a half centuries, especially those of a literary turn of mind. Milton is, *par excellence*, the poet of the academic world, which delights in his verse for the melodious flow of its long, sustained paragraphs, for its classical allusions, and for what Arnold termed its 'high-seriousness'. No poet ever succeeded in forging from such diverse and intractable materials a style more sonorous and beguiling. In doing so, he imposed his will upon the language of poetry, and achieved an influence hardly second even to that of Shakespeare. But this achievement had its price. Milton banished, from his own and from much of the most admired English poetry after his time, the natural rhythm of common speech. There is very little in the whole body of his poems which sounds like the direct utterance of spontaneous feeling; while throughout the century which followed his death the style of 'official' English poetry was hardening into an artificial idiom divorced from natural speech, sincere poetic feeling was obliged to discover for itself new directions and re-discover forms and accents overlooked by Milton and his imitators.

CHAPTER EIGHT

The Age of Satire 1660-1745

THE temper of the age in which Milton spent his later years was very different from that into which he had been born. The political and social tensions of the time and the violence through which men had lived had had a hardening effect upon their sensibilities. Cromwell's despotism had made the Puritan rule universally unpopular, and the Restoration of the monarchy under Charles II was hailed with grateful relief throughout the nation, especially in London, the centre both of court life and of literature. A spirit of hard-headed and self-seeking rivalry invaded the literary world. The sense of chivalry which had proved so disastrous to the fortunes of the Royalist poets was replaced by an attitude of realism, and even of cynicism. The gentlemen-poets who thronged the extravagant and pleasure-loving court of Charles II at Whitehall in search of patronage had inherited the smooth, neat, epigrammatic manner of the Cavaliers, but not their warmth and ardour. Sir Charles Sedley and Charles Sackville, Earl of Dorset, were the authors of a number of light and graceful songs; and the Earl of Rochester, in his lyrics and satires, combined brutal cynicism with wit and good sense. With him, as with the other Restoration song-writers, love was sex. The conventions of *amour courtois* were turned inside out, and the mistress was not so much a goddess as an animal. The only inviolable marriage was between wit and bawdry. The opening stanzas of Rochester's amusing lampoon on Charles II are characteristic of Rochester and the whole courtly school.

> Chaste, pious, prudent, Charles the Second,
>   The miracle of thy Restoration
> May like to that of quails be reckoned
>   Rained on the Israelitish nation;
> The wished-for blessing from Heaven sent
> Became their curse and punishment.

The virtues in thee, Charles, inherent,
  Although thy countenance be an odd-piece,
Proves thee as true a God's vicegerent
  As e'er was Harry with the codpiece:
For chastity and pious deeds
His grandsire Harry, Charles exceeds.

Our Romish bondage-breaker Harry
  Espoused half a dozen wives;
Charles only one resolved to marry
  And other men's he never strives.
Yet hath he sons and daughters more
Than e'er had Harry by threescore.

Wit and good sense were indeed the distinguishing marks of
the literature of this period, and they all but killed poetry. The
age was opposed to idealism, enthusiasm, extravagance, the
inspired frenzy which had once been taken for granted as of the
essence of poetry. Yet some of the poets of the time, notably
Dryden, desired consciously to preserve the heroic strain in
English poetry. How were they to do this when the heroic
temper, except in the mind of Milton, had perished in the Civil
War and the Protectorate? How was the old Spenserian
magnanimity to be regarded by a generation which derived its
philosophy from the self-regarding materialism of Hobbes?
Dryden's response to this problem was the epic satire; Pope's
was the mock-heroic. Since heroic love was no longer possible
(Dryden reduced it to an absurdity in *All for Love*), heroic hate
might replace it. The emotional element in poetry took the form
of a hatred which, with Dryden, had about it something noble,
and with Pope deteriorated into a sick man's malice. There was,
about the satirical spirit of the age, something purely negative
and destructive; its positive effect, indirect though it was, lay in
helping towards the establishment of that attitude of tolerant
good sense and humane materialism which characterised British
politics in the eighteenth and nineteenth centuries.

A very popular work during the last decades of the
seventeenth century was Samuel Butler's *Hudibras*, a poem of
10,000 octosyllabic lines which appeared in 1662–3 and 1678.
This is a grotesque and crudely composed attack on the Parlia-
mentary party, and especially on religious enthusiasts with
Puritan leanings. It is a strange rigmarole with a certain

Skeltonic impetuosity, abundance of invention and uncon-
ventionality of form. Butler ridicules extravagance of all kinds,
including the excesses of Metaphysical imagery to be found in
contemporaries such as Cowley.

> The sun had long since in the lap
> Of Thetis taken out his nap,
> And like a lobster boiled, the morn
> From black to red began to turn,
> When Hudibras, whom thoughts and aching
> 'Twixt sleeping kept all night and waking,
> Began to rouse his drowsy eyes
> And from his couch prepared to rise.

Of all the writers who pushed and scrambled for patronage
during the Restoration period, however, by far the most eminent
was JOHN DRYDEN (1631–1700). He dominated his age as no
poet had done before, achieving during his lifetime something
like the esteem accorded to Chaucer during the century after
his death, and more influence than even Ben Jonson during
Jacobean and Caroline times. He was the first English poet to
live almost wholly by his pen, and during the period of his working life this involved considerable adaptability and compromise.
We are accustomed to think of a writer as writing for the public –
in effect, the middle classes. No such thing was possible in the
seventeenth century. Writers were obliged to court the favour of
men of power, influence and usually title, by flattering odes and
dedications. This would secure for their works the attention of
the reading public, who were mainly upper class. It would also
secure for the poet, if he was fortunate, a position of dependence
in the household of a patron, to whom he might become
secretary, tutor or chaplain. It was not until the eighteenth
century that writers could appeal substantially to a wider
audience, and so gradually achieve independence from
patronage. Addison, during the reign of Queen Anne, was one
of the first to deliberately write for a new middle class. The age
of Dryden was one of intense political controversy and intrigue,
and writers became identified with one or other of the two great
political parties. It was at this time that political, religious and
social differences decisively hardened into the division between
Whigs and Tories which dominated British politics for over two

centuries. During a literary life of over forty years Dryden maintained his position and earned a livelihood by trimming his sails
to the prevailing wind. The necessity for doing this gradually
engendered in him a profound contempt for politics, and it may
have been responsible also for a certain coldness and insincerity in
his work, which has been read with admiratión but never with
affection.

He was born in 1631 of a Northamptonshire family with
Puritan leanings. He was educated at Westminster and Trinity
College, Cambridge. During the Protectorate he supported
Cromwell, after whose death he published, in 1659, a set of
'heroic stanzas'. The following year he published *Astraea Redux*,
'A Poem on the Happy Restoration and Return of His Sacred
Majesty Charles the Second'. It was in this poem that Dryden,
whose early work had been in the Metaphysical style, first
adopted the heroic couplet as his medium of expression. This is a
series of iambic pentameters rhymed in pairs and having a
consciously balanced and antithetical character. Chaucer had of
course used rhymed iambic pentameters, and many writers
between him and Dryden had written, as it were by chance,
couplets which could be called 'heroic'. But the term is properly
reserved for the form perfected by Dryden and adopted by Pope
and his imitators in the following century. Dryden himself
admitted the influence of Sir John Denham and Edmund
Waller, who are usually accorded a place in the literary histories
on this account. Waller had certainly written heroic couplets at
an early date, and Denham's four charming lines to the River
Thames in *Cooper's Hill* may serve as a prototype, and as a
statement of the prosodic ideals of the period.

> O could I flow like thee, and make thy stream
> My great example, as it is my theme!
> Though deep yet clear; though gentle yet not dull;
> Strong without rage, without o'erflowing full.

It was Dryden's adoption of the heroic couplet, however, as
his principal, if not exclusive, medium that gave it its supremacy
at least until the death of Pope. The effect of this on the course of
poetry was decisive.

It is interesting that Dryden's *Annus Mirabilis*, a patriotic piece
with a fulsome dedication to the City of London, should appear

in 1667, the same year as *Paradise Lost*. Of these two very different poems there is no doubt that Dryden's was the more 'contemporary' in form and spirit. In it, however, Dryden temporarily forsook the couplet and adopted what later came to be known as 'Gray's Elegy metre'.

Dryden was always under the necessity of writing for a livelihood, and much of his abundant energy went into the composition of heroic tragedies and licentious artificial comedies. He was not a very good dramatist, and himself conceded the field to Congreve, in which time has endorsed his judgement. As a man of the theatre he was immortalised as Bayes in the Duke of Buckingham's witty burlesque, *The Rehearsal*. For this, Dryden got back at him by portraying him as Zimri in *Absalom and Achitophel*. In 1670 his pre-eminence in the 'establishment' was signalised by his appointment as Poet Laureate. He was the first to be formally so appointed. In 1681 he wrote the first part of his great satire, *Absalom and Achitophel*, in which Monmouth is depicted as the misguided Absalom and the Earl of Shaftesbury as Achitophel. It achieved immediate popularity as the finest political satire which had yet appeared in English. The famous satirical portrait gallery shows Dryden in his best vein. There is something heroic – if only mock-heroic – about these caricatures, in which Dryden rises above pettiness and personal spite and achieves a sort of grandeur in ridicule.

> Of these the false Achitophel was first:
> A name to all succeeding ages curst.
> For close designs and crooked counsels fit;
> Sagacious, bold, and turbulent of wit:
> Restless, unfixed in principles and place;
> In power unpleas'd, impatient of disgrace.
> A fiery soul, which working out its way,
> Fretted the pigmy body to decay:
> And o'er informed the tenement of clay.
> A daring pilot in extremity;
> Pleas'd with the danger when the waves went high
> He sought the storms; but, for a calm unfit,
> Would steer too nigh the sands to boast his wit.

So begins the cartoon of Shaftesbury. Dryden has been said to lack warmth; yet he is not without passion, if political ardour may be called passionate.

Of the same quality, though narrower in range, is *MacFlecknoe* (1682), an attack on the rival poet and dramatist, Thomas Shadwell, a supporter of the Whigs. Here again, though the description of Shadwell as chief among the sons of Dulness is caricature, it is great caricature by virtue of Dryden's technical mastery of the medium. Dulness, King of Nonsense, speaks thus:

> Shadwell alone my perfect image bears,
> Mature in dulness from his tender years;
> Shadwell alone of all my sons is he
> Who stands confirmed in full stupidity.
> The rest to some faint meaning make pretence,
> But Shadwell never deviates into sense.
> Some beams of wit on other souls may fall,
> Strike through and make a lucid interval;
> But Shadwell's genuine night admits no ray,
> His rising fogs prevail upon the day.

In 1682 Dryden also published *Religio Laici* in support of the Anglican Church; but in 1685 he was converted to Roman Catholicism and two years later produced *The Hind and the Panther*, a long defence of the Church of Rome, allegorised as 'a milk-white hind, immortal and unchanged'. These two didactic works are serious attempts to versify theology, and show Dryden's power to sustain an argument in heroic couplets. But apart from some imaginative flights *The Hind and the Panther* remains as unattractive as the theological books of *Paradise Lost*.

Apart from these major works Dryden showed his versatility by composing, not only many graceful songs in the late Cavalier tradition, which he incorporated in his plays, but also elegies and epitaphs, prologues and epilogues, epistles and commendatory verses, and the two fine odes in the Pindaric manner, *St Cecilia's Day* and *Alexander's Feast*. These have gained him the reputation of being the best lyrical poet of the period. The last decade of his life was largely occupied in making copious translations from the Greek and Latin. It became Dryden's aim to raise the dignity of English literature by bringing it into conformity with classical standards. His critical work, which falls outside the scope of this book, reveals him consciously attempting to re-mould English prose; it is to his credit, and perhaps a greater title to fame than anything he did as a poet, that he was the first to achieve a distinctively modern prose style. There had been poets in other times who had written well, or at any rate effectively, in prose – Shakespeare, Sidney, Jonson, Milton; but little that was done before Dryden's later phase gave promise of the harvest soon to be reaped in this field.

Dryden's life was a hard struggle to maintain himself and the dignity of poetry, according to his lights, in an essentially un-poetic age. Here is how, in his sixty-second year, he summed up his life's work.[1]

> 'Tis a vanity common to all writers to over-value their own pro-ductions; and 'tis better for me to own this failing in myself than the world to do it for me. For what other reason have I spent my life in so unprofitable a study? Why am I grown old in seeking so barren a reward as fame! The same parts and application which have made me a poet might have raised me to any honours of the gown, which are often given to men of as little learning and less honesty than myself. No government has ever been, or ever can be, wherein time-servers and blockheads will not be uppermost. The persons are only changed, but the same jugglings in state, the same hypocrisy in religion, the same self-interest and mis-management will remain for ever. Blood and money will be lavished in all ages, only for the preferment of new faces with old consciences. There is too often a jaundice in the eyes of great men; they see not those whom they raise in the same colours with other men. All whom they affect look golden to them; when the gilding is only in their own distempered sight. These considerations have given me a kind of contempt for those who have risen by unworthy ways. I am not ashamed to be little when I see them so infamously great. Neither do I know why the name of poet should be dishonourable to me, if I am truly one, as I hope I am; for I will never do anything that shall dishonour it.

He died in 1700, and was buried in Westminster Abbey. He had lived long enough to see the opening of a new century. One of his last works was the libretto for *The Secular Masque*, in which he writes with terse and humorous contempt the epitaph on his times. Momus, the spirit of mockery, addresses first Diana, goddess of hunting; then Mars, god of war; and then Venus, goddess of love.

> All, all of a piece throughout:
>   Thy chase had a beast in view;
> Thy wars brought nothing about;
>   Thy lovers were all untrue.
> 'Tis well an old age is out,
>   And time to begin a new.

[1] Dedication to the *Examen Poeticum*, 1693.

Never has an age been more tellingly epitomised.

It is in the seventeenth century that we can first note a marked cleavage between formality and familiarity of style in verse. The familiar style gained in favour partly as a reaction against the grand style of Cowley, Dryden and others, partly also by infection from the more familiar and relaxed character of prose after the Restoration. The familiar poets of the Augustan age have, on the whole, been underrated by critics, who would rather see a poet in the bardic mantle than in his shirt-sleeves. This is what Scott meant when he said that Swift was deficient in sublimity. But there was little in the age of Swift to inspire a sense of the sublime.

There was, on the other hand, much to encourage the development of what is called *vers de société* – relaxed, colloquial poetry which sounds like conversation between friends, and whose lightness of tone and touch does not necessarily imply superficiality or frivolity.

One of the best of the Augustans to make poetry out of good sense and good humour, rather than spleen and malice, was MATTHEW PRIOR (1664–1721). His good sense occasionally verged on insipidity, and his good humour sometimes lapsed into sentimentality. But if we are not looking for the sublime, Prior is one of the most readable poets of his day, with the gift of making what he does supremely well sound supremely easy.

JOHN GAY (1685–1732), the friend of Swift and Pope, is remembered as the author of *The Beggar's Opera*, which, in our own day, after two hundred years has regained the popular success it enjoyed when first performed in 1728. In the sparkling lyrics, so perfectly wedded to popular melodies, Gay showed himself to be the heir to all the song-writers from Tudor times to the Restoration.

The most considerable poet in the familiar style during this period was JONATHAN SWIFT (1667–1745). Three circumstances have combined to bring about the general neglect of Swift as a poet. After the eighteenth century he was found too coarse for middle-class taste; he was, moreover, deficient in sublimity – his was indeed the poetry of a thoroughly earthy realism; lastly, Swift's reputation as the greatest of English prose satirists has thrown his verse into the shade. Yet he was the most productive poet of his age, even including Pope if the translations from Homer are omitted. Most of it is informal, lucid, natural, and rhythmically expressive. Only its subject matter is often of small interest to modern readers. Swift began as a writer of florid and bombastic Pindarics. On reading them, Dryden, to whom he was related, said: 'Cousin Swift, you will never be a poet.' Whether or not this helped to persuade Swift to radically alter his style, he did so with admirable results. Adopting the Hudibrastic couplet as his principal form, he turned out easy, fluent and ironic verses for the rest of his life, especially after his fiftieth year. Among the best are *On Poetry: a Rhapsody*, *Mrs Frances Harris's Petition*, and the superb *Verses on the Death of Dr Swift* (1731). Like Suckling's *Ballad* this loses its effect, which is a cumulative one, if quoted in part; it must be read as a whole. It was part of Swift's success that he had an instinctive understanding of the proper provinces of prose and verse. Being a master of prose, he was able to use it for purposes of argument, exposition and controversy. He was thus able to reserve verse, on the whole, for appropriate occasions. His great contemporary Pope, on the other hand, had no talent for prose, and used verse as the medium for subjects better treated in prose – theology and ethics, among others. Swift was the master of the informal style, Pope of the formal.

ALEXANDER POPE (1688–1744) was born in London, the son of a Roman Catholic linen-draper. His Catholicism was important, because it prevented his ever taking a public appointment, as he might otherwise have done. Even more important was the chronic ill-health and physical disfigurement which followed a serious illness at the age of twelve. His education was irregular and indifferent. These three circumstances combined to determine the course of his life. He was left free to devote all his time to literature. His restless intelligence developed precociously; and his diseased body produced in him a sense of injury which later grew into a persecution mania. Moreover, his incapacity for normal physical pleasure, while it enfeebled his visual and sensory imagination, must have nourished in him the desire to excel in intellectual pursuits. There is about his work as a whole that sense of strain which comes from a perpetual compulsion to over-compensate for some basic deficiency or privation.

One of his basic deficiencies was in creative imagination. He had little originality. On the other hand, he had a voracious appetite for books, a prodigious memory, and a sensitive ear for the musical and rhetorical qualities of language. His early preceptors encouraged him to imitate the classics, especially Virgil, and to aim at what was called 'correctness' – that is, perspicuity and aptness of phrasing combined with metrical smoothness and regularity. The young Pope determined, by sheer application combined with his natural gifts, to shine as the master of a correct and classical style.

In 1709, at the age of twenty-one, he published his *Pastorals*, which he said he wrote at sixteen. All such statements coming from Pope are unreliable. Once their essential unreality, their bookish and derivative character is accepted, the *Pastorals* are charming.

> Resound, ye hills, resound my mournful lay!
> Beneath yon poplar oft we passed the day,
> Oft on the rind I carved her amorous vows,
> While she with garlands hung the bending boughs:
> The garlands fade, the vows are worn away;
> So dies her love, and so my hopes decay.

There is about this a vein of elegiac melancholy which, though the language may in part be borrowed, reveals romantic undertones in Pope's nature. These undertones were gradually to be all but silenced by the harsher music of his later writing. The romantic strain was not often heard again.

Windsor Forest, which was published four years later, contains pleasant descriptive writing in the same manner; but although it appealed to many critics on account of its political implications, it represented something of a blind alley in Pope's own development. It is worth noting that the artificial diction which was so widely imitated by his followers, and for which he was so severely censured by later critics, is a feature of this early work, and is steadily replaced by a more direct vocabulary as his art matures. The periphrases – 'the scaly breed' for 'fish', and 'fleecy care' for 'sheep' – are a feature of *Windsor Forest* and the *Pastorals*, not of the later satirical writings.

Meanwhile, in 1712 Pope published *An Essay on Criticism*, his own *ars poetica* in the tradition of Horace and Boileau. In this he begins to show the penchant for didacticism and moralising which later had more portentous results. It is a witty and lively per-

formance, and contains much good sense of a superficial kind.
Pope had already decisively elected to adopt the heroic couplet
of Dryden as his all but exclusive medium, and the *Essay on
Criticism* demonstrates how readily it lends itself to the framing of
moral tags and maxims.

> A little learning is a dang'rous thing;
> Drink deep, or taste not the Pierian spring:

and

> True wit is nature to advantage dressed,
> What oft was thought, but ne'er so well expressed.

Pope set himself to refine and perfect the couplet which
offered a workable alternative to the prosodic uncertainty that
had prevailed until the time of Dryden, and still to some extent
persisted. He made this instrument his own in a unique manner;
at the same time, he was in another sense only polishing and
strengthening the bars of a prison. What the couplet was capable
of at its best, he demonstrated in his own mature work; but there
were whole areas of experience from which the addiction to such
a limited and restrictive medium would exclude any poet,
however ingenious. About such an addiction there is something
narrow and even vulgar, since serious thought is inevitably
degraded into a kind of nutshell wisdom.

> For forms of government let fools contest:
> Whate'er is best administered is best.

A comparison between the flexibility of Homer's hexameters
and the mincing movement of the heroic couplet would have
convinced anyone not committed to the two irreconcilable
notions of the supremacy of the ancients and of the superiority of
the heroic couplet over other English verse forms, of the absurdity
of rendering the *Iliad* and the *Odyssey* in such a medium. Pope
began the publication of his translations from Homer in 1715;
and such was the essential vulgarity of Augustan taste, however
comme il faut it might be on the surface, that they were regarded
during his lifetime as his principal title to fame. They brought
him in a small fortune which enabled him to retreat in comparative affluence to Twickenham for the rest of his life.

To modern readers the most undoubted success of this early

period is *The Rape of the Lock* (1712), a mock-heroic account of a society quarrel. Readers have at all times delighted in the vivacity and sparkle of this exquisite *tour de force*. It reveals two things – Pope's absolute mastery of his medium, and his growing misogyny. It is true that he merely mocks his Belinda, and does not flay her in the manner of his later treatment of Lady Mary Wortley Montagu and other women. But the germs of his maturer attitude are there. Nevertheless, full credit must be given for the astonishing virtuosity of this performance by a young man of twenty-four. It was perhaps Pope's most original poem. As for the mock-heroic as a literary type, it is evident that this was to be Pope's solution to the problem first encountered by Dryden: how was poetry to find heroic themes, as it had always done hitherto, in an anti-heroic age? Pope and his friends became involved in politics more closely even than Dryden. They identified themselves with the Tory interest, and became the intimates and counsellors of the most influential statesmen of the day. With the fall of the Tories and the triumph of the house of Hanover in 1714, their influence was at an end. They consoled themselves by satirising their political and literary enemies, the apostles of Dulness.

The Rape of the Lock contains a proportion of mock-Homer; the translations of the *Iliad* and the *Odyssey* contain more; and the famous conclusion to *The Dunciad*, sometimes regarded as the crown of Pope's achievement, is mock-Milton.

It is interesting to notice how deftly and simply Pope converts the heroic couplet to the uses of the mock-heroic attitude.

> Close by those meads for ever crowned with flowers
> Where Thames with pride surveys his rising towers
> There stands a structure of majestic frame
> Which from the neighb'ring Hampton takes its name.
> Here Britain's statesman oft the fall foredoom
> Of foreign tyrants, and of nymphs at home;
> Here thou, great Anna! whom three realms obey,
> Dost sometimes counsel take – and sometimes tea.
>   Hither the heroes and the nymphs resort
> To taste awhile the pleasures of a Court;
> In various talk th'instructive hours they past,
> Who gave the ball or paid the visit last:
> One speaks the glory of the British queen,
> And one describes a charming Indian screen;

> A third interprets motions, looks and eyes;
> At ev'ry word a reputation dies.
> Snuff or the fan supply each pause of chat,
> With singing, laughing, ogling, and all that.
>   Meanwhile declining from the noon of day
> The sun obliquely shoots his burning ray;
> The hungry judges soon the sentence sign,
> And wretches hang that jurymen may dine;
> The merchant from th'Exchange returns in peace,
> And the long labours of the toilet cease.

The deflatory effect of this depends solely on one trick well known to comic writers in all ages, the trick of bathos; Pope's skill is shown in the subtle and manifold ways in which he varies the device.

In 1725 he published an edition of Shakespeare, an undertaking for which he was not well equipped. His errors were advertised by the scholar Lewis Theobald, who was accordingly chosen as the hero of *The Dunciad*, in which Pope pillories his poetical rivals and critics. The idea of this satire on Dulness is borrowed directly from Dryden's *MacFlecknoe*, and it is crammed with malicious portraits in the manner of Dryden's Shadwell. *The Dunciad* first appeared in 1728; in a later, expanded edition Colley Cibber replaced Theobald as hero. It is a tasteless though amusing work and must have afforded Pope infinite satisfaction. In such lines as those against Avidien (Wortley Montagu) the reader is spell-bound at the precision of the technique and shocked at the ignoble end it serves.

> Avidien, or his wife (no matter which,
> For him you'll call a dog, and her a bitch),
> Sell their presented partridges and fruits
> And humbly live on rabbits and on roots:
> One half-pint bottle serves them both to dine,
> And is at once their vinegar and wine.
> But on some lucky day (as when they found
> A lost bank-bill, or heard their son was drown'd),
> At such a feast, old vinegar to spare,
> Is what two souls so generous cannot bear:
> Oil, though it stink, they drop by drop impart,
> But souse the cabbage with a bounteous heart.

Pope's final phase as arbiter of taste and moral preceptor to his age began with an *Essay on Man* and the *Moral Essays* (1733–34), and continued with the *Imitations of Horace*, including such things as the familiar epistles to Arbuthnot and to Augustus, the latter a brilliantly ironical address to George II. As a heroic coupleteer, as a malicious misanthropist, Pope continued in this last phase to coruscate with undiminished virtuosity. Once he had decided that his rôle in society was to be the great hater, he could bend his whole intellect to practising the keenest satirical art ever perfected by an English poet. As the guardian of virtue and the Christian philosopher, he is neither original nor truthful. The accents of conscious rectitude are only tolerable when they are sincere.

'Ask you what provocation I have had?' Pope says to the unnamed 'Friend' of the dialogue entitled *Seventeen Hundred and Thirty-Eight*, and answers himself:

> The strong antipathy of good to bad.
> When truth or virtue an affront endures,
> Th'affront is mine, my friend, and should be yours.
> Mine, as a foe profess'd to false pretence,
> Who think a coxcomb's honour like his sense;
> Mine, as a friend to ev'ry worthy mind;
> And mine as man, who feel for all mankind.

Literary and political controversy was a dangerous game in the Augustan age, and it was played with the weapons of personal slander and ridicule; Pope had played it with zest and with an unrivalled technique. But the note of self-exculpation which is heard in much of his later writing sounds rather like the voice of an uneasy conscience, or at least of a fundamental self-doubt. It is always alleged in Pope's favour that he was generous in compliments to his friends. Undoubtedly his compliments were magnificently phrased; and if this is a virtue, it cannot be denied to Pope.

This is an unsympathetic but not unjust account of a poet who has aroused more controversy and inspired more contradictory criticism than any other. Equally reasonable critics have on the one hand accorded him almost unqualified praise and on the other denied him the right to be called a poet at all. This can only be because of temperamental affinity or dyspathy between poet and reader. The truth is that Pope was a complicated man, and his varied achievements are very unequal in quality. No simple judgement can be passed on either the man or his writing. The defence of Pope rests on admiration for his brilliance as the greatest English classical poet and his supremacy over all others of his kind, on account of which are to be excused the defects of character which were accentuated by disease and the savage temper of the age. Dislike of Pope springs from a temperamental antipathy to a character which displays such a morbid vanity, such jealousy and suspicion, such dishonesty, and such delight in sheer malice. Pope had great gifts, but he misused them. One cannot help wondering whether most of what he laboured so diligently to do was worth doing. Undoubtedly many of his now forgotten enemies were worthy of the scorn and spite he poured upon them. But as literature do the results make good reading? We would be more willing to applaud Pope as the champion of reason and virtue against stupidity and vice if he did not, so constantly and obsessively, proclaim himself such. His case is curiously like that of Milton. Both poets felt themselves set apart at an early age for some important destiny; both were gifted with great verbal and prosodic skill, without abundant creative imagination and originality; both read the work of their immediate predecessors with close attention and adapted for themselves a personal style out of hints and borrowings; both were disappointed men with a grievance against society; both were consumed by ambition to excel and the lover of power; both were vain, both suffered from serious physical defects, and both were misogynists who ended as misanthropists and built their final works upon a foundation of revenge for disappointed hopes; finally, both put a stamp on the poetry of future times which was not easily effaced. Milton, however, had no wit, but Pope had it in abundance. Milton had a sense of grandeur, which he expressed in the form of a heroic epic. Pope had only a sense of the pettiness of society, and his pose of standing outside it on a lonely eminence was sheer humbug. He was as deeply committed to the social rat-race as anyone, and he was bitterly hurt by it. He does indeed stand outside the contemporary ruck by virtue of being the greatest comic poet in English; if his admirers would admit this, without making more extravagant claims, they and his detractors would have less to quarrel about.

There was, indeed, a different Pope, who had once been outside the scramble; but this part of his nature – the melancholy, retiring and romantic part – had been suppressed. After all, his first surviving poem, said to have been written at about the age of

twelve, is the *Ode on Solitude*, with its advocacy of a quiet, un-
ambitious self-sufficiency.

> Blest, who can unconcern'dly find
> Hours, days, and years slide soft away,
> In health of body, peace of mind,
>   Quiet by day,
>
> Sound sleep by night; study and ease,
> Together mixt; sweet recreation:
> And innocence, which most does please
>   With meditation.
>
> Thus let me live, unseen, unknown,
> Thus unlamented let me die,
> Steal from the world, and not a stone
>   Tell where I lie.

True, the theme was not original; but in adapting it, Pope no
doubt expressed something in his own boyhood nature. This
romanticism broke out again on a few occasions, as in *Eloisa to
Abelard* and the *Elegy to the Memory of an Unfortunate Lady*. Had
there been more of this man, and less of the high priest of reason
and correctness, the poetry of the age would have been different.
As a harbinger of romanticism with a taste for the Gothic, Pope
was before his time. It is not easy to realise that that strange piece
of medievalism, *Eloisa to Abelard*, which for once it would be
mistaken to call 'mock', was written at least as early as 1717. It
implies an imaginative range and a power of suggestion far
beyond the usual compass of the heroic couplet.

> The darksome pines that o'er yon rocks reclined
> Wave high, and murmur to the hollow wind,
> The wand'ring streams that shine between the hills,
> The grots that echo to the tinkling rills,
> The dying gales that pant upon the trees,
> The lakes that quiver to the curling breeze;
> No more these scenes my meditation aid,
> Or lull to rest the visionary maid.
> But o'er the twilight groves and dusky caves,
> Long-sounding aisles and intermingled graves,
> Black melancholy sits, and round her throws
> A death-like silence, and a dread repose:
> Her gloomy presence saddens all the scene,
> Shades ev'ry flower and darkens ev'ry green,
> Deepens the murmur of the falling floods,
> And breathes a browner horror on the woods.

CHAPTER NINE

The Age of Prose 1725-1785

HISTORY is an account of the past, viewed from the present. It is therefore relative, since the standpoint is constantly changing; and it distorts the past because it inevitably anticipates. A historian looking back over the literature of the eighteenth century from the time of the triumph of Romanticism in 1798 is bound to view it in a different light from that in which it had appeared to one of the so-called forerunners of Romanticism fifty or sixty years earlier. Thomson, Gray and Collins are often referred to as if they knew they were pre-natal influences on a movement whose birth they did not live to see. It is better to try to view these poets as they appeared during their lifetime, and to assess their work for its intrinsic merits. For it must be admitted that, while the reaction against the eighteenth century has now lost much of its force, most readers still find its poetry less attractive than that of the Romantics; and that the renewed appeal of late Augustan poetry is rather to the critic and the scholar. The latter argue that we must not judge late Augustan poetry by the standards of Romanticism, and that it has its own peculiar attractions. This is true; yet the nineteenth-century view that eighteenth-century poetry is somehow 'un-poetic' compared with that of other periods has its justification. During the Renaissance poetry enjoyed a central and pre-eminent position in all European cultures. But in the seventeenth century it gradually lost this pre-eminence. Its slow and imperceptible decline corresponded with the rise and development of prose as a medium for imaginative literature. The history of the novel from Defoe to Scott is an illustration of this. In the fourteenth century Chaucer had written in verse certain tales which he would probably have written in prose had prose existed for this purpose. But in the seventeenth century writers such as Dryden, Defoe and Hobbes, and later Steele, Addison and Swift, perfected a prose which made it unnecessary, and even anachronistic, to use verse for narrative, philosophical and moralistic subjects. Reason, moderation, good sense, and the scientific outlook were the ideals of the eighteenth century; they require the existence of a perspicuous and flexible prose, but they are apt to produce dull poetry.

It might be said that poets were now free to concentrate on subjects especially suited to poetry. In a sense this is true; but the decline in aristocratic patronage of literature which followed the death of Queen Anne and the triumph of the Hanoverians,[1] threw writers back on the support of the booksellers and the new middle-class reading public. Johnson and Goldsmith were obliged to eke out their inadequate income from imaginative writing by doing a variety of hackwork.

With the death of Queen Anne there came also the end of the domination of the type of social or 'city' poetry which is noticeable during the age of satire. There was a reaction against this domination, and poets could give in to the urge to look more closely at nature and at their own feelings as individuals rather than as social animals. The vogue for the 'Ode to Solitude' during the early eighteenth century would make an interesting study. Pope's boyhood attempt has already been referred to, and we have seen how this side of Pope's nature was atrophied or suppressed. A much more fruitful expression of the same idea is to be found in *The Petition for an Absolute Retreat* by Anne Finch, Countess of Winchelsea, which appeared as early as 1713.

> Give me, O indulgent fate!
> Give me yet before I die
> A sweet but absolute retreat
> 'Mongst paths so lost and trees so high
> That the world may ne'er invade,
> Through such windings and such shade,
> My unshaken liberty.

The Countess was something of a pioneer of naturalism, though there is a good deal of Virgilian pastoralism mixed up with her genuine observation of nature. Nevertheless, her *Nocturnal Reverie*, of the same date, suggests the faithful realism of a later period. The Welshman, John Dyer, also is remembered

---

[1] George I's remark, 'I hate all boets and bainters,' might be taken as symptomatic of the attitude of the whole Whig aristocracy towards art for the next two centuries, and as a motto for British philistinism.

for his long descriptive poem, *Grongar Hill* (1726), which despite Miltonic echoes is closely in touch with rural nature.

But of all Pope's contemporaries the one who, without know-ing it, did most to counter his influence was the Scotsman JAMES THOMSON (1700–1748). His *Hymn on Solitude* (1729) connects his name with the vogue just referred to, but hardly shows him at his best. However, the notion that there is virtue, as well as contentment, to be found in solitude is significant.

> Hail, mildly pleasing solitude,
> Companion of the wise and good.

Thomson was born in Scotland, the son of a minister whose father had been a gardener. James studied for the ministry in Edinburgh, but gave up this course at the age of twenty-five and repaired to London to become a poet. His descriptive poem in blank verse on *Winter* (1726) was a success, and by 1730 he had written the three remaining books of *The Seasons*, which became one of the most popular of all eighteenth-century poems. It is a mixture of natural description based on personal observation; moral, religious and sentimental reflection; and descriptive reminiscences from works of travel and topography. It was the sort of book which accorded exactly with eighteenth-century middle-class taste. There was nothing embarrassingly personal or passionate, only a gently melancholy but charming – if at times bookish – appreciation of rural life, combined with meditations which could in no way outrage the sentiments of a commercial Whig public. Technically, two points about *The Seasons* are important. Written in blank verse, it offered to its imitators, of whom there were many, an alternative to the tyranny of the heroic couplet, and established Milton as a model for diction and structure. It also fostered that tendency to periphrasis and Latinism which endangered English verse style after the example of Milton and the early Pope. The following lines from *Spring* are fairly characteristic.

> The blackbird whistles from the thorny brake;
> The mellow bullfinch answers from the grove:
> Nor are the linnets, o'er the flowering furze
> Poured out profusely, silent. Joined to these
> Innumerous songsters, in the freshening shade
> Of new-spring leaves, their modulations mix
> Mellifluous.

Thomson's other popular poem was *The Castle of Indolence*, an allegorical poem in two cantos, closely modelled on Spenser. This may be now no more than a curiosity but, like nearly everything else about Thomson, it was a portent. Spenser had never fallen into neglect; but Thomson's elaborate pastiche, which has been called 'perhaps the most successful imitation in English literature', was symptomatic in three distinct ways: it marked a stage in the growth of the influence of Spenser as 'the poet's poet'; it exemplified the taste for the antique, and especially the mock-medieval as distinct from the Graeco-Roman, which became such an important feature of Georgian culture; and it revealed, although indirectly and under a disguise, the poet's enjoyment of day-dreaming, which was the very breeding-ground of the Romantic sensibility.

Thomson was the first Scottish writer of importance to emerge after the Act of Union in 1707. Much of his writing is inspired by British patriotism, of which the most ardent and best-known expression is his song, 'Rule, Britannia'. If his historical importance far outweighs his intrinsic interest for modern readers, that is due, in part at any rate, to the poetically unpropitious climate of Thomson's period.

The 1740's, which were the last years of Pope, Swift and Thomson, were a decade of voluminous, but to the modern reader not very rewarding, poetic production. This decade represents the aftermath of the Augustan movement, but it is too early to show much promise of a revival of sensibility. It shows the interest in solitude and nature which has already been noticed, combined with a habit of reflection on life in general. This encouraged the fashion for abstraction and personification which characterises the poetry of the mid-eighteenth century. It is perhaps no accident that the one line by which the Rev. Edward Young is now remembered is

Procrastination is the thief of time.

Young's *Night Thoughts*, a long poem in blank verse published between 1742 and 1745, won immediate popularity on account of its strain of gloomy soul-searching. Robert Blair's 800-line blank verse moralistic meditation, *The Grave* (1743), is in similar vein, and may be said to extract the Gothic elements from *Macbeth* for eighteenth-century readers.

In 1744 appeared the first edition of Dr Mark Akenside's *The Pleasures of Imagination,* later enlarged to four books in blank verse written under Miltonic influence. This is a typically discursive, moralistic-topographical work containing descriptive passages which show considerable powers of observation and a talent for smooth and harmonious blank verse. Akenside died in 1770, the year of Wordsworth's birth, and it is impossible to ignore the influence of such passages as the following from Book IV of *The Pleasures of Imagination* on Wordsworth's mature style.

> O ye Northumbrian shades which overlook
> The rocky pavement and the mossy falls
> Of solitary Wensbeck's limpid stream;
> How gladly I recall your well-known seats
> Beloved of old, and that delightful time
> When all alone, for many a summer's day,
> I wandered through your calm recesses, led
> In silence by some powerful hand unseen.
> Nor will I e'er forget you, nor shall e'er
> The graver tasks of manhood, or the advice
> Of vulgar wisdom, move me to disclaim
> Those studies which possessed me in the dawn
> Of life, and fixed the colour of my mind
> For every future year.[1]

A poet of the 1740's who reacted against Augustan didacticism was WILLIAM COLLINS (1721–1759). In 1747 he published his Odes, of which *To Evening, To Simplicity* and *How Sleep the Brave* are the best. Of his later poems the *Dirge in Cymbeline,* the *Ode on the Death of Thomson* and the unfinished *Ode on the Popular Superstitions of the Highlands of Scotland* are also good. Collins himself was a pathetic figure, the victim of a hypochondria which in the end sent him mad. Under the influence of his friend, Joseph Warton, whose odes were published together with his own, he believed in the importance of imagination as opposed to reason and in the example of Milton rather than Pope. It is evident that the figure of Lycidas, the drowned poet of Milton's elegy, had a fascination for Collins. His *Ode on the Death of Thomson,* whom he greatly admired, and the unrhymed *Ode to Evening* have a power of romantic suggestion and a delicate music almost entirely alien to the poetry of the period.

[1] I am indebted for this instance to the editor of *The Oxford Book of Eighteenth Century Verse,* D. Nichol Smith.

But when chill blust'ring winds, or driving rain,
Forbid my willing feet, be mine the hut
    That from the mountain side
    Views wilds and swelling floods,
And hamlets brown, and dim-discovered spires,
And hears their simple bell, and marks o'er all
    Thy dewy fingers draw
    The gradual dusky vale.

The *Ode to Evening* shows Collins' ability to make his personifications live, an ability in which he excelled all his contemporaries.

A similar fastidiousness of spirit is to be found in the best of THOMAS GRAY (1716–1771). Educated at Eton and Cambridge, Gray combined a retiring and scholarly temperament with an inbred emotional reserve. As a consequence of the popularity of his *Elegy written in a Country Churchard* (1750) he was offered but declined the Laureateship after the death of Cibber. He was appointed Professor of History at Cambridge but never delivered a lecture. He was a friend of Horace Walpole, the dilettante and connoisseur of Strawberry Hill, a mansion in the mock-Gothic style. Gray published the first of his odes in 1742, including that *On a Distant Prospect of Eton College*, which reflects the emotional atrophy, the sense of futility which had afflicted him ever since youth. This motif is again discernible in the *Elegy*, which Gray spent many years in polishing and correcting. This has appealed to generations of readers on grounds of both form and sentiment: the luminous melancholy of its diction and imagery, the tranquil solemnity of its cadences; and its chivalrous advocacy of the cause of the under-privileged. These sentiments cannot fail to appeal to any Englishman with a spark of radical feeling.

Gray has been underrated by critics despite – or perhaps because of – the popularity of the *Elegy*. As a Whig, he was attacked by Dr Johnson, a Tory, who had no patience with his reserved and over-sensitive nature. Gray believed in inspiration, an 'affectation' which the sturdy Doctor would have no truck with. 'He had a notion,' wrote Johnson, 'not very peculiar, that he could not write but at certain times, or at happy moments; a fantastic foppery to which my kindness for a man of learning and of virtue wishes him to have been superior.' This is a revealing exposure of the attitude of the age of prose towards poetic vocation. But Gray's reticence as a poet was based, not on purely personal grounds, but on the intellectual conviction of the difficulty of being a poet in his day. In his Pindaric ode *The Progress of Poesy* (1754) he recounts allegorically how the Pindaric or imaginative conception of poetry descended from Greece and Rome to England, where it expired with Dryden. Clearly he regarded the Augustanism of Pope as abortive. Gray's other Pindaric ode, *The Bard*, which has never been popular, but which has intellectual strength and integrity, is an attempt to express in concrete terms the belief that authority is the enemy of genius.

Possibly Gray's sense of frustration owed something to an awareness of having been born into an age of prose. The high priest of this age was Samuel Johnson, whose verse tract, *The Vanity of Human Wishes* (1749), was a belated attempt to continue the Augustan tradition. Its heroic couplets compare badly with Pope's, but the poem can still be read as an expression of Johnson's dignified pessimism. He is at his best in a later and less ambitious poem *On the Death of Mr Robert Levet, a practiser in physic.*

> Condemn'd to hope's delusive mine,
>   As on we toil from day to day,
> By sudden blasts or slow decline
>   Our social comforts drop away.
>
> Well tried through many a varying year,
>   See Levet to the grave descend;
> Officious, innocent, sincere,
>   Of every friendless name the friend.

These two opening stanzas show some of the merits and shortcomings of eighteenth-century occasional verse. Its compression of form and neatness of language represent the neo-Augustan couplet pruned of superfluities; but this very language, somewhat erudite and reminiscent of Latin, keeps the writer firmly based on the prose in which he was more at home. A contemporary example of poetry brought to the verge of the ridiculous by its cultivation of the prose virtues is George Bubb Dodington's famous *Ode* (1761), an epitome of certain aspects of the eighteenth century.

Love thy country, wish it well,
    Not with too intense a care,
'Tis enough that, when it fell,
    Thou its ruin didst not share . . .

Void of strong desire and fear,
    Life's wide ocean trust no more;
Strive thy little bark to steer
    With the tide, but near the shore . . .

Keep thy conscience from offence
    And tempestuous passions free,
So when thou art called from hence
    Easy shall thy passage be.

This is a characteristic expression of the prudential morality, half-sensible, half-cynical, preached by Lord Chesterfield; but poetry and the instinct of self-preservation do not live together.

A much better poet than Johnson, but still essentially a man of prose, was his friend OLIVER GOLDSMITH (1728–1774). This gentle, charming Irishman was educated at Trinity College, Dublin, and, after training as a doctor, spent some years abroad, but returned penniless, to take up the life of a literary hack in London. His varied output reflects his unsettled life and his tendency to drift from one place or occupation to another. He wrote miscellaneous prose works, including some graceful essays and many forgotten pages on history and politics. He achieved lasting popularity in three distinct fields – fiction, stage comedy, and moralistic verse. The Traveller (1764), a rambling, didactic poem based on his experiences abroad, has lost the popularity it attained on its first appearance; but The Deserted Village (1770) has remained a favourite. Written in heroic couplets on the Johnsonian, neo-Augustan model, it describes the spoliation of the countryside by rapacious landlords. Goldsmith undoubtedly attacks a very real social evil, that of enclosure, and his 'sweet Auburn, loveliest village' is under the shadow of the approaching industrial revolution; but it is tinged also with the golden after-glow of the lost happiness of youth. Goldsmith was the perennial wanderer, and the imaginary village he describes with such pathos is the archetypal 'home', the Ithaca or Hesperides, of the wanderer's return. Despite its didacticism and its sentimentality, The Deserted Village emerges as one of the most attractive poems of a singularly barren period.

> In all my wanderings round this world of care,
> In all my griefs – and God has given my share –
> I still had hopes my latest hours to crown,
> Amidst these humble bowers to lay me down;
> To husband out life's taper at the close,
> And keep the flame from wasting by repose.
> I still had hopes, for pride attends us still,
> Amidst the swains to show my book-learned skill,
> Around my fire an evening group to draw,
> And tell of all I felt and all I saw;
> And as an hare whom hounds and horns pursue
> Pants to the place from whence at first she flew,
> I still had hopes, my long vexations past,
> Here to return – and die at home at last.

Little has been said of the topographical and descriptive poetry of the eighteenth century, because not much space can be spared for minor writers; it has been indicated, however, that an important feature of poetic theory was that no subject was outside the range of verse, provided it was understood that the less obviously poetic the subject, the more poetic must be the language. We are accustomed nowadays to hear the cry, 'Poetry must deal with reality; it must concern itself directly with men's everyday interests'. Accordingly, in the 1930's a not very convinced attempt was made by a few poets to bring into their verse the physical manifestations of contemporary technology – express trains, aeroplanes and pylons. The well-meant futility of this might have been realised sooner had the poets considered the awful example of Erasmus Darwin, a much more determined modernist than they. Between 1789 and 1796 Darwin rendered the latest scientific doctrines in copious and florid heroic couplets. His *The Botanic Garden* makes excellent reading if it is not taken seriously, and affords a fitting epilogue to the history of Augustan poetry. In the second part of *The Botanic Garden*, published in 1792 as *The Economy of Vegetation*, Darwin makes a spirited attempt to poeticise the new discovery of steam power.

> Soon shall thy arm, unconquered steam! afar
> Drag the slow barge or drive the rapid car;
> Or on wide-waving wings expanded bear
> The flying-chariot through the fields of air.
> – Fair crews triumphant, leaning from above,
> Shall wave their fluttering kerchiefs as they move;
> Or warrior-bands alarm the gaping crowd,
> And armies shrink beneath the shadowy cloud.

A belated writer in the descriptive tradition of Goldsmith was the Aldeburgh clergyman, George Crabbe, whose poem in heroic couplets in the manner of Pope, *The Village*, appeared in 1783. But it was not until the early nineteenth century that Crabbe's best work was published – the verse narratives of *The Parish Register*, *The Borough*, and *Tales*. With faithful and unsparing realism he describes the lives of ordinary people, especially the poor and afflicted. His sombre truthfulness was highly regarded by discriminating critics in his own day, and has recently been the subject of renewed interest. Nevertheless, those who find Crabbe lacking in lyrical appeal and in the poetic virtues have some justification. Crabbe might have been a great novelist, but in his prime the novel had hardly yet become respectable; his wife discouraged his attempts at prose fiction, which were in consequence put on the fire.

A stream of purer poetry than any other in the eighteenth century flowed from a source not so far mentioned – the hymn. Ever since the development of a distinctively English church liturgy, whether by the Anglican or by the Nonconformist denominations, hymns have been a source of some excellent, and much bad poetry. Many seventeenth-century hymns were paraphrases of the Psalms, and the tradition of making metrical versions of parts of the scriptures for singing in church is a long and honourable one. The eighteenth century is the golden age of the English hymn. Isaac Watts, one of the first and best of the hymn writers, composed a fair amount of somewhat ridiculous homiletic verse for children, appropriately parodied by Lewis Carroll in *Alice*. But his *Psalms of David Imitated* (1719) contains dignified and workmanlike metrical versions. The finest of these, 'Our God, our help in ages past', has achieved unsurpassed popularity.

Charles Wesley, author of 'Jesus, lover of my soul', was a poet of greater emotional intensity. His *Psalms and Hymns* (1740) contains the fine *Morning Hymn*, 'Christ, whose glory fills the skies'. Mention should also be made of the Rev. Augustus Montague Toplady, the writer of 'Rock of ages cleft for me' (1776) and the Rev. John Newton, celebrated for 'How sweet the name of Jesus sounds' (1779), and for the baneful influence of his repressive evangelism on the mind of William Cowper.

But the greatest religious poem of the eighteenth century (unless we include some of Blake's lyrics) was Smart's *Song to David* (1763). CHRISTOPHER SMART (1722–1771) was born in Kent and educated at the expense of a wealthy Durham family. He went to Pembroke College, Cambridge, where he was elected to a fellowship. He soon became notorious for riotous living, and in 1749 he went to London to earn a living as a hack writer. He turned his hand to every kind of poem then fashionable – odes, epigrams, translations, fables, satires, complimentary addresses – and excelled at none of them. At about the age of thirty-four he was shut up in a madhouse; the cause of his mental disorder, which took a religious form, is obscure. On this subject Johnson said to Boswell, 'I did not think he ought to be shut up. His infirmities were not noxious to society. He insisted on people praying with him; and I'd as lief pray with Kit Smart as anyone else. Another charge was that he did not love clean linen; and I have no passion for it.'

After his release, Smart's constitutional instability continued, and in 1769 he was imprisoned for debt. He died two years later. His *Song to David* is a prolonged paean of praise for him who, as the supposed author of the Psalms, was the father of religious poetry. Its eighty-six stanzas are composed in a lofty yet simple style, using the diction and imagery of the Bible. They show no signs of insanity, unless religious exaltation and an almost total break with current poetical fashions is thought to have been insane in the 1760's.

> Strong is the lion – like a coal
> His eyeball – like a bastion's mole
>   His chest against the foes:
> Strong, the gier-eagle on his sail,
> Strong against tide, th'enormous whale
>   Emerges as he goes.
>
> But stronger still, in earth and air,
> And in the sea, the man of prayer,
>   And far beneath the tide;
> And in the seat to faith assigned,
> Where ask is have, where seek is find,
>   Where knock is open wide.

In an ironical and provocative essay, *The Name and Nature of Poetry*, A. E. Housman maintained that most of the true poetry of the eighteenth century was written by madmen. It is certainly a notable feature of the age of reason that creative power was so often accompanied by melancholia verging on insanity. WILLIAM COWPER (1731–1800) is connected with the foregoing group by his contribution to the Rev. John Newton's *Olney Hymns* (1779), of which the best known is his 'God moves in a mysterious way'. He wrote in order to keep depression from the door, and to dispel the shades of the asylum, where he had been kept for a time after an attempt at suicide. His mental instability has been ascribed to early bullying, but at Westminster he was happy enough. He was something of a social figure, and had connections with the aristocracy. His early poems were *vers de société* in the manner of Prior. He was called to the bar, but a professional career was prevented by the onset of mental disorder. His cure was accompanied by conversion to evangelical Christianity. After his brief but agitating association with the Calvinistic Newton, what was almost a second existence began for Cowper at the age of fifty – a simple, cheerful life in the country. Under the ministrations of the widowed Mary Unwin and other sympathetic gentlewomen, he became a prolific and versatile poet. Among his most popular pieces are *The Diverting History of John Gilpin*, *On the Loss of the Royal George*, and the lines suggested by the adventures of Alexander Selkirk, 'I am monarch of all I survey'. His *Table Talk* (1782) is an attempt at didactic satire in the tradition of Pope. His translation of Homer was not a success, but *The Task* (1785), a series of descriptive and moralistic reflections in six books of blank verse, achieved lasting popularity. Pleasant as much of it is for its pictures of rural and domestic life, *The Task* now seems tepid poetry. The fact is that to Cowper poetry, like tea, is a 'cup that cheers but not inebriates'. Despite his hypersensitive nature and his command of a plain and concrete verse style, Cowper was a man of prose. All the virtues of his verse – its familiarity, its humour, its eye for the immediate and telling detail, its somewhat apprehensive cheerfulness – are to be found to greater advantage in the beautiful prose of his letters. As a poet, however, Cowper is still remembered for the simple and touching verses *To Mary*, and for *The Castaway*. Mary Unwin's death in 1794 plunged him into the abyss of despair on the brink of which he had lived for so long.

CHAPTER TEN

Romanticism: The First Phase

1785-1810

> I thought of Chatterton, the marvellous boy,
> The sleepless soul that perished in his pride;
> Of him who walked in glory and in joy
> Following his plough, along the mountain-side:
> By our own spirits are we deified:
> We poets in our youth begin in gladness;
> But thereof come in the end despondency and madness.
> *(Resolution and Independence)*

WRITING at the age of thirty-two about Chatterton and Burns, Wordsworth was expressing the admiration which he and his circle felt for poets of an earlier generation whom they regarded as forerunners. These early Romantics – and we may add Blake, whom Wordsworth may or may not have read – were esteemed more highly, since the triumph of Romanticism, than their established contemporaries. While the Augustan tradition was running to seed in prose and didacticism, a new growth was springing up, unacknowledged by the age in general. Different as they are, these three poets have something in common – they were all of humble origin. The majority of the poets of the establishment from the Elizabethans to the late eighteenth century were educated at Public Schools and Oxford or Cambridge. It is no accident that the new spirit in poetry should draw some of its vitality from social classes which had hitherto made little direct contribution. It was as if the radicalism of Gray, and his prophetic vision of 'the youth to fortune and to fame unknown', was being fulfilled; and although the later Romantic poets were mostly from the educated classes, they no longer felt themselves to 'belong' socially. They regarded the kind of poetic ideal for which they stood as having no place in the established order. Poetry itself was thenceforward an exile from the social scheme.

Thomas Chatterton, who was born in 1752 of a Bristol schoolmaster, received a fair education as a boy and was articled to a lawyer. His interest in literature was inseparably and fatally connected with antiquarianism, a pursuit much in favour in the mid-eighteenth century. We have seen how Thomson went back to Spenser for inspiration, and how Gray drew on ancient Welsh history and legend. It was as if they were seeking an extension of eighteenth-century sensibility by exploring the past. The boy Chatterton discovered in himself a talent for medieval penmanship and a real insight into the atmosphere and language of the fifteenth century. When he was twelve or thirteen, he began to write fake medieval ballads which were passed off as genuine. Soon afterwards he published a collection of these imitations as if edited from the manuscripts of an imaginary fifteenth-century Bristol poet, Thomas Rowley. In 1770 he went up to London where, despite a brief and limited success, he could not make ends meet. In destitution and despair, he took poison and died before he was eighteen. Almost nothing he wrote is now enjoyable for its own sake. His imitations must be regarded as literary curiosities. Nevertheless, mixed up with all the sham Gothic is a sincere lyric impulse. Chatterton really lived more in the Middle Ages than in his own day, and we may thus see him as one of the transmitters of an almost forgotten past to the poets who came after him. What he found in the antique was romance, a lyricism not evident in the poetry of the 1760's. Chatterton began writing his Rowley ballads before the publication of Bishop Percy's important *Reliques of Ancient English Poetry* (1765), parts of which they closely resemble. There is in both a mixture of the authentic medieval idiom and a somewhat stilted literary quality which suggests later editing and 'improvement'. Percy's *Reliques* were the most important printed source of traditional English and Scottish ballads until the appearance of Child's great collection, well over a century later. Another important collection was Sir Walter Scott's *Minstrelsy of the Scottish Border* (1802–3). Romanticism was made up of several strands, of which one of the chief was a taste for the popular ballads of the past, which have always been disparaged by the devotees of correctness as 'rude'. They gave a vital impetus to the poetry of the Romantics.

ROBERT BURNS (1759–1796) has sometimes been regarded as a forerunner of Romanticism, but he is not easy to place historically. From the point of view of Scottish poetry he represents, in some respects, not the beginning of a new movement, but the culmination – even the close – of a tradition going back to the fifteenth century. All the elements of Dunbar's poetry are to be found in Burns – satire and invective, lyricism, bawdry, vigorous and pungent narrative, even the religious strain, though there is nothing in Burns of the same elegiac splendour as in the best of Dunbar. His poetry has many qualities which have endeared it to generations of readers, both Scottish and non-Scottish, but it lives chiefly by its abundant and full-blooded vitality. By an inevitable reaction against the nineteenth-century view of Burns as the writer of sentimental Scots songs, it is now the fashion to praise him for the unrestrained license of *The Merry Muses*, composed for convivial gatherings of the less polite elements in Edinburgh society. Excellent as these are of their kind, there is in the better known of Burns' poems just as much of his characteristic warmth of feeling and *joie de vivre*.

Burns was the son of a poor Ayrshire farm-worker, who educated him to the best of his ability. The boy grew up with an uncommon love of literature, and a taste for dissipation. It was the aim of educated Scotsmen to write good English, and Burns' early satirical and sentimental verse is in the polite English of the time. It was not until he abandoned this and took up the native tradition of vernacular poetry that he wrote anything for which he is now read. The language he evolved was a mixture of English and Scots, with the latter predominating. In 1786 appeared the famous Kilmarnock edition of his early poems. He achieved fame, went to Edinburgh where he was fêted and lionised, and was enabled to become a small farmer in his own right. He married Jean Armour, one of the many girls to whom he had made love. He contributed about two hundred songs to James Johnson's *Scots Musical Museum*, a compilation in which traditional melodies were served up for the polite world with new or re-written words. Among these are *Auld Lang Syne*, *A Red, Red Rose* and *Scots Wha Ha'e*. Some of his best known lyrics, such as *Coming through the Rye*, are bowdlerised versions of bawdy folk songs. It is probably by his songs above all that Burns became the Scots national bard. Tenderness and sentimentality on the one hand, wit and good sense on the other, strong local patriotism and a satirical tang give them a permanent appeal.

Burns was not a passionate poet, as were Donne and Shelley, but he was one of the best of social and convivial poets. Indeed, his genius was essentially comic – the creator of fine humorous narratives such as *Tam o'Shanter* and moralistic and satirical addresses such as those *To the Deil* and *To the Unco Guid*. The conflict in Scots society between the ultra-respectable repressive morality of the Calvinistic church, and the healthy and exuberant paganism that burst out from below the surface, was the mainspring of Burns' satire. But what makes it supreme of its kind is not any bitterness or rancour but the frank delight in conviviality and spontaneous well-being.

Burns' versification is springy and regular – too regular, perhaps, for the expression of intimate personal feeling, but entirely appropriate to witty social comment. How well adapted it is to this purpose is shown by the closing stanzas of the *Address to the Unco Guid*.

> Ye high, exalted, virtuous dames,
>   Tied up in godly laces,
> Before ye gie poor frailty names,
>   Suppose a change o'cases;
> A dear-loved lad, convenient snug,
>   A treacherous inclination –
> But let me whisper i' your lug,
>   Ye're aiblins[1] nae temptation.
>
> Then gently scan your brother man,
>   Still gentler sister woman;
> Though they may gang a kennin wrang,[2]
>   To step aside is human:
> One point must still be greatly dark,
>   The moving Why they do it:
> And just as lamely can ye mark
>   How far perhaps they rue it.
>
> Who made the heart, 'tis He alone
>   Decidedly can try us,
> He knows each chord, its various tone,
>   Each spring, its various bias:

[1] *aiblins*: perhaps.
[2] *a kennin wrang*: a little wrong.

> Then at the balance let's be mute,
>   We never can adjust it;
> What's done we partly may compute,
>   But know not what's resisted.

If Burns belongs, after all, to his own century rather than to the age of Romanticism, WILLIAM BLAKE (1757–1827) seems rather to belong to no time, or to a timeless region of pure lyricism owing nothing of its essential quality to any historical influences. This is perhaps only to say that he was profoundly original. Critics have presented him as, on the one hand, a mystic and a visionary, and on the other a child of the Industrial Revolution. In some respects he was both; in more important respects he was neither. He was a poet of the purest inspiration, at once a man and a visionary. There is about his best lyrics a rightness of tone and feeling, an inevitability of rhythm and language which give them a kind of authenticity, even authority, that we accept without question. It is as if their creator were transcribing the utterance of some inner or outer voice – one cannot say which – without the necessity of following the processes of composition which a writer ordinarily carries out.

> How sweet I roamed from field to field
> And tasted all the summer's pride,
> Till I the prince of love beheld
> Who in the sunny beams did glide!
>
> He showed me lilies for my hair,
> And blushing roses for my brow;
> He led me through his gardens fair
> Where all his golden pleasures grow.
>
> With sweet May dews my wings were wet,
> And Phoebus fired my vocal rage;
> He caught me in his silken net,
> And shut me in his golden cage.
>
> He loves to sit and hear me sing,
> Then, laughing, sports and plays with me;
> Then stretches out my golden wing,
> And mocks my loss of liberty.

Of this lyric, written before the age of fourteen, one may say that it owes something to the popular hymnody of Watts and others, and even more to the anonymous folk songs of tradition; one may detect in the language a trace of contemporary poetic diction and a trace of the Bible. But these influences count for little beside the original contribution of a gifted boy writing at one of the barrenest moments in the history of English poetry.

> The languid strings do scarcely move!
> The sound is forced, the notes are few!

This is the conclusion of a poem *To the Muses*, in which Blake laments the poetic situation in the 1770's.

He was born in London, where he remained for most of his life. An unusually sensitive and imaginative child, he grew up in an unsympathetic family atmosphere, and in physical surroundings which repelled him. His poems abound in references to the dirt and squalor of the city, as compared with the charm of the countryside on the northern outskirts. This contrast, forced upon the impressionable mind of a boy, coloured all his later thinking.

He received no formal primary education, and at ten years old, in recognition of his precocity as a draughtsman, he was apprenticed to an engraver. This profession remained his life-long source of income. He made almost nothing by his writings, which were not printed and published in the ordinary way, but hand-engraved by himself.

In 1782 he married the uneducated daughter of a grocer, Catherine Boucher, whom he taught to read and write, and who proved to be a devoted and sympathetic wife. In 1783 he issued his *Poetical Sketches*, containing, among others, the early lyric quoted above. He remained poor, and nothing he turned his hand to was in the least profitable. He had no material success, either as painter or as writer, but he enjoyed the friendship and regard of men of talent in the artistic and literary world. He associated himself with the political radicalism of Godwin and Paine, but was less interested in politics than in his inner visions. He began to see life as a tissue of contraries – joy and pain, energy and reason, creation and destruction, innocence and experience: that is, happiness and misery. He saw that the co-existence of these contraries was a necessary condition of life, and that peace was to be sought in their reconciliation.

In 1789 he engraved *Songs of Innocence* and five years later *Songs of Experience*. The poems in these two books are complementary and contrasting – 'Infant Joy' and 'Infant Sorrow', 'The Lamb' and 'The Tiger', 'The Divine Image' and 'The Human Image'.

In 1804, Blake began to engrave the symbolic or prophetic poems which he was writing under the influence of mystical and esoteric philosophers. As explorations of Blake's personal philosophy these books have aroused the curiosity of scholars, but as poetry they have never inspired unqualified enthusiasm. On the other hand the lyrical poems which he wrote mainly in his youth and early manhood are among the most precious things in English poetry. In later life Blake became increasingly detached from the outer world; he persisted in living, thinking and acting with simple sincerity, so that he gained a reputation for eccentricity. His old age was outwardly uneventful, and at his death his genius was little recognised.

No one would deny that the prophetic books have great power of suggestion and a magnificent, though apparently formless, abundance. It is fair to call their author an undisciplined writer, as he was an undisciplined painter. This in his case is no disparagement; he was a revolutionary, living at a time when the whole of Europe and the American colonies were in turmoil with revolutionary ideas, breaking the bonds of despotism. There was no artistic or literary discipline he could accept, other than that of his individual intuition. There are times in the history of society when accepted ideas and forms have become rigid and sterile, and when the only possibility of new growth lies in the capacity of gifted individuals to renew the contact between the human mind and the primary sources of experience. This is what gives Blake's lyrical poems their perennial freshness. They charm by their childlike spontaneity and simplicity of thought and vision, but the permanence of their appeal is due also to their formal qualities. Their rhythm and rhyme have the irregular formality of a folk song, never mechanical, always subject to variations dictated by meaning or emotion. It is this formality which, it seems to me, the prophetic books lack: the English ear cannot easily accustom itself to a rhythmical pattern which departs far from the iambic norm. In his earliest work Blake, by an absolute rightness of instinct, renewed the sources of inspiration by returning to native forms. But in the prophetic books it was as if he had lost patience with these forms, or had found them in the end restrictive, and had introduced an alien note, aiming at, but missing, the cadence of the Bible.

No poem can be fully satisfying if the rhythm is mechanically regular. The ear demands flexibility. On the other hand, when a poet of Blake's imaginative power and rhythmic subtlety is impelled by emotional pressure to adopt a tighter and more regular cadence, the effect is overwhelming.

> My spectre around me night and day
> Like a wild beast guards my way.
> My emanation far within
> Weeps incessantly for my sin.
>
> A fathomless and boundless deep,
> There we wander, there we weep;
> On the hungry craving wind
> My spectre follows thee behind.
>
> He scents thy footsteps in the snow,
> Wheresoever thou dost go
> Through the wintry hail and rain.
> When wilt thou return again?

This, like *The Tiger*, has an incantatory quality unmatched for sheer intensity outside the fifteenth-century *Lyke-Wake Dirge*.

Much of what Blake was discovering instinctively during the 1780's was expressed with conscious dogmatism by Wordsworth and Coleridge towards the end of the following decade. WILLIAM WORDSWORTH (1770–1850) was born in Cumberland, the son of an attorney, and educated at Hawkshead Grammar School and St John's College, Cambridge. A not very happy childhood induced in him that habit of brooding introspection which was essential to his most characteristic poetry. He visited the Continent in 1790, and a year later returned to France. Here he was fired with revolutionary ardour, and his association with some republicans involved him in a *liaison* with Annette Vallon, who bore him an illegitimate daughter. After his return to England, he experienced a sense of revulsion against the excesses of the French Revolution and against the emotional temerity which had entangled him with Annette. This was the first stage in the onset of respectability which gradually overcame Wordsworth. For the time being, however, he remained a rebel, though his rebellion was against the literary, not the political, establishment.

His earliest poems were conventional enough. *An Evening Walk* and *Descriptive Sketches* (1793) are exercises in the manner of the late eighteenth-century topographical poets. In 1795 he received a legacy which freed him for the time being from material worries, and he went to live with his sister Dorothy at Alfoxden in Somerset. Shortly before this he had made the acquaintance of Coleridge, who was now living at Nether Stowey in the immediate neighbourhood. So began one of the most important friendships in the history of literature.

SAMUEL TAYLOR COLERIDGE (1772–1834) was the son of a Devonshire parson-schoolmaster. He was a precocious and sensitive child, and to leave home at an early age to go to a boarding school in far-off London helped to destroy his sense of security. Christ's Hospital did something to foster his great intellectual gifts, and he was less unhappy there than lonely. He went to Jesus College, Cambridge, where an inner craving for attention and companionship made him the centre of a circle of intelligent admirers. He became interested in radical politics, and the neglect of what he considered a fossilised academic curriculum gave him cause to fear for the outcome of his college career. He ran away and joined a regiment of Dragoons. This was characteristic of his improvidence where his own interests were concerned. He came to regard all actions as essentially futile, and was constitutionally incapable of adopting a course which was not more or less disastrous for him. Paradoxically, he was one that had it in him to be practical. After his discharge from the army, he made friends with a young man from Oxford, Robert Southey, who, like Coleridge, had poetic ambitions. Of Southey's poems it need only be said that they were sufficiently admired in the right quarters, and their author was thought sufficiently respectable, to earn him the Laureateship. But this was not till much later. For the present Southey was un-conventional enough to agree to join Coleridge in a political scheme which must have seemed reasonable enough in 1794. This scheme, to which Coleridge gave the name 'Pantisocracy', was none other than the setting up of an ideal communistic republic in America. The plan did not materialise, but after its failure Coleridge found himself married to Sara Fricker, whose sister became the wife of Southey. A condition of Pantisocracy was that each of the emigrating young men should take a wife. Coleridge married Sara from a sense of honour, and the two proved as incompatible as two partners could be.

At first, however, Coleridge was happy. In 1795 he and his bride took a cottage at Nether Stowey, and the friendship with Wordsworth and his sister continued.

There followed two of the most fruitful years in the lives of either poet. Coleridge wrote his *Rime of the Ancient Mariner*, *Kubla Khan* and the first part of *Christabel*. Of these only *The Ancient Mariner* was included in the first edition of *Lyrical Ballads*, published anonymously in Bristol in 1798. Wordsworth's contribution included *The Idiot Boy*, *Goody Blake and Harry Gill*, *The Thorn*, and *Tintern Abbey*. The book was prefaced by an 'Advertisement', in reality a manifesto and a challenge to contemporary taste.

> The majority of the following poems are to be considered as experiments. They were written chiefly with a view to ascertain how far the language of conversation in the middle and lower classes of society is adapted to the purposes of poetic pleasure. Readers accustomed to the gaudiness and inane phraseology of many modern writers, if they persist in reading this book to its conclusion, will perhaps frequently have to struggle with feelings of strangeness and awkwardness: they will look round for poetry, and will be induced to enquire by what species of courtesy these attempts can be permitted to assume that title.

Lyrical Ballads was received unfavourably, but was re-issued in a revised form in 1800 with the famous Preface in which the poets elaborated their theory. This involved a rejection of specialised poetic diction and a recognition of the lives and speech of the humble and uneducated as a source of poetic material. Sophistication and book-learning were regarded as inhibiting that direct communion with nature which was a necessary condition of mental and spiritual health.

> Books! 'tis a dull and endless strife:
> Come, hear the woodland linnet,
> How sweet his music! on my life,
> There's more of wisdom in it.
>
> And hark! how blithe the throstle sings!
> He too is no mean preacher;

> Come forth into the light of things,
> Let Nature be your teacher.

> She has a world of ready wealth,
> Our minds and hearts to bless –
> Spontaneous wisdom breathed by health,
> Truth breathed by cheerfulness.

> One impulse from a vernal wood
> May teach you more of man,
> Of moral evil and of good,
> Than all the sages can.

> Sweet is the lore which Nature brings;
> Our meddling intellect
> Misshapes the beauteous forms of things;
> – We murder to dissect.

> Enough of science and of art;
> Close up those barren leaves;
> Come forth, and bring with you a heart
> That watches and receives.

So run the defiant stanzas of *The Tables Turned*.

Criticism has not always been kind to Wordsworth's experimental poems – that is, ballads such as *The Idiot Boy* and *Simon Lee, the Old Huntsman* – but, if they do at times descend to bathos, they have true simplicity and directness, such as it is difficult to find elsewhere in the poetry of the period, unless in Blake's *Songs of Innocence*. It might be claimed, however, that Wordsworth was more himself when he forgot theory and the ballad form, and, in *Tintern Abbey*, returned to the blank verse of Akenside and a mood of introspective calm.

In *Lines written in Early Spring* Wordsworth wrote:

> Through primrose tufts, in that green bower,
> The periwinkle trailed its wreaths;
> And 'tis my faith that every flower
> Enjoys the air it breathes.

> The birds around me hopped and played:
> Their thoughts I cannot measure,
> But the least motion which they made,
> It seemed a thrill of pleasure.

Such an extreme view of the self-consciousness of nature can have no rational foundation; yet the central importance of nature in Wordsworth's poetry, where it was raised to the level of a divinity, had a crucial effect on most of the poetry written during the following century.

Coleridge was far less committed to the critical theory behind *Lyrical Ballads* than was Wordsworth, even though he may have had an equal or greater share in formulating it. Indeed, it is likely that Coleridge's more fertile intellect evolved the theoretical basis of Wordsworth's experimental practice at this period. Whatever he may have thought good for his friend, for whose poetry he had an unbounded and generous admiration, he himself had small use for the lives and language of uneducated peasants. He was, however, aware of the possibilities of the ballad form. *The Ancient Mariner* was begun as a deliberate pastiche of the traditional ballads in collections such as Percy's *Reliques*, much in the manner of Chatterton's Rowley poems. But it is one of the mysteries of the creative faculty at its highest that it can transform what is outwardly mere imitation into something better and greater than its models.

Writing later about *Lyrical Ballads*, Coleridge explained that, in contrast to Wordsworth, whose object was 'to give the charm of novelty to things of every day', his own 'endeavours should be directed to persons and characters supernatural, or at least romantic; yet so as to transfer from our inward nature a human interest and a semblance of truth sufficient to procure for these shadows of imagination that willing suspension of disbelief for the moment which constitutes poetic faith'. *The Ancient Mariner* is thus a story of the supernatural and the romantic, but it is at the same time an exploration of the soul of man. The mariner's journey, narrated in language even more striking and unforgettable than that of the travellers' tales which Coleridge had drawn on, is the journey of the human spirit from innocence through guilt and remorse to expiation and reconciliation. Not only has Coleridge's evocation of the isolation of the human soul through a sense of guilt permanent validity –

> Alone, alone, all, all alone,
> Alone on a wide, wide sea!
> And never a saint took pity on
> My soul in agony –

but the poem is unequalled in literature for its terrifying dramatic power and for its bold and startling imagery.

It is undoubtedly one of the phenomena of Romanticism that its best poets wrote their best poems when comparatively young. *The Ancient Mariner*, written in Coleridge's middle twenties, was never equalled again, except perhaps in *Kubla Khan*, composed at the same period. He later called this 'A Vision in a Dream: a Fragment'. He did not publish it until 1816, and all his life he tended to write it off as a strange aberration. To others, however, it is an almost perfect expression of the joy of creativity, in language of the utmost splendour and sensuous suggestion.

In the same year, 1797, Coleridge wrote the first part of *Christabel*, a narrative poem of deliberately medieval character. It is a magnificent fragment, but Coleridge was never able to finish it, though he later achieved a second part. Its seminal force was perhaps greater even than its immediate appeal. How much Keats' medievalism, and later that of Tennyson and the Pre-Raphaelites, owed directly to Coleridge it is impossible to say. At any rate it is clear that Coleridge anticipated Scott as a romantic medievalist.

After the appearance of *Lyrical Ballads* the friendship between Coleridge and the Wordsworths lost something of its pristine intimacy, though the cracks did not show at first. The three of them went to Germany, where Wordsworth and his sister parted from Coleridge. Wordsworth began to write *The Prelude*, his long autobiography in blank verse. He also wrote the poems on 'Lucy Gray' which are among his finest lyrics. In 1799 he settled with Dorothy at Grasmere in the Lake District, where he spent the rest of his life. In 1802 he married Mary Hutchinson, and the remainder of his long life was passed calmly in the heart of his family. By about 1807 he had done all his significant work, and with increasing recognition by a younger generation of poets and by the more discriminating of the public he gradually became a national institution, until in 1843 the respectability of his life and connections, and the uninflammatory character of his later verse, were rewarded with the Laureateship.

After *Lyrical Ballads* the best of Wordsworth's poems are *Michael, Resolution and Independence*, the *Ode on the Intimations of Immortality*, certain shorter pieces, and *The Prelude* (including a separate episode called *Nutting*). *Michael* is a long, bare narrative of great dignity and pathos. What Wordsworth admired in the peasant character was its granite-like stoicism, the witness it bore to human dignity in the midst of adversity. The same quality is displayed by the old leech-gatherer who is the hero of *Resolution and Independence*. I have called the leech-gatherer the 'hero', but the real hero is Wordsworth himself, as in all his principal works. The poem is an exploration of the theme which obsessed him in the years of his maturity – what to make of life after the animal spirits of youth have subsided and its naked vision become obscured by habit, experience and reflection. We can but accept, he seems to say, the life of stoical resignation, of duty without complaint. Wordsworth had dedicated himself to his belief in the life of instinct, of primary experience – in other words, the worship of nature. In the early part of *The Prelude* he endeavours to recapture his sensations and experiences as a boy amidst the wild scenery of the Lake District, and so to re-live and preserve that instinctual life which alone seems to him worth living. He describes his early home, his expeditions on foot or by boat, his boyhood games. In the best passages he achieves a vivid and striking actuality.

> O! when I have hung
> Above the raven's nest, by knots of grass
> And half-inch fissures in the slippery rock
> But ill sustained, and almost, as it seemed,
> Suspended by the blast which blew amain,
> Shouldering the naked crag; O! at that time,
> While on the perilous ridge I hung alone,
> With what strange utterance did the loud dry wind
> Blow through my ears! The sky seemed not a sky
> Of earth, and with what motion moved the clouds!

Such a state of 'innocence', to use Blake's word, could not last, and the *Intimations Ode*, published in 1807, is a lament for its passing.

> There was a time when meadow, grove and stream,
> The earth, and every common sight,
> To me did seem
> Apparelled in celestial light,
> The glory and the freshness of a dream.

It is not now as it hath been of yore; –
Turn whereso'er I may,
By night or day,
The things which I have seen I now can see no more.

Wordsworth recognises and accepts the failure of nature as a permanent source of inspiration. The philosophy he had rejected in early manhood must be called in again to repair the loss. He must reconcile himself to the 'years that bring the philosophic mind'. He must assume the stoic calm of one of his solitary peasant figures. In the *Ode* he composed his own poetic epitaph. There were a few fine things later – some of the sonnets, and the beautiful *Extempore Effusion upon the Death of James Hogg* – but if Wordsworth had died at forty instead of eighty, his poetic reputation would be even higher than it is.

After his return from Germany Coleridge moved with his wife and child to Keswick in order to be near the Wordsworths. His incompatibility with his wife could no longer be ignored; he found in Sara none of that intellectual and spiritual companionship he craved, and which he received so abundantly from Wordsworth and Dorothy. Sara, though a good mother, was jealous of his success with the Wordsworths, and exasperated by his continued failure to provide a regular income. Domestic unhappiness combined with chronic ill-health increased the addiction to opium which had gradually taken hold of him ever since he first discovered its narcotic properties. Judicial separation from his wife was unthinkable, for he was a sincere Christian; and he drifted into a hopeless and unfulfilled attachment to another Sara, the sister of Wordsworth's wife. To Sara Hutchinson he addressed several love poems under the guise of 'Asra'. In 1802 he sent her an impassioned verse-letter which he later re-cast as *Dejection: an Ode*. Two years later, in order to get some relief from ill-health and domestic unhappiness, he went to Malta and Italy. On his return he remained in London, endeavouring to earn a living by journalism and lecturing. He did not return to his wife, and in London his health grew steadily worse. He was now estranged from the Wordsworths, and the breach was never completely healed. At length, on the verge of utter despair and broken in health, he took up residence with a kindly physician, James Gilman, and his wife in Highgate. Here he remained from 1816 until his death in 1834.

From the point of view of worldly success and the fulfilment of early promise, no career was a greater failure than Coleridge's. He was a man of unequalled intellectual gifts, and his discoveries in the fields of literary criticism, metaphysics, theology, education and psychology, as recorded in his voluminous notebooks, show him to have been an intellectual pioneer far in advance of his time. He had a genius for friendship, and the capacity to arouse admiration and affection in others to a degree which was dangerous, because it weakened the will to fend for himself. Despite his subtlety of intellect and his wide and varied interests, his was an essentially simple nature, craving only the affection and loyalty he gave so freely to others.

> To be beloved is all I need,
> And whom I love, I love indeed.

So runs his confession at the end of an agonised self-examination, *The Pains of Sleep*.

Coleridge's was a warmer and more impulsive nature than his friend Wordsworth's. Wordsworth was at his best as a gaunt and solitary devotee of nature. Coleridge needed human sympathy and understanding. His best poem, *The Ancient Mariner*, is concerned with the essential loneliness of the human spirit; the best of his other poems are all concerned with domestic love, as in *Frost at Midnight*, or friendship, as in *This Lime-Tree Bower my Prison*. The greatest of these confessional monologues is the *Dejection* letter addressed to Sara Hutchinson. *Dejection*, like Wordsworth's *Intimations Ode*, is an outpouring of grief for lost hopes: Wordsworth consoles himself for the failure of nature to fulfil its early promise; Coleridge grieves for the loss of his creative power, the power which five years earlier had conceived his finest poems, through a withering of sensibility at its very centre, the domestic hearth.

> But now ill tidings bow me down to earth,
> Nor care I that they rob me of my mirth –
> But Oh! each visitation
> Suspends what nature gave me at my birth,
> My shaping spirit of imagination!

Coleridge had staked his happiness, not on external nature,

but on family and marital affection. When these failed, he was adrift, as hopelessly and completely as his becalmed Mariner.

> These mountains too, these vales, these woods, these lakes,
> Scenes full of beauty and of loftiness
> Where all my life I fondly hoped to live –
> I were sunk low indeed, did they no solace give;
> But oft I seem to feel, and evermore I fear,
> They are not to me now the things which once they were

> O Sara! we receive but what we give,
> And in our life alone does nature live.
> Ours is her wedding garment, ours her shroud –
> And would we aught behold of higher worth
> Than that inanimate cold world allowed
> To that poor loveless, ever anxious crowd,
> Ah! from the soul itself must issue forth
> A light, a glory, and a luminous cloud
> Enveloping the earth!

Coleridge was peculiarly vulnerable to disappointment, and his sensibility appeared to have no power to harden itself against the repeated attacks of utter hopelessness. Accordingly, long after his first exultant creativity had been crushed by illness and misery, he could still occasionally compose poems and fragments instinct with living emotion.

> All nature seems at work. Slugs leave their lair –
> The bees are stirring – birds are on the wing –
> And winter slumbering in the open air
> Wears on its smiling face a dream of spring!
> And I, the while, the sole unbusy thing,
> Nor honey make, nor pair, nor build, nor sing.

So Coleridge began, at the age of fifty-seven, the lines entitled *Work without Hope*.

The achievement of Wordsworth and Coleridge before their lives were half spent transformed English poetry. It is difficult to sum up the nature of this transformation, which was indeed not apparent for some years. In what was poetry different after 1810 from what it had been before? The dominant view of poetry before their time was that it was concerned with man in society. The poet was the spokesman of a ruling class – or at any rate, he felt that he should have some influence on the course of human affairs. Wordsworth and Coleridge did indeed write poems about public affairs, but they were more in the nature of occasional and personal protests against tyranny and injustice than constructive appraisals of the political situation. Romanticism involved a separation between the poet and society: he could only be himself in solitude, or within the confines of his personal life. True, there had been premonitions of this revolution in ideas for some time before the birth of Wordsworth. Gray in particular felt himself to be dispossessed in the poetical hierarchy. He expressed more than once this feeling, that the poet did not 'belong' any more in the social order. Eighteenth-century materialism, and the philistinism of the ruling class, had driven him to a lonely eminence where he could mourn the loss of prestige in solitude, or in the company of other aloof and retiring spirits.

Wordsworth and Coleridge realised that the establishment had cut itself off from the sources of spiritual renewal, and believed, in the climate of revolutionary radicalism of their time, that renewal must come from contact with the poor and dispossessed. They believed also that poetic growth must spring from a rejection of the aristocratic tradition and a re-discovery of the medieval and romantic past. In the former belief they were anticipated by Blake, and in the latter by the exponents of the Gothic revival. But it was they who drew together the diverse strands of incipient Romanticism, formulated a critical programme for their faith, and above all, left an enduring body of poetry as witness to its potentiality. Wordsworth revealed the scope of the individual vision in the contemplation of outward nature; Coleridge pointed to the 'shaping spirit of imagination' as it explores remote time and place; both demonstrated that henceforth the proper sphere for poetic investigation was no longer sophisticated society but the privacies of the human heart and mind.

On the technical side, the innovations of the two poets were not conspicuously revolutionary. Their most experimental contribution to poetic technique was Wordsworth's adoption of the bare simplicity of some of the *Lyrical Ballads*. Even he, after the turn of the century, dropped this extreme form of anti-poetic diction, and became increasingly conservative. By the time he was writing the *Intimations Ode*, he derived far more from the language of Spenser and Milton than from that of unlettered peasants. Coleridge was at no time a great technical innovator, but he had a superb ear, and was content to make a personal music out of whatever he found attractive in the poetic language of the present and the past. What they achieved, more indirectly, was a general loosening of rhythmic restriction, and an enrichment of imagery. The Romantic use of language was far less precise, far more suggestive than that of the Augustans. The diction of Keats, for instance, writing less than a generation after Wordsworth, is often more in the spirit of the eighteenth century than was the older poet's; both he and Shelley indulged in personification reminiscent of the typical mid-eighteenth-century ode. But both enjoyed a rhythmic freedom, a sense of unhampered rhetorical utterance experienced by no one between the later Elizabethans and Coleridge. The style of Keats, even in his more eighteenth-century vein, as compared with that of, say, Goldsmith, is a measure of the revolution consummated by Wordsworth and Coleridge.

CHAPTER ELEVEN

Romanticism: The Second Phase

1805-1830

IN the period between the best of Wordsworth and Coleridge and the appearance of Byron, the narrative poems of Sir Walter Scott achieved enormous popularity. Indeed, viewed historically, it was Scott's chief function to have popularised romance. However low in critical estimation Scott has now sunk as a poet, we have to recognise the influence of his antiquarian and historical interest – passion, one might almost call it. A Tory in sympathies, he had no use for the radicalism which had fired his contemporaries. He lived in the past, and his lasting claim to esteem is his evocation, in the *Waverley* novels, of Scotland's romantic history. He is important also as a collector, editor and (it must be admitted) restorer of the old Scots ballads. It was this early antiquarian work which nourished his love of the past and inspired his efforts as a poet. His first long poem, *The Lay of the Last Minstrel* (1805), was written in imitation of the metrical romances of the middle ages; but its form and language were directly inspired by the first part of *Christabel*, which Scott had heard read. This transmission by a minor artist of the romantic spirit is a signal instance of the seminal power of Coleridge's genius, then unrecognised except by a small circle.

The immediate and phenomenal success of *The Lay* encouraged Scott. *Marmion* appeared in 1808 and *The Lady of the Lake* in 1810. But in 1814, admitting the supremacy of his more youthful compatriot, Lord Byron, he published the first of his *Waverley* novels. He thus discovered his true vocation as a writer of historical prose fiction. He has been extravagantly praised for the songs occurring throughout the novels. At best these are competent pastiche of other men's styles and are among the most readable of lyrics composed by non-poets.

We have had occasion previously to make a distinction between writers of great intrinsic worth and small historical importance, and those whose historical importance far outweighs the permanent value of their work. Pre-eminent among these is the man who ousted Scott in popular favour towards the end of the long Napoleonic wars. To a considerable extent Byron created the taste by which he was appreciated, and when that taste changed his popularity declined. It is doubtful if even his most fervent admirer today would accord him a fraction of the praise lavished on him during the last ten years of his short life. Nevertheless, though everyone is now acutely aware of his shortcomings, we have to admit the potency of his appeal to his own generation and that which immediately succeeded it.

GEORGE GORDON, LORD BYRON (1788–1824) was born in London, the only child of a profligate father and a vain, hysterical mother. He was brought up – if that is the right expression – by his mother, through whom he inherited Stuart blood. He inherited also a passionate nature, which was half fascinated, half chilled by the beauty of the Scottish scenery in which he grew up, and the repressive atmosphere of Scots Calvinism. He had great personal beauty, combined with the physical deformity of a club foot. His upbringing made him introspective, precocious, self-centred, eager for love and admiration. He inherited his title when he was ten, and at thirteen he went to Harrow and later to Trinity College, Cambridge. He enjoyed close friendships with men of discernment and intelligence. He published his juvenilia in 1809 under the title, *Hours of Idleness*. These attracted the indulgent notice of some critics, but a savage attack in *The Edinburgh Review* provoked his Popian satire, *English Bards and Scotch Reviewers*.

From 1809 to 1811 he travelled in Europe and the Levant. On his return he entered the House of Lords, where his maiden speech, which indicated strong radical sympathies, attracted favourable comment. Had his interest lain in that direction, he might have had a brilliant political career. In fact, however, his interest lay in no particular direction for very long. The political atmosphere had changed since the youth of Wordsworth and Coleridge. Napoleon, heir to the French Revolution so loudly acclaimed in 1789 as the hope of every lover of liberty, had subjected Europe to an even more reactionary despotism. In

England the wars had been so costly that the poor were worse off than they had been for generations, and the government was correspondingly harsh and repressive. Byron was not so much a lover of liberty as had been the older poets in their youth, but a hater of tyranny, a rebel against government, and ultimately against society itself. In 1812 he published the first two Cantos of *Childe Harold*, a long, impassioned account of the wanderings of a restless soul amid the splendours of European scenery and civilisation. Nothing like it had been read before; this kind of declamatory travelogue exactly answered the needs of popular taste, and Byron became famous overnight. Five editions were called for during the year. The public had never accepted the poems of Wordsworth and Coleridge, and were accustomed to the moral rectitude and prosiness of the imitators of Pope, the comparatively tepid graces of Cowper, Rogers and Erasmus Darwin. Even the lays of Scott seemed colourless beside *Childe Harold*. Here was something new, something altogether absent from English poetry since the time of Marlowe – passionate rhetorical utterance, gorgeous imagery and hyperbolical language, an unhindered sweep of bold and dashing invention.

For the next four years Byron enjoyed a literary and social success unparalleled since the reign of Pope himself, and spreading far beyond the London clubs and drawing-rooms where he was fêted and lionised. He was hailed on the Continent also as a new literary star, and his influence on German and French romanticism was even greater than in his own country. An affair with Lady Caroline Lamb began the series of scandalous episodes for which he soon became notorious.

But this fame and these adventures were not, in all likelihood, what he really craved. The essence of Byronism is that the hero, or victim, is torn by conflicting desires, in the pursuit of which he is possessed by gloomy self-questionings and a sense of futility, a *Weltschmerz*, from which he cannot escape. He attains what he pursues, only to find that it was not what he really desired. He is never sure what he truly wants, or what he sincerely feels. He is a rebel against all authority, moral and social; the only law he knows is the law of self-gratification. Only what he wills is right. With part of himself Byron undoubtedly craved something he never had – domestic peace and security. In 1815 he married Anne Milbanke, an heiress; after a brief and turbulent marriage she sought a separation the following year. The grounds have never been made entirely clear, but it is probable that Byron misused her cruelly, and made it impossible for her to remain with him. The society which had idolised him now ostracised him, and in 1816 he went abroad, never to return. He joined the Shelleys, with whom he travelled to Switzerland and Venice. He lived in Italy for the remainder of his life, enjoying an immense poetic reputation and a series of sensational love affairs. He became identified with the cause of Italian liberation, and his name was revered there, as elsewhere, as that of a noble and fearless champion of the oppressed. He became interested in the cause of Greek independence against their Turkish masters; in 1823 he went to Greece to join the insurgents, but the following year he died of a fever at Missolonghi. His funeral in London was the occasion of nation-wide mourning.

Byron's career has been dwelt on at some length because of the importance of the Byron legend. Undoubtedly the splendid immorality of the poet had much to do with the popularity of his work; but the poems themselves were the expression of the man. Those which follow the first two Cantos of *Childe Harold* – *The Giaour*, *The Bride of Abydos*, *The Corsair*, *Lara*, and *The Siege of Corinth* – enjoyed an even greater popularity. *The Corsair* sold 10,000 copies on the day of publication. These Turkish tales introduced an exotic note into the poetry of a nation too long confined within its own island by the Napoleonic wars. The yearning for foreign travel, for scenes of oriental magnificence, and unfettered wandering had much to do with Byron's appeal.

> There is a pleasure in the pathless woods,
> There is a rapture on the lonely shore,
> There is society where none intrudes,
> By the deep sea, and music in its roar!
> I love not man the less, but nature more,
> From these our interviews, in which I steal
> From all I may be, or have been before,
> To mingle with the universe, and feel
> What I can ne'er express, yet cannot all conceal.

These lines from *Childe Harold*, Canto IV, are a fair sample of Wordsworthian or Shelleyan romanticism served up in a more flamboyant form for ordinary middle-class readers. Take Byron's romantic poetry where you will, and it is the sort of intoxicating stuff which easily persuades immature or un-discriminating minds that they are enjoying fine poetry. The lines on Waterloo, for instance, are claptrap, but they have a kind of tawdry magnificence which, like the shop-soiled melodies of Tchaikovsky, are all right in their place and justly popular.

> On with the dance! let joy be unconfined;
> No sleep till morn, when youth and pleasure meet
> To chase the glowing hours with flying feet –
> But hark! – that heavy sound breaks in once more,
> As if the clouds its echo would repeat;
> And nearer, clearer, deadlier than before!
> Arm! arm! it is – it is – the cannon's opening roar!

In his lyrics, though they are derivative, Byron even achieved a certain lightness and grace.

> The mountains look on Marathon –
>   And Marathon looks on the sea;
> And musing there an hour alone,
>   I dreamed that Greece might still be free;
> For standing on the Persians' grave,
> I could not deem myself a slave;
>   (*The Isles of Greece*)

Not to respond to a music like that is perhaps to show a certain deficiency in sympathies.

Perhaps, however, the musical analogy is not with Tchai-kovsky but with Sullivan. To regard Sullivan as a composer of great religious music in the idiom of Bach may be wrong; but to deny him outstanding talent as a creator of light, melodious, comic music would be absurd. During the last six years of his life Byron dropped the romantic posturing, the passionate heroics, the rôle of the world-weary misanthropist and discovered his true bent as a comic poet. In 1818 he began to compose *Don Juan*, which he left unfinished at the seventeenth Canto at the time of his death. This is a scandalous, amusing and slangy mock-heroic version of *Childe Harold*, in which the traveller is no longer a Byronic hero but a sensual, intelligent, worldly philanderer. Byron shows himself to be, not the heir to Marlowe, the rival of Wordsworth and Shelley, but the true successor to Pope: he has the satiric gift, the sense of the mock-heroic. But he has none of Pope's fastidious verbal elegance; instead, he is racy and colloquial, deliberately flouting the literary proprieties as in England he had flouted social propriety. Byron's most assured success in the comic vein was *The Vision of Judgement*, in which he attacks the Tory Poet Laureate, Southey, who had written a pretentious elegy on the death of George III. Here is Byron's gaily irreverent account of the King's arrival at the gate of Heaven.

> Saint Peter sat by the celestial gate,
>   And nodded o'er his keys: when, lo! there came
> A wondrous noise he had not heard of late –
>   A rushing sound of wind, and stream, and flame;
> In short, a roar of things extremely great,
>   Which would have made aught save a saint exclaim;
> But he, with first a start, and then a wink,
> Said, 'There's another star gone out, I think!'
>
> But ere he could return to his repose,
>   A Cherub flapped his right wing o'er his eyes –
> At which Saint Peter yawned, and rubbed his nose:
>   'Saint porter,' said the angel, 'prithee rise!'
> Waving a goodly wing, which glowed, as glows
>   An earthly peacock's tail, with heavenly dyes:
> To which the saint replied, 'Well, what's the matter?
> Is Lucifer come back with all this clatter?'
>
> 'No,' quoth the Cherub: 'George the Third is dead.'
>   'And who *is* George the Third?' replied the apostle:
> '*What George? what Third?*' 'The King of England,' said
>   The angel. 'Well! he won't find kings to jostle
> Him on his way; but does he wear his head?
>   Because the last we saw here had a tustle,
> And ne'er would have got into Heaven's good graces,
> Had he not flung his head in all our faces.'

Gone are the pretentious solemnity, the sham profundities, the awkward inversions of *Childe Harold*; instead, there is a careless lightness, a natural and easy colloquialism; and it is this tone and manner which are Byron's real contribution to the resources of modern poetry.

There are some poets and writers of humble origin who are of an essentially aristocratic sensibility – Hardy, for instance, or Clare – and there are others, born in the aristocratic class, who are as naturally vulgarians. Brought up to write for the violin, Byron discovered his true medium in the brass band. It is to the credit of his good sense, his intelligence and a kind of ingrained integrity that he made the discovery.

The reputation of Byron's younger friend, Shelley, has fluctuated widely during the past century and a half. He has been more misunderstood and misrepresented than most other poets. Critical opinion of his work has always been, and still is, divided: about his historical influence there can be no question. During and immediately after his life he was regarded by society in general as a monster of immorality, anarchy and atheism. He was anathema to the respectable; Browning was obliged to pursue his boyhood admiration of his poetry as if it were a secret vice. When the scandal died down, Shelley's serious scientific and political interest was forgotten, and he was read as a lyric poet of extreme but fragile beauty – an 'ineffectual angel', as Arnold called him. Later he came to be regarded as the type of the Romantic poet – vague, untidy, lax in morals, inhabiting a rarefied atmosphere not of this world. Reaction set in, and only recently has a more sober and balanced view prevailed.

PERCY BYSSHE SHELLEY (1792–1822) was the misfit son of a titled family of no special distinction, the kind of prodigy recurrently put forth by the English aristocracy. At a private boarding school he was made hypersensitive by insensitive treatment; at Eton he formed a passionate interest in experimental science; and at University College, Oxford, he came under the influence of the writings of William Godwin, the radical atheist. He was sent down for publishing a pamphlet on *The Necessity of Atheism*. In the same year, at the age of nineteen, he married the sixteen-year-old Harriet Westbrook, whom he deserted three years later. In 1812 he left England with Godwin's daughter, Mary Wollstonecraft, a woman much nearer his own intellectual level; and when Harriet committed suicide by drowning, Shelley and Mary were married. His early writings in prose and verse did not show great promise. His first long poem of any quality was *Alastor* (1816), whose sub-title, *The Spirit of Solitude*, is significant. For despite Shelley's attachment to certain friends and his need for human – especially feminine – companionship and devotion, he was essentially a solitary spirit. There was about him something remote: it was not society which exiled him, so much as he who rejected society. Paradoxically, he had a sincere, even fanatical, passion for humanity in the abstract; he was the kind of idealist whose contact with reality is always painful. As a young rebel and anarchist, he detested kings and priests, whom he regarded as the cause of all society's miseries: possibly he was actuated by a detestation of all forms of paternalism, whether in politics or religion, because of his personal revolt against his father. In any case it was the age of revolt, and Shelley was profoundly responsive to the spirit of the age. In his years of comparative maturity he came to regard the world's ills as due less to external oppressors than to man's own inherent failures.

Inevitably perhaps, he came into contact with Byron, the other notorious outcast from society. The poets met in 1816, and two years later they went to Italy together. Shelley began to be interested in the writings of Plato, whose views on society and the arts he found increasingly attractive. In 1819 he wrote *The Mask of Anarchy*, an attack on the reactionary government of the English Prime Minister, Castlereagh; and *Peter Bell the Third*, a light-hearted satire on Wordsworth, surprisingly witty in places, considering he had small gift for comic verse. There followed his verse-tragedy, *The Cenci*, and *Prometheus Unbound*, an ambitious lyrical drama embodying his ideas on the perfectibility of man; he wrote also at this period his best and most successful lyrics, among them the *Ode to the West Wind*, *To a Skylark*, and *The Cloud*. In 1821 he published his *Defence of Poetry*, a vindication of the poet against a spirited and forthright attack by his friend Peacock. In this he develops certain ideas which were of central importance to him: the supremacy of the artist's imagination as an agent for moral good, and the importance of poets as the 'unacknowledged legislators of the world'. In the same year he heard of the death of his younger contemporary, John Keats, through consumption; he had generously offered to help Keats, but nothing was able to save him. Hearing that Keats' illness had been aggravated by the attacks of hostile reviewers – a belief which was, to say the least, grossly exaggerated – Shelley composed *Adonais*, a lament for the dead poet and a triumphant assertion of the transcendent power of poetry to soar beyond the calumnies and miseries of the world.

> He has outsoared the shadow of our night;
> Envy and calumny and hate and pain,
> And that unrest which men miscall delight,

Can touch him not and torture not again;
From the contagion of the world's slow stain
He is secure, and now can never mourn
A heart grown cold, a head grown grey in vain;
Nor, when the spirit's self has ceased to burn,
With sparkless ashes load an unlamented urn.

He lives, he wakes – 'tis Death is dead, not he;
Mourn not for Adonais. – Thou young Dawn,
Turn all thy dew to splendour, for from thee
The spirit thou lamentest is not gone.

These are the high notes of Shelleyan rhetoric, the mature utterance of Romanticism both in form and in substance. Shelley began by desiring the regeneration of mankind after the doctrines of Godwin, and ended by renouncing it in the name of Platonic mysticism.

Shelley's own death followed that of Keats, little more than a year later. In 1822 he was drowned in a sudden storm while sailing in the Gulf of Spezzia. He was cremated, as the law then required, on the beach; his ashes were buried in Rome near the tomb of Keats. He had loved both storm and sea, and his end was tragically symbolic. Of the three poets of his immediate generation who died young, Shelley's death perhaps represents the greatest loss to poetry. The point will of course always be hypothetical, but at least the promise of Shelley's poetry at the time of his death seems to have been more defined and certain than that of either Byron's or Keats'.

It must be said, without hesitation, that the charge of 'in-effectuality' is wholly inappropriate to Shelley. It has been pointed out[1] that all the political ideals for which he and Mary strove, during a peculiarly inauspicious decade, have since become the commonplaces of British political theory and practice – the rights of women, to name only one. Nevertheless, while we can read his political and philosophical poems with interest and respect, we cannot read them with unmixed pleasure. Poetry is not the right medium for the kind of general ideas Shelley sought to promulgate. We may respect him as a wholly 'committed' poet, but we must recognise that a poet cannot serve two masters – poetry and philosophy. It is the

[1] See the Introduction to *Selected Poems of Percy Bysshe Shelley*, by John Holloway (Heinemann 1960).

greatest proof of Shelley's growing promise that he came to
realise this himself, and to understand that imagination, not
dogma, is the sphere of the poet.

> A man, to be greatly good, must imagine intensely and com-
> prehensively; he must put himself in the place of another and of
> many others; the pains and pleasures of his species must become his
> own. The greatest instrument of moral good is the imagination.

So he wrote in *A Defence of Poetry*, and it is as an imaginative
artist of a high order that we most value him.

In effect, however, the imagination was not to Shelley the
agency by which he experienced 'the pains and pleasures of his
species' – as it was with Shakespeare. It was the agency by which
he was transported from the contemplation of his own isolation
and misery to an ideal world, a world of pure beauty, ideal love
and celestial harmony.

> The keen stars were twinkling,
> And the fair moon was rising among them,
>   Dear Jane!
> The guitar was tinkling,
> But the notes were not sweet till you sung them
>   Again.
>
> As the moon's soft splendour
> O'er the faint cold starlight of Heaven
>   Is thrown,
> So your voice most tender
> To the strings without soul had then given
>   Its own.
>
> The stars will awaken,
> Though the moon sleep a full hour later,
>   To-night;
> No leaf will be shaken
> Whilst the dews of your melody scatter
>   Delight.
>
> Though the sound overpowers,
> Sing again, with your dear voice revealing
>   A tone
> Of some world far from ours,
> Where music and moonlight and feeling
>   Are one.

In these lines *To Jane*, the words 'some world far from ours' are characteristic. The world of Shelley's imagination was one of swift movement, aerial insubstantiality, remote and immeasurable vastness. Nature was the free and spacious element which compensated for man's own restricted existence. The words 'vast', 'eternal', 'ethereal', 'swift' and 'dream' occur constantly in his poems; this is not to say that the insubstantiality of the world of his thought is matched by any insubstantiality of language and imagery. To say this would be like saying that the paintings of Turner use vague and airy means to convey an impression of vague airiness. This is not so. Turner is the pictorial counterpart of Shelley. Few painters, and few poets, have ever conveyed more surely and by such subtle and inimitable means the sense of illimitable space and dazzling light. There is nothing cloudy about the language in which Shelley conveys the idea of a cloud. Typical of his attitude to nature is his passion for storms – clouds, wind, thunder, lightning, hail and rain; and in the *Ode to the West Wind*, perhaps his most completely realised imaginative creation, he conveys the sense of the destructive and regenerative forces of nature – forces of which he desires, as an inspired poet, to be the agent. The eighteenth century produced much excellent descriptive writing, based on direct sensuous perception; but compared with Shelley even Wordsworth is a painter of still life. Shelley's poetry, like the man, is restless, conveying as no other poetry does, the sense of nature, not as a picture, but as a power, active, vital and quickening. He was the first completely nineteenth-century poet. The nature he realises in his best work is an embodiment of the dreams, the healthy idealism of youth, its undefined imaginings and its buoyant aspirations. We may not wholly approve of nineteenth-century libertarian and perfectionist aspirations, but we cannot deny their power. Shelley was their prophet. When we think of the part that socialism has played in our own century, of fabianism and the influence of Ruskin, then of Browning's optimism and the influence Shelley had on Browning – then Shelley's claim to be regarded as an 'unacknowledged legislator' may not seem so absurd as some have found it. That the ideas which have struggled into fulfilment in our time were born of nineteenth-century aspirations there can be no doubt; that such aspirations were by their nature vague is also true. But the language in which Shelley realised his world of the imagination, where aspirations are born, was far from vague. If it had been, it must have had less influence. From such generalities we can always return to the actual poems for proof of Shelley's unique power to convey the dynamic aspects of nature.

> . . . The thunder-smoke
> Is gathering on the mountains, like a cloak
> Folded athwart their shoulders broad and bare;
> The ripe corn under the undulating air
> Undulates like an ocean; – and the vines
> Are trembling wide in all their trellised lines –
> The murmur of the awakening sea doth fill
> The empty pauses of the blast; – the hill
> Looks hoary through the white electric rain,
> And from the glens beyond, in sullen strain,
> The interrupted thunder howls; above
> One chasm of Heaven smiles, like the eye of Love
> On the unquiet world . . .
>
> (*Letter to Maria Gisborne*, 1820)

By contrast, the descriptive poetry of Keats represents in some ways a return to the eighteenth century. It is static, rich in detail and in classical allusion. But of course it is very seldom merely descriptive; it is usually charged with personal emotion, that of a man keenly alive to the beauties of the natural world. Keats was not, like most of his contemporaries, a didactic poet. He reacted against the idea that poetry should have a message. He was, for most of his brief life, in love with poetry for its own sake.

JOHN KEATS (1795–1821) was born in London, the son of a livery-stable keeper. Before he was nine years old, his father died, and two months later his mother re-married. When he was fourteen, his mother died, leaving him virtually in charge of the welfare of his two brothers and his sister, under the not very sympathetic guardianship of their step-father. After a passable education, Keats was apprenticed to an apothecary, and later to a surgeon; but after a short hospital training, he fell in love with literature, to which he devoted his remaining years. In 1816 he met the poet and radical journalist, Leigh Hunt, and also Hazlitt. He was immediately influenced by the lush descriptive style of Hunt's poems, and by his cultivation of the Italian renaissance. Through his association with Hunt he was regarded as one of the so-called 'Cockney School' of writers who were abused for their radicalism by Scottish Tory reviewers. No one was, in fact, less interested in politics than Keats. In the same year he made the acquaintance of Shelley, and began to write the poems on which his fame is based. From the first his poems were concerned with poetry. In the sonnet *On first looking into Chapman's Homer* he expresses the rapture of his discovery of Greek literature; in *Sleep and Poetry* he reveals his ambition to be a poet.

> O Poesy! for thee I grasp my pen,
> That am not yet a glorious denizen
> Of thy wide heaven; yet, to my ardent prayer,
> Yield from thy sanctuary some clear air,
> Smoothed for intoxication by the breath
> Of flowering bays, that I may die a death
> Of luxury, and my young spirit follow
> The morning sunbeams to the great Apollo
> Like a fresh sacrifice.

In this same poem he declares his faith in the Romantic conception of poetry, and pours scorn upon the followers of Pope, with their slavery to pedantic rules of prosody. His own masters were Spenser, from whom he derived a penchant for allegory, Shakespeare and Milton. Early in 1817, he published his first volume of poems. This failed. He at once began on a far more ambitious project, the long romantic allegory, *Endymion*. This is concerned with the search for ideal beauty and love, but Keats' interest was not so much in his theme as in the opportunities it gave him for voluptuous description and luxuriant imagery. When it was published in 1818, *Endymion* was severely censured, but the fact remains that, despite its weaknesses, it is one of the most genuinely promising poems ever produced by a man as young as twenty-one. Keats shows himself to have had that exuberance of creativity and profusion of utterance which, once they are controlled by experience and artistry, produce the best poetry.

Keats next finished *Isabella, or the Pot of Basil*, based on a story from Boccaccio, and began on *Hyperion*, an epic narrative in the manner of Milton. In the autumn of 1818 he first met Fanny Brawne, the daughter of a Hampstead neighbour. He fell passionately in love with her, and the two became engaged at

Christmas. Before that, however, Keats had nursed his younger brother Tom through the consumption which ended his life. It was not long before he discovered in himself the unmistakable symptoms of the same fatal hereditary disease. From January 1819 until September 1820, when he left England for the last time, Keats' life was a mounting fever, in which poetry, love and death were the recurrent themes. In *The Eve of St Agnes* he adopts a medieval theme reminiscent of *Christabel*, and aims at an ever greater richness of sensuous appeal. In April 1819 he met Coleridge at Hampstead, and Coleridge recorded his presentiment of Keats' approaching death. *Lamia* and *La Belle Dame sans Merci* are inspired by the compulsive passion for Fanny Brawne. *Lamia*, a story derived from Burton's *Anatomy of Melancholy*, tells of a deadly witch-serpent transformed into a beautiful maiden, and of Lycius' infatuation with her, despite the arguments of the philosopher Apollonius. *La Belle Dame sans Merci* is, on the surface, a pastiche medieval lyric, but with as profoundly personal a significance as *The Ancient Mariner*. It is a work of pure inspiration, in which are fused Keats' sorrowful despair at the death of his brother, and his sense of the devastating effects of obsessive passion. It is the solemn and heart-rending elegy upon himself of a man aware that he is doomed by hereditary illness, the love of woman, and the ambition for fame. It is perhaps Keats' most unquestionable poetic success.

There is no space in which to deal with Keats' sonnets, fine as some of them are, nor with his lighter verse, which abundantly shows itself to be the work of a true poet in moods of relaxation. The crown of his work is generally agreed to be the great Odes – *To Psyche, On Melancholy, To a Nightingale, On a Grecian Urn,* and *To Autumn.* In these he explores the theme of the serenity and permanence of great art in contrast to the misery and brevity of life. In *To a Nightingale* he is poignantly aware of his personal situation, and of the world of ideal beauty to which he is transported by the bird's song. In *On a Grecian Urn* he sees a work of classic art as a thing of chaste and serene tranquillity symbolising the identity of truth and beauty, which before had seemed to Keats irreconcilably opposed. The *Ode to Autumn* evokes in three stanzas the spirit of the season of calm fruition, and breathes a sense of reconciliation on the part of Keats with the fate which had made his life one with the harvested sheaves. Nowhere is

Keats' power of sensuous suggestion better illustrated – a power which is now under the control of a subdued and self-disciplined mind. In the first stanza Keats describes the sights of autumn, the ripe fruits and the late flowers; in the second, he personifies the spirit of Harvest and evokes the scents of the hayfield and the cider-making; in the last stanza he describes to perfection the sounds of autumn.

> Where are the songs of Spring? Ay, where are they?
>   Think not of them, thou hast thy music too, –
> While barrèd clouds bloom the soft-dying day;
>   And touch the stubble-plains with rosy hue;
> Then in a wailful choir the small gnats mourn
>   Among the river sallows, borne aloft,
>   Or sinking as the light wind lives or dies;
> And full-grown lambs loud bleat from hilly bourn;
> Hedge-crickets sing; and now with treble soft
>   The red-breast whistles from a garden-croft;
>   And gathering swallows twitter in the skies.

It may be fanciful, though the temptation is irresistible, to link this final image of the 'gathering swallows' with Keats' conviction of the urgency, for himself, of going south into the sunshine with the swallows to escape the fatal cold and damp of an English winter. He did in fact survive one more winter in London, but in February 1820 his fatal illness began. The following autumn he sailed for Italy, accompanied by his friend, Joseph Severn. He died in Rome in February 1821.

Keats' poems, considered, as they should be, in conjunction with his letters, and with what we know of his lovable and attractive personality, are the work of a great man and a poet of extraordinary gifts. As a man – and he enjoyed only a few years of full manhood – Keats was generous, conscientious about family responsibilities, a loyal friend, and a companion full of zest, enthusiasm and humour. His character rises altogether superior to the rather ordinary circle of friends who surrounded him. He was fired by a single-minded devotion to poetry, in the pursuit of which he burnt himself up; his reflections and intuitions on the nature of poetry, as expressed in letters to friends, are almost, if not quite, the finest flowers of his genius. 'I am certain of nothing,' he wrote, 'but the holiness of the heart's affections and the truth of imagination. What the imagination seizes as beauty must be truth.' And again: 'Poetry should surprise by a fine excess. . . . It should strike the reader as a wording of his own highest thoughts and appear almost as a remembrance.' In these and many other passages he put into memorable form his forthright and uncompromising conviction of the supreme worth of poetry. The felicitous phrases which abound in his critical utterances have been for over a century, and will continue to be, the *loci classici* of a profoundly imaginative view of poetry. These utterances are of greater pregnancy than those of any of his contemporaries except Coleridge at his most inspired. They are the result of his daily concern with his chosen vocation, not only as a writer but as a reader. His share in the poetic revolution of his time was to focus attention once more on the capacity of poetry to embody lofty and splendid conceptions, a capacity somewhat in abeyance since Elizabethan times. Even in *Endymion* and *Hyperion*, which must be accounted great failures, he was in search of the kind of large and heroic conceptions which would have engaged the efforts of Spenser.

Keats was a ceaseless experimenter, keenly self-critical, but not to the point where creativity was inhibited or dammed. It will be remembered how the heroic conception of poetry died with Milton, and was replaced by the mock-heroic. In attempting to revive the Spenserian allegory, in the hope of re-creating a heroic poetry, Keats was bound to fail. The Romantic era was not, after the false fire of the early revolutionary period, heroic. What the poet had to celebrate was no longer the possibility of a great society but the capacity of the individual for heroic suffering. Individual sensibility was the theme of poetry from Wordsworth onwards. Keats did not believe in the rôle of the poet as a moral philosopher, or an 'unacknowledged legislator': he believed that he was dedicated to the exercise of imagination in the pursuit of beauty and truth – truth not in the moralist's but in the artist's sense. Knowledge of his personality and his tragic fate has coloured most views of his poetry from the publication of *Adonais* to our own day. Taken by themselves, the poems inadequately represent the true quality of Keats. Nevertheless, the finest poems of the great year, 1819, are of the quintessence of Romanticism. *La Belle Dame sans Merci* and the ode *To Autumn* approach perfection, and many consider that *On a Grecian Urn* also is perfect. On strictly critical considerations, few of the poems, even the best, are without flaws; yet everywhere we find the Shakespearean phrase, the rounded felicity of expression which is the mark of the best in English poetry.

What Keats came finally to discover, perhaps without knowing it, was the use of all the suggestive power of words – their music, their associations, their romantic and sensuous appeal – to convey a personal mood, whether of melancholy, of heart-ache, of serenity, or of exaltation. His poems are very rarely autobiographical in any direct sense, as Coleridge's often were; yet we feel that his best things are informed throughout by his personal joys and sufferings. He stands, therefore, it seems to me, for the emotional integrity of poetry, for truth of feeling, and against frigidity, artifice and meanness.

The chief poets of the Romantic period have demanded treatment at considerable length, and little space is available for the many minor poets of the time. There is, however, another and a better reason why they need not concern us: unlike the minor poets of the Elizabethan age, they are not particularly interesting. But it would be wrong to deny that there were poets who were, in their day, considered as important as Wordsworth and Coleridge, and more important than Shelley or Keats. Leigh Hunt, whose influence on Keats is so questionable, enjoyed some popularity; even more popular were the *Irish Melodies* of Byron's friend, Tom Moore. These admirable, though artificial, lyrics were written to be sung to traditional Irish airs, much as Burns had composed words for the airs of Scotland; they are easy, graceful and mellifluous, and have something of the facile beauty of the songs of the Cavaliers. Thomas Campbell, Thomas Hood, George Darley, Felicia Hemans and Anna Laetitia Barbauld all had their vogue and wrote at least a few pieces which have retained some popularity. Walter Savage Landor, whose long life spanned the whole of the Romantic and early Victorian era, is one of the most interesting minor figures of the time; his lapidary lyrics, far more classical than romantic in spirit, have outlived most of the work of his lesser contemporaries. The brief lyric of formal perfection has always seemed to English poets worth achieving: the very unruliness and profusion of the language in comparison with that of Horace or of the Greek Anthology have provided a challenge. If Landor's *Rose Aylmer* and *Past ruin'd Ilion Helen lives* have something of the stiffness of a wax flower, they never-

theless deserve to be remembered with the brief masterpieces of
Herrick and Housman.

Of far more lasting appeal, however, than any of these is
JOHN CLARE (1793–1864), who outlived both his fame and
his period, and spent almost half his life in the dreary seclusion
of a madhouse.

> I am: yet what I am none cares or knows,
>   My friends forsake me like a memory lost;
> I am the self-consumer of my woes,
>   They rise and vanish in oblivious host,
> Like shades in love and death's oblivion lost;
> And yet I am, and live with shadows tost
>
> Into the nothingness of scorn and noise,
>   Into the living sea of waking dreams,
> Where there is neither sense of life nor joys,
>   But the vast shipwreck of my life's esteems;
> And e'en the dearest – that I loved the best –
> Are strange – nay, rather stranger than the rest.
>
> I long for scenes where man has never trod,
>   A place where woman never smiled or wept,
> There to abide with my creator, God,
>   And sleep as I in childhood sweetly slept:
> Untroubling and untroubled where I lie,
> The grass below – above, the vaulted sky.

So he wrote during his last years as a man forgotten and
neglected, and the lines are the final statement of the isolation of
the Romantic poet. Clare was to discover, as Shelley and Keats
discovered, that the poet in modern times has no place in the
social order and that he possesses nothing but his individual
sensibility. Shelley and Keats died young; Clare alone was left to
bear the burden of his identity in solitude. His work was for the
most part forgotten until the present century; but if we turn back
to 1820, the year when Shelley, Keats and Byron were at the
zenith of their creative effort, we find that Clare achieved also a
sudden meteoric popularity. He was then twenty-seven, and if
he had died before he was thirty, his fame might have remained
as bright as that of his contemporaries.

Born in 1793, the son of a very poor Northamptonshire farm
worker, John Clare received a rudimentary education, and
spent the greater part of his working life eking out a mere sub-
sistence on the land. In his adolescence he became infected with

the passion for poetry, and gave himself an informal education in the literature of the day by spending all his earnings on books. He fell obsessively in love with a country girl of rather superior station, Mary Joyce, to whom he proposed marriage. Her rejection of him preyed on his mind, but became one of the leading motives in the poems which with unparalleled fluency he began to pour out. These were mostly descriptions and evocations of nature, outwardly in the manner of the late eighteenth-century topographical writers, but with a marked fidelity and individuality of vision. His marriage to a farmer's daughter brought no satisfaction to his restless and sensitive nature, and resulted in a growing family who were always on the verge of starvation. In 1819 his poems attracted the notice of a London publisher, John Taylor, who issued them the following year as the work of an unlettered 'peasant poet'. In the literary atmosphere of the day this ensured their immediate success, but hastened the neglect into which Clare's poems subsequently fell. This early success was bad for him, but not for his poetry. Failure and material difficulties gradually increased his mental instability, and in 1837 he was confined to a private asylum. From thence he drifted home four years later, but the causes of his malaise remained. In 1841 he was confined in Northampton Asylum, where he spent the remainder of a long and harmless life. The poems he wrote there are among his finest. He died in 1864.

Most of Clare's best work was never corrected for the press, and he wrote in almost total isolation from the literary currents of his time. He had no Coleridge, nor even a Leigh Hunt, to guide and advise him. His work, as it is now preserved, is full of the faults of over-profusion and under-correction, but the best of his poems are the result of pure inspiration. One is inevitably reminded of Robert Graves' *Lost Love*:

> His eyes are quickened so with grief,
> He can watch a grass or leaf
> Every instant grow; he can
> Clearly through a flint wall see,
> Or watch the startled spirit flee
> From the throat of a dead man . . .
>   This man is quickened so with grief,
> He wanders god-like or like thief
> Inside and out, below, above,
> Without relief seeking lost love.

Clare experienced nature with preternaturally heightened sensibility, and his inborn integrity as an artist led him to record his experience with the utmost fidelity. Yet his descriptive power was no merely photographic talent; a fresh and delicate perception informs his vision of the Midlands landscape in which he grew up, loved, and suffered.

In their manifesto of Romanticism, the Preface to *Lyrical Ballads*, Wordsworth and Coleridge had described the poet in these words:

> What is a poet? To whom does he address himself? And what language is to be expected from him? – He is a man speaking to men: a man, it is true, endowed with more lively sensibility, more enthusiasm and tenderness, who has a greater knowledge of human nature and a more comprehensive soul than are supposed to be common among mankind; a man pleased with his own passions and volitions, and who rejoices more than other men in the spirit of life that is in him; delighting to contemplate similar volitions and passions as manifested in the goings-on of the Universe, and habitually impelled to create them where he does not find them.

Clare was an infant when these words were written, but it was as if he came into existence to act the part of the poet as here described. He was a conscientious craftsman with high critical standards, but he was no theorist: when all else had failed him, he believed in the power of poetry to interpret life and give it meaning.

CHAPTER TWELVE

The Middle-Class Muse

1830-1892

THE death of Byron in 1824 marks the end of a phase in English literature. Aristocracy and poetry had hitherto been connected, even though the connection had often been tenuous. The fact that Clare had been advertised in 1820 as the 'peasant poet' was symptomatic. Wordsworth, though of fairly humble origin, had been in a position of dependence on influential patronage, and his championship of those of lowly station had had in its turn a somewhat patronising air. But since the nobility, with stray exceptions, had little real interest in poetry, poets enjoyed, during the Romantic period, an unwonted independence. They felt themselves exiled from society, and this gave them comparative freedom of utterance. Shelley's anarchism would have been unthinkable for a poet fifty years before or after his time.

But the age of democracy – which in Victorian times meant the rule of the middle classes – began with the passing of the Reform Act of 1832. From now on the poet had to consider the opinions of the wealthiest, most numerous and in some respects most tyrannical patron he had ever known – the great British public. How did poetry thrive under its new master?

The poets of the nineteenth century found themselves heirs to the rich and varied discoveries of Romanticism. Some of them explored the regions of private sensibility; but on the whole there was a move away from subjectivism, as being slightly unhealthy, or at any rate unmanly. Some followed the more promising paths opened up by Romantic interest in medieval and classical legend. Some attempted to grapple, but not very successfully, with the social and intellectual problems of the day. The poets of the Victorian age, however varied their themes, have for the modern reader one thing in common – a certain thinness of technical interest. They were mostly satisfied to write in Miltonic or Wordsworthian blank verse, or in the lyric forms of Byron, Shelley and Keats, and to echo the rhythm and diction of one or more of these poets. If we read any typical early Victorian lyric – for instance, Clough's 'Say not the struggle nought availeth' – we are aware of a certain generalised poetic diction, which gives the lines a vaguely poetic sound which probably answered the needs of a not very discriminating public. That opening line alone contains one inversion and two archaisms which, without being otherwise justified, make it sound rather solemn and impressive. The lyric as a whole appears to be concerned with the spiritual doubts and uncertainties by which sensitive Victorians were assailed when they reflected on the effects of Darwinism on religious dogma. But it does not strike us as having the force of more than a pathetic and ineffectual sigh. Arthur Hugh Clough, the friend of Tennyson and of Arnold, was a minor poet, and in perspective the Victorian age is best considered as a long age of minor poets, many of them popular in their day, and most now regarded as having been over-rated.

It is difficult to believe how popular Lord Macaulay's *Lays of Ancient Rome* (1842) once were, but their vigorous and manly rhythm, and their simplified view of human actions recommended them warmly to a philistine and expansionist nation. A complete contrast is offered in the lyrical and dramatic writings of Macaulay's contemporary, Thomas Lovell Beddoes, who was afflicted by insanity and committed suicide in 1849. He continued the tradition of the Jacobean drama from the point where Webster and Tourneur had left off. He was a poet of marked power and originality, but he stands far outside the main stream of nineteenth-century poetry.

William Barnes's *Poems of Rural Life*, which appeared between 1844 and 1863, are in the Dorset dialect, and convey a picture of idyllic rural tranquillity. It was one of the successes of Romanticism to have accommodated poetry to the rural scene, and it was part of the Victorian tragedy to have exiled man from nature through the influences of industrialism. England became most poignantly aware of the beauty of nature at a time when it was being increasingly threatened by industry. In such an atmosphere the poems of such nature lovers as Barnes had a peculiarly nostalgic appeal.

Many readers of Emily Brontë will feel that her great novel is by far her finest poem, but the lyrics she published in 1846 have a peculiar bleak intensity and integrity which shine through the conventional early Victorian diction we have already noted in connection with Clough.

Another woman poet, and one who attempted valiantly to accommodate the problems of the day to a voluminous but inadequate poetic gift, was Elizabeth Barrett, already famous before Browning's celebrated courtship. It is difficult to see what Browning or the larger reading public saw in Miss Barrett's undistinguished verse, but it was the kind of verse well calculated to appeal to a middle-class intelligentsia whose real literary needs were catered for by the prose novel. This intelligentsia was earnest, puzzled, and a prey to doubts about man's ultimate destiny despite the assurances of progressive liberal thinkers. To them, therefore, the frankly fatalistic hedonism of the Persian poet Omar Khayyám, whose *Rubáiyát* was translated by Edward Fitzgerald and published anonymously in 1859, must have come with a shock of relief. Fitzgerald's poem, written in facile rhymed pentameters, represents one of the efforts of the Victorian intelligentsia to escape from the consequences and the atmosphere of commercial materialism and the feelings of guilt it engendered. The 'sorry scheme of things' which the eleventh-century Persian poet desired to shatter might well come to mean the whole dismal structure of Victorian industrialism which oppressed the conscience of the age.

MATTHEW ARNOLD (1822–1888) must be accounted more than a minor figure in the literary and critical world of his day; if he must be regarded as no more than a minor poet, his work is nevertheless among the most rewarding of the period. It is of considerable psychological interest, and breathes a quiet, though somewhat nerveless, charm of language and atmosphere. Before, and even after, he became the apostle of 'sweetness and light' and the high priest of culture against anarchy in government and barbarism in taste, all that he wrote is informed by his gentle, sometimes wistful, spirit; his polemical writings have a satirical toughness and humour not found in his poetry, and his criticism, mostly the outcome of his Professorship of Poetry at

Oxford, had a salutary effect on educated taste towards the end of the century.

He was the son of the Rev. Dr Thomas Arnold, historical and religious controversialist and founder of the modern Public School system, with its emphasis on strenuous Christianity, sound classical scholarship, liberal idealism and the striving towards self-perfection. The system to some extent reformed the landed gentry and civilised the commercial barbarians from the new manufacturing class. It would perhaps be an exaggeration to say that Matthew was the first victim of the Public School system; but there can be no doubt that, on a gentle, poetic spirit, the severe, though benevolent paternalism of Dr Arnold's views had a somewhat repressive influence. At all events, it is possible to trace, throughout the poems, the signs of an inner conflict between Puritanism and duty on the one hand and the Hellenistic paganism of his intellectual background on the other.

Matthew Arnold was educated at Winchester, Rugby and Oriel College, Oxford, where he became a Fellow. He travelled on the Continent, and has left in some of his less-known lyrics the record of an attachment to a young woman he calls 'Marguerite'. The pictures of her contained in a number of poems which he entitled *Switzerland* are charming, but it is probable that he found her frivolous and worldly. Some internal inhibition, rather than external prohibition, seems to have ended the affair, which involved some sort of renunciation in the name of some sort of duty. In a poem called *The Lake*, which describes a reunion after separation, he says:

> Again I spring to make my choice;
> Again in tones of ire
> I hear a God's tremendous voice –
> 'Be counselled, and retire!'

Could it have been that Marguerite was a Catholic, with whom union to a disciple of Dr Arnold's broad church Protestantism was unthinkable? At all events the renunciation coloured all his later thinking: the confessional passages in his poems abound in references to man's loss of what he most desires, to the isolation of human souls, to 'the salt, unplumbed, estranging sea' which divides them. 'We rush by coasts where we had lief remain', he sighs in *Human Life*; and both *The Forsaken Merman* and *The New Sirens* are concerned, allegorically and indirectly, with a conflict between paganism and Christianity involving grief and renunciation.

The total volume of Arnold's poems is, for a Victorian, slight. He had neither great originality nor great creative strength; his imagery is not forceful and his technical accomplishment is uneven. For all that, he was a constant striver after a poetic utterance which would express his restless spirit and satisfy his classical ideals of clarity and grace. He read and imitated the Greeks for their charm and for the sunny sweetness of their lost Mediterranean world rather than for their primitive vigour and tragic splendour. His evocations of the English countryside in *The Scholar Gipsy* and in *Thyrsis*, the elegy on his friend Clough, are full of pastoral beauty. When Arnold writes of contemporary life with 'its sick hurry and divided aims', and refers elsewhere to the social ills of his time, he is perhaps projecting upon society some of the malaise in his own nature. When he is preaching Swift's ideal of 'sweetness and light', and the advancement of classical standards in culture and education, he is perhaps compensating for the frustrations in his own life. The autobiographical strain in his poems is muted and often disguised, but if we hear it correctly, there is, behind the mask of the moralist, the true poet repressed by the social and personal forces which shaped him. The best known of his later poems, *Sohrab and Rustum*, is an imaginary Persian episode related in the manner of a Homeric epic. Critics have been more concerned either to praise the stateliness and dignity of its manner or to censure the artificiality of the Homeric similes than to notice the theme. The poem relates the accidental killing of a son by a venerated father. If this subject was not chosen quite arbitrarily, surely it is impossible to overlook the connection, oblique though it is, with Arnold's own case.

There is about all his more ambitious poems, especially those inspired by Greek models, this same obliquity of statement. There is about much Victorian poetry something of this form of concealment, as if only in this way could the unregenerate poet come to terms with middle-class standards of morality. More significant, and altogether more alive than these 'dramatic' pieces are some of the earlier lyrics, where Arnold seems to be speaking directly and with his own voice, not that of a Professor of Poetry or a purveyor of Hellenistic culture.

Of those poets who came to maturity during the first half of the Victorian period only Tennyson and Browning have serious claims to be considered major poets. On the score of its relevance to contemporary life, its bulk and its popularity, their work is bound to loom large in any study of nineteenth-century literature. When we come to consider it in the context of English poetry as a whole, however, we have doubts.

ALFRED TENNYSON, later LORD TENNYSON (1809–1892), enjoyed the greatest popularity ever accorded to an English poet during his lifetime. He came to be regarded almost as the 'unacknowledged legislator' of Shelley's manifesto, as an arbiter or oracle on the questions of the day. It is clear that such unprecedented popularity was not due to the merits of his poetry alone. Other poets in his time, though less widely read, also enjoyed considerable favour. We can only say that cultural conditions in the later nineteenth century favoured the existence, if only temporarily, of a widespread demand for poetry. Nor was Tennyson's popularity attained without artistic sacrifice.

Tennyson was born at Somersby in Lincolnshire, the son of a country parson of slender means. He went to Louth Grammar School where, on hearing of the death of Byron, he was overcome by a tragic sense of loss. As a boy he was a fluent and precocious writer. In 1827 his earliest poems were printed locally, in company with those of his brother, Charles. At Trinity College, Cambridge, he was one of a circle of promising young literary men, and in 1829 he wrote his prize-winning poem, *Timbuctoo*, under the influence of Milton. The following year appeared his *Poems Chiefly Lyrical*, which included such things as *Mariana*, *Claribel* and *The Owl*. These show the essential qualities for which he was later to become famous – notably an astonishing combination of visual perceptiveness and verbal melody, as in the opening of *Mariana*.

> With blackest moss the flower-plots
> Were thickly crusted, one and all:
> The rusted nails fell from the knots
> That held the pear to the gable-wall.
> The broken sheds look'd sad and strange:
> Unlifted was the clinking latch;

Weeded and worn the ancient thatch
Upon the lonely moated grange.
    She only said, 'My life is dreary,
        He cometh not,' she said;
    She said, 'I am aweary, aweary,
        I would that I were dead!'

True, the poem has not much to say, and is no more than Tennyson's version of the medievalism of Keats and Coleridge. But it shows that a wide reading of poetry had made his ear abnormally sensitive to the cadences of the English tongue, and that a boyhood among the fens and wolds had made his eye keenly aware of the visual appeal of the countryside. *Poems Chiefly Lyrical* contains also a certain amount of pretentious and tumid writing, pardonable in a young man of twenty-one, but revealing a capacity for vulgarity which was never wholly suppressed.

In 1832 Tennyson published a further volume, which contained several of the poems which have always been among his most admired – *The Lady of Shalott, A Dream of Fair Women, Oenone, The Lotos-Eaters*. In these he surpassed his earlier work in sheer descriptive power, investing imaginary worlds of Arthurian and Greek legend with colour, warmth, and the magic of verbal melody. *The Lady of Shalott* suggests the cool lucidity of a medieval illumination; *Oenone* presents a glowingly romantic version of the myth of the judgement of Paris; *The Lotos-Eaters*, based on an episode in the *Odyssey*, goes as far as Tennyson ever went in depicting the yearning towards a life of sheer sensuous pleasure: it is as if he were trying to echo Keats' cry, 'O for a life of sensations rather than of thoughts!'

In much of this early poetry there is a dream-like quality. Tennyson is aware of his own physical sensations and of his growing technical accomplishment, and of little else. It might be described as Romanticism in search of a subject. Like the Romantics, Tennyson ranged over the whole field of imaginative literature in search of subject-matter; but whereas at the centre of their poems is always the romantic ego striving for self-expression, there seems to be at the centre of Tennyson's fantasies nothing but an unusually clear eye and a superb ear. What, one may ask, did the story of Elaine or the fate of Oenone mean to Tennyson? It is as if in fact he shrank from the life of sensations by which Keats had been consumed, and as if his experience was literary – sheer words. To progress from this position, a change had to come over his work.

A period of crisis ensued. His close friend, Arthur Hallam, who was engaged to marry Tennyson's sister, died suddenly in 1833; this plunged the poet into a gulf of gloom and despair, and greatly aggravated a natural tendency to hypochondria. Moreover, his poems had not been well received by the critics, and he was always sensitive to criticism, to the point of morbidity. He began work on the Arthurian poems which came later to be called *Idylls of the King*, and on some of the sections of *In Memoriam*, an extended series of elegiac lyrics commemorating his dead friend. He was engaged to be married, but the engagement was indeterminately protracted owing to his poverty. At last in 1842 a new two-volume edition of his poems brought him wider recognition, and it was not long before he was accepted as the leading poet of his time. The new edition contained certain poems which exhibited a more strenuous, even moralistic, turn of mind: *Sir Galahad* and the *Morte d'Arthur*, besides some poems more specifically English in background and inspiration, notably *Dora* and *Locksley Hall*.

Fame, however, did not bring him wealth, and in 1845 he was granted a Civil List pension. He still suffered from prolonged bouts of melancholy. He next tackled a subject of public interest, the higher education of women; but *The Princess* was not well received.

Gradually his work began to make more concessions to public taste. In 1850 came the real turn in his fortunes. He published *In Memoriam*, and was made Poet Laureate in succession to Wordsworth. He was also enabled to marry. The remainder of his life was uneventful. Despite his immense popularity, Tennyson craved seclusion, and when his house in the Isle of Wight became the haunt of sightseers, he built for himself a more inaccessible home in Hampshire.

He took his Laureateship seriously, and in 1852 published his grandiloquent *Ode on the Death of the Duke of Wellington*. Other patriotic poems followed, including *The Charge of the Light Brigade*. *Maud* (1855) represents something of a return to his earlier mode. Although it was dramatic in form, it showed greater subjectivity than other poems of this period, and even a strain of passionate morbidity. Tennyson thought highly of it himself, and when the public received it badly, his feelings were wounded. He atoned for this affront to public opinion by publishing in 1859 the *Idylls of the King*. With the possible exception of some of Scott's and Byron's works, this was the most popular book of poems ever published in English. 10,000 copies were sold in a month. Tennyson was in his fiftieth year and at the height of his fame. In these disconnected tales in blank verse based on Malory, the modern reader can recognise a charm and grace of narration, a certain attractive portrayal of character, and a serene other-worldliness in the delineation of a medieval dream-landscape. But the unprecedented popularity of the *Idylls* is not to be explained by their intrinsic quality so much as by their immediate appeal to middle-class mid-Victorian minds. This dream world of turreted castles, brave and chivalrous knights, fair ladies, quests and enchantments offered an irresistible contrast to the urban materialism, the struggle for wealth, the spiritual doubts that oppressed the Victorian conscience. There is this to be said for the nineteenth century – it did want poetry: that it also wanted poetry to be respectable, idealistic, and unembarrassing was a fact to be taken into account by any poet desiring to secure a wide hearing. To provide poetry that was all these things, as well as supremely readable, was Tennyson's public duty.

In 1862 he was presented to Queen Victoria, and in the same year he published more poems, including a domestic idyll, *Enoch Arden*. This was once taken very seriously by a public which had by now learned from Browning to enjoy psychological problems in verse form. He followed it with further Arthurian and patriotic poems. In 1884 he accepted the offer of a peerage, which he had more than once refused. In 1892 he died, and was buried in Westminster Abbey. Unlike Wordsworth, Tennyson had not started as a rebel, and it is therefore in his case less to be wondered at that he ended as an institution. He remained poetically alive to the last decade of his life. Some of his final poems, which deal with the social problems of his time, have been greatly admired; even if one cannot be enthusiastic about them, one can at least admit that Tennyson was never content to rest on his laurels, even though they were so well deserved.

It is difficult to sum up his achievement. His poems are not particularly attractive to the present generation, but they have in them qualities which may well recommend them to future readers. All can agree on their command of language, their variety, their sincerity. Yet few would now concede to them anything like the importance they seem to pretend to. After reading, say, *Enoch Arden* or *Tithonus*, one feels like asking what all the fuss is about. A great deal of technical mastery has been called into play for the illustration or demonstration of an idea or a truth which seems comparatively trite or unimpressive. The opening lines of *Tithonus* (1860) are, from the point of view of word-magic and sensuous suggestion, among the most purely beautiful ever written.

> The woods decay, the woods decay and fall,
> The vapours weep their burden to the ground,
> Man comes and tills the field and lies beneath,
> And after many a summer dies the swan.
> Me only cruel immortality
> Consumes: I wither slowly in thine arms,
> Here at the quiet limit of the world,
> A white-haired shadow roaming like a dream
> The ever silent spaces of the East,
> Far-folded mists, and gleaming halls of morn.

The carefully wrought and solemn melody of this induction surely portends something of surpassing importance. The poem is based on the legend of the mortal, Tithonus, on whom his wife Aurora had conferred immortality; he is now weary with life, and begs the goddess to withdraw her gift. That is all. What is the purpose of the poem – to illustrate the truism that we can have far too much of a good thing, or to give expression to a mood of weariness and disillusion? In either case, the means adopted – the solemn opening, the apparatus of classical mythology, the ornate diction and elaborate descriptive vignettes – seem excessive. There is an unreality about the whole thing, as if we were contemplating an exquisite stucco façade covering an inner emptiness. The crux of Tithonus' argument comes at the point where he says that immortality is not for mortals.

> Why should a man desire in any way
> To vary from the kindly race of men,
> Or pass beyond the goal of ordinance
> Where all should pause, as is most meet for all?

Here the hollowness beneath the façade is most apparent, and betrays itself in the utter unreality of the language. Who ever *spoke* like this? Tennyson is using a language that is neither the speech of his day nor any other recognisable idiom, but a hotch-potch of vaguely impressive phrases.

Tennyson is said to have admitted that he never had anything to say. Yet even this admission hardly satisfies. We do not look for a message, a dogmatic assertion, a didactic intention in poetry; in any case, his poems are perhaps at their least satisfy-ing when they come nearest to having a message. Is it rather that he lacks feeling, not thought? His poems abound in dramatised feeling, as in *Maud*; yet one is never convinced that there is a man of flesh and blood behind the passionate utterances. Many readers have placed *In Memoriam* at the head of Tennyson's achievement; but in the even flow of its quatrains there is an almost cold perfection which half expresses, half inhibits the out-burst of personal passion. There is a sense in which a superb technique is the enemy of true feeling. Tennyson is always too much in control of his poems: they never carry him away. In the work of any poet whom we regard as among the greatest there is at times the feeling that he is in the possession of an over-mastering experience which takes his poem out of his hands and writes it. Tennyson has nothing of this poetic frenzy; he is a Parnassian, undeniably a classic, but a minor classic. Even Arnold's uneven achievement is essentially more interesting. Despite all his variety, Tennyson never surprises us. But in Arnold's less well known pages we can often find some line or stanza, some turn of phrase, some unexpected overtone by which we recognise that the poem has a life of its own, that it is not just a superbly wrought artefact but the manifestation of an inner emotional urge working through the poet's conscious art.

Almost as difficult to assess as Tennyson is his friend and rival, Browning. Looking back at him from a time when poetry has no general appeal, it is not easy to visualise the atmosphere in which Browning was lionised by London literary circles, awarded honorary degrees, and made the centre of a learned society which bore his name. Like Tennyson, he dedicated his whole life to poetry, but unlike him, he had private means and never had to face the alternatives of poverty or writing for a living. He must be the last considerable poet in England who has enjoyed such freedom. Even now it is difficult to disentangle the poetry from the cult. Seventy years have passed since his death, and there can be few now living who were brought up in the full tide of his popularity. The fresh assessment of his work which is now being made is not altogether favourable, and critical opinion is strongly divided. There are those who accord him the status of a major, or a great, poet, and those who deny him any status at all. It is difficult to call a 'minor' poet anyone who once commanded such a following and who achieved such an immense mass of work; but disregarding mere quantity, and forming an estimate in and for our own day, we are bound to take a sober view of Browning's poetry. The fact is that the tide has turned against it. Nevertheless, there is still much to be enjoyed amidst the somewhat discouraging bulk of his poems.

ROBERT BROWNING (1812–1889) was the son of a Bank of England clerk, and lived with his family in London until the day of his marriage. His father was a minor poet, a lover of books, and a dilettante in several spheres. He indulged his only son's dislike of regular education, and after he left school at fourteen Robert was more or less self-taught. He acquired a heterogeneous and unsystematic mass of knowledge, literary, historical and artistic. He also retained all his life a more than ordinary love of animals. As a boy poet of some precocity, his first master was Byron; but he soon discovered Keats, and especially Shelley. He was carried away by Shelley's passionate libertarianism at a time when respectable middle-class circles regarded him with utter abhorrence. There was in Browning's life something of a conflict between the lover of natural life and all its destructive and anarchic forces, as embodied in Shelley, and the dutiful and well-conducted son of a bourgeois father and a mother of Scottish descent.

The poem he wrote under Shelley's influence, *Pauline*, was published anonymously in 1833. Later he suppressed it, and destroyed all the copies he could collect. It is of considerable autobiographical interest, but not at all recognisable as the work of the Browning whom everyone knows. In his next two poems, *Paracelsus* and *Sordello*, he concerned himself with the problem of artistic genius and the psychology of the creative mind. These long, obscure works earned for him some very adverse critical comment, and the support of a few readers of discernment, who saw in them promise of great originality and power. In one respect these two apprentice works are characteristic: they adopt the dramatic form – that is, they express Browning's views indirectly, through the agency of a historical or semi-historical character. This habit of mind, for so it became after *Pauline*, was not unlike the Tennysonian mask. Browning did, indeed, make a number of serious attempts to succeed as a writer for the theatre; whether or not he had the necessary gifts it is hard to say, since there was in his time no stage capable of calling them forth. Probably even Shakespeare would not have excelled if there had been no living stage tradition. Browning had the dramatist's capacity for projecting his ideas into the personalities and utterances of imaginary characters. He also had some, but not much, understanding of the clash of temperaments; he had no great gift for creating significant dramatic situations. Circumstances obliged him to seek some sort of compromise, and this he did in the form he made peculiarly his own – the dramatic monologue. In this he could expatiate upon art and literature; he could moralise and preach, he could describe and gossip and speculate to his heart's content without the fear of being called to account for his views.

Between 1841 and 1846 he published a series of pamphlets entitled *Bells and Pomegranates* – the bells representing the musical, the pomegranates the intellectual side of poetry. He began to make influential friends among literary men and women, and to receive wider recognition. His public was, however, still a select and limited one.

In 1846 occurred what was, in effect, the sole significant event of his life. Two years earlier a poem by the celebrated Elizabeth Barrett, six years his senior, contained a flattering reference to his work. Browning at once sought out the poetess, rescued her from the sick room in Wimpole Street where she was languishing, psychologically rather than physically a chronic invalid, and married her. The risk he took was considerable, for had her health really been such as to succumb to the shock of a clandestine marriage and a secret flight to Italy, society would never have forgiven him. As it was, the two enjoyed fifteen years of domestic happiness, mainly in Italy: Elizabeth began a new life, and Browning wrote what are now considered to be his best poems.

These were contained in the two volumes of *Men and Women* (1855) and *Dramatis Personae* (1864).

After his wife's death in 1861, Browning returned to England to supervise the education of their only son. His fame and popularity increased. They were crowned by the appearance of *The Ring and the Book* (1868–9). This was long considered his masterpiece. It was certainly a *tour de force* of unprecedented magnitude, consisting as it does of twelve separate versions of the same event, the trial of a Roman nobleman for the murder of his wife. The fact is, however, that Browning's psychological penetration is simply not adequate to sustain such an undertaking: he is more within his limits when he writes shorter pieces – pieces whose drift and quality can be grasped at a sitting – such as *The Bishop Orders his Tomb at St Praxed's Church*, *My Last Duchess* and *How it Strikes a Contemporary*.

The remaining twenty years of his life were spent in further strenuous poetical effort, in enjoying the recognition of his achievements, and in the pleasures of friendship and travel. Like Tennyson, whose fame he rivalled but never surpassed, he became an institution, admired for the range of his metaphysical and ethical speculations, and for the inscrutable depth and obscurity of much of his poetry. He died in Venice on a visit to his son, and was buried in Westminster Abbey.

The esteem in which Browning was held during the late Victorian age was due largely to the themes he investigated with such copious and original industry – the integrity of the artist, the duality of human nature, its sincerity and humbug, love between husband and wife, failure and success, spirituality and worldliness, self-fulfilment and conventional morality. His poetry was also admired for its fictional qualities – like the novels of Dickens, it was a crowded panorama of assorted characters, comic, pathetic, grotesque, noble or base. The typical Browning hero was the futile grammarian ceaselessly striving towards an unattainable goal which was desirable not for itself but for its unattainableness; the typical Browning sentiment for which the middle classes loved him was the hearty and virile optimism of *Rabbi ben Ezra*.

> Grow old along with me!
> The best is yet to be,
> The last of life, for which the first was made:

Our times are in His hand
Who saith 'A whole I planned,
Youth shows but half: trust God: see all nor be afraid!'

We no longer admire the expression of optimism, we regard a
love of effort for its own sake as sentimental, we do not read
poetry which slaps us on the back and jollies us along. We care
nothing for Browning's metaphysics, his ethics, his æsthetics.
We find his psychology superficial, his history amateurish. But
it may take a ton of ore to yield an ounce of pure metal; and in
the poetry of Browning's middle period there is a vein of true
poetry, unpretentious, alive and original. In such things as *Love
Among the Ruins*, *Up at a Villa – down in the City*, *Two in the Campagna*
and *A Toccata of Galuppi's* we can discover the best of Browning –
a Browning worth discovering, though perhaps an acquired taste
to modern palates. Wherever we find him at his best, his writing
is distinguished by a certain spontaneous lightness of touch,
familiarity, and genuine sweetness of tone and accent. He is at
his best when writing of Italy, which he always loved because of
the serenity and warmth of its climate, and the natural capacity
of its people for enjoying life. When Browning was gratifying the
taste of the Victorian middle classes for moralistic reflections, for
'profundity', for soul-searching and for the strenuous life, there
is a false note in his voice; but when he is writing of Italy and her
pleasure-loving, easy-going people, he is natural, colloquial and
genuine. He drops the back-slapping manner and the falsetto
voice, and a slight – almost delicate – poetry emerges.

Ere you open your eyes in the city, the blessed church-bells begin:
No sooner the bells leave off than the diligence rattles in:
You get the pick of the news, and it costs you never a pin.
By-and-by there's the travelling doctor gives pills, lets blood, draws
      teeth;
Or the Pulcinello-trumpet breaks up the market beneath.
At the post-office such a scene-picture – the new play piping hot!
And a notice how, only this morning, three liberal thieves were shot.
Above it, behold the Archbishop's most fatherly of rebukes,
And beneath, with his crown and his lion, some little new law of the
      Duke's!
                          (*Up at a Villa – Down in the City*)

Some account must now be given of the first considerable body
of poetry in English to be produced outside the British Isles.

Space does not allow of a full and detailed treatment of American poetry, but no general account of poetry written in our language can ignore the fact that for a century American poets have been included in English anthologies and have, without in any way losing their national identity, been regarded as belonging to the English tradition. There has been, indeed, at least one period – about the second decade of the present century – when the contribution made from the other side of the Atlantic has been more vital and influential than ours.

American poetry began unobtrusively with English-born colonists of the seventeenth century. The most important of these were ANNE BRADSTREET (1612–1672) and EDWARD TAYLOR (1644–1729), whose manuscripts were not discovered until more than two hundred years after his death. Anne Bradstreet's husband, whom she had married in England at the age of sixteen, was twice governor of the Massachusetts Bay Colony. During the colonial period America was too busy establishing herself as a nation to be much concerned with poetry, and Anne Bradstreet's poems were in fact first published in England, under the title, *The Tenth Muse Lately Sprung Up in America*. There was not, it must be said, anything specifically American about these poems: instead, they are for the most part a studied reconstruction of English poets, particularly of Spenser, Raleigh and Quarles. The chief influence upon them, appropriately enough, was the didactic and highly artificial French poet, du Bartas, who had already left his mark on English poetry.

Edward Taylor was more original, and the publication of his poems in 1939 was rightly hailed as something of a literary event. Although Taylor's poems – of which he expressly forbade publication after his death – closely resemble those of Herbert and the later Donne of the religious poems, his chief inspiration was derived from his peculiarly American situation, that of a Puritan parson engaged in the task of establishing a spiritual code in a new country. Although a man of complex intellect, Taylor sought plainness both as a poet and as a theologian:

> I fain would have a rich, fine Fancy ripe
> That curious polishings elaborate

Should lay, Lord, on thy glorious body bright
  The more my lumpish heart to animate.
  But searching o'er the Workhouse of my mind,
  I but one there; and dull and meagre find.

Hence, Lord, my Search hand thou from this dark Shop
  (It's foul, and wanteth Sweeping) up unto
Thy Glorious Body whose bright beams let drop
  Upon my heart: and Chant it with the Show,
  Because the Shine that from thy body flows,
  More glorious it than is the brightest rose.

Taylor is most original in his curious poem, *Upon a Wasp Chilled With Cold*; here passionate devotion vivifies a highly elaborate conceit with complete success.

It was not, however, until the early nineteenth century that anyone emerged who can be called a professional poet. Some of the poems of the New Jersey poet PHILIP FRENEAU (1752–1832) dealt with regional subjects, but he was entirely dependent on English models. The ballads and folk-songs exported by emigrants from Britain continued to be sung and modified by American usage, but a distinctively and consciously national style was slow to develop. The first truly American poems were written by WILLIAM CULLEN BRYANT (1794–1878), who is often called 'the father of American poetry'. The landscape that Bryant so gracefully celebrates, like the tone of his poems, is unmistakably American. His generous spirit found its most enduring expression in his simple nature poems, such as *To a Waterfowl* and *To the Fringed Gentian*.

Whatever the intrinsic merits of their work, the three New England poets, RALPH WALDO EMERSON (1803–1882), JOHN GREENLEAF WHITTIER (1807–1892) and HENRY WADSWORTH LONGFELLOW (1807–1882) were the first to write in a wholly American style. With the exception of Longfellow, they have never appealed strongly to English readers; and for this reason, perhaps, the extent of their influence has often been underestimated in England. As great a maker of aphorisms as La Rochefoucauld, Emerson was a clergyman who protested throughout his life against orthodoxy and dogma, and who eloquently pleaded the cause of American cultural independence. His poetry, although it lacks texture and is extremely uneven, is at its best warm and immediate in its appeal to forthright, pantheistic emotions.

There is no better verdict on Whittier than that of his contemporary New Englander, James Russell Lowell, another who exercised a great influence on American poetry:

> . . his failures arise (though he seems not to know it)
> From the very same cause that has made him a poet:
> A fervour of mind which knows no separation
> 'Twixt simple excitement and pure inspiration.

Nevertheless, Whittier's homespun and often prosaic verse has a kind of native strength about it, as is evident in his most famous poem, *Snowbound*. Though far less good a poet than, say, Bryant, his influence on the course of American poetry was probably much greater.

Modern criticism represents Longfellow as an adolescent balladist and romancer; yet his popularity in his lifetime was as great as that of Tennyson. Longfellow is the classic case of a poet who would have been better had he found it more difficult to express himself in verse. Unfortunately, his mechanical facility spoils almost all his work, and it is difficult to find more than a few poems that are readable today. *Hiawatha*, the first genuinely native epic in American poetry, is ruined for the modern reader by its unvaried and monotonous trochaic metre; attempts have been made to rehabilitate it as a poem, but it must be conceded that its importance lies in what it attempted, and the influence it exercised, rather than in what it achieved. In his ceaseless experimentation with classical measures, as in the heady hexameters of *Evangeline*, Longfellow may be said to have anticipated his descendant, Ezra Pound.

Another New England poet worth mentioning, as having preserved in some of his work the distinctive idiom of New England speech, is Oliver Wendell Holmes. But until the birth of Edgar Allan Poe in 1809, the same year as Tennyson, no poet appeared who is of much consequence outside America.

Poe was a precocious and imaginative youth whose first poems appeared when he was eighteen. Some of his work achieved popularity during his short life, and after his death in 1849 his reputation for romantic decadence increased, especially in France. This reputation, however, rested more upon his prose tales and upon the example of his unhappy and drunken life, than upon his poems. He played no small part in the formation of the mind and character of the French poet Baudelaire, another and more gifted romantic decadent, and because of this Poe may be said to have exercised a far-reaching influence on both English and American poetry – for T. S. Eliot and Ezra Pound, to name only two, were strongly influenced, in their turn, by Baudelaire and the French symbolists. However, not too much should be made of this: the sort of French decadence that interested Pound and Eliot and their contemporaries was indigenous, and it was something of a coincidence that the neurotic American, Poe, happened to provide them with a model. Poe's poetry as a whole is a mixture of the tawdry and the inspired, and was ruined both by the increasing toll taken on him by his dissipation and by his obsession with the idea of poetry as a kind of magical incantation. He left a small body of lyrics such as *The City in the Sea* and *To Helen*, of genuine imaginative power; but too often his work is vulgarized by tinkling rhymes and jingling rhythms.

WALT WHITMAN (1819–1892) was, by contrast, deliberately and stridently American, seeking to express in his sprawling and voluminous poems the heart and soul of the nation. He identified himself with the cause of an independent American culture, and with the Union as personified by his hero, Lincoln. It is very easy to be exasperated by the noisy egotism of Whitman's free verse, and by its aggressive flouting of literary decorum.

> I celebrate myself, and sing myself
> And what I assume you shall assume,
> For every atom belonging to me as good belongs to you.
>
> I loafe and invite my soul,
> I lean and loafe at my ease observing a spear of summer grass.
> *(Song of Myself)*

But there is another Whitman – a keen observer of nature and a warmly sympathetic lover of humanity. At his best, as in *Memories of President Lincoln* and some of the less pretentious lyrical pieces, as well as the sketches of the Civil War, he is very good indeed. *Leaves of Grass* (the title under which he published all the successive editions of his poems, beginning with that of 1855) fully repays exploration.

Whitman represents the authentic and unbridled American spirit, although it took his compatriots a long time to realise this. Far more than Whittier or Emerson he exemplified and put into practice what Emerson had asked for when he wrote: 'We have listened too long to the courtly Muses of Europe. We will walk on our own feet; we will work with our own hands; we will speak with our own minds'. Few poets, perhaps, could be as bad as Whitman at his worst—and this was simply because he characteristically rejected outright the bonds of rhyme and regular rhythm; but few American poets, it must be admitted, have been as good at their best. This is the poet who asked the Muse

> to cross out please those immensely overpaid accounts,
> That matter of Troy and Achilles' wrath, and Aeneas',
> Odysseus' wanderings . . .

And who could achieve such profundity and wit as:

> I project my hat, sit shame-faced, and beg.
> Enough! Enough! Enough!
> Somehow I have been stunn'd. Stand back!
> Give me a little time beyond my cuff'd head,
> slumbers, dreams, gaping,
> I discover myself on the verge of a usual mistake.

Whitman has been underrated in England and admired for the wrong reasons by some Americans. His influence on English poets has perhaps been unfortunate, and it may have led critics to suppose that formlessness, for its own sake, is a feature of Whitman rather than of the poet who has been imitating him – very often because he himself has a weak ear, and has been fondly taking comfort from his American model. In America, too, some younger poets have tried to make Whitman's work into a reason for literary nonconformity. In fact, Whitman's so-called formlessness was as essential to his achievement as was Hopkins's sprung rhythm to his.

Another nineteenth century American poet who should be

mentioned is HERMANN MELVILLE (1819–1891). Most famous, of course, for *Moby Dick* and the other novels, Melville's poetry has been consistently underrated, especially in England. He was, in fact, probably the most original nineteenth century poet after Whitman and Emily Dickinson, and his work is well worth studying. Perhaps he reached his peak in *Billy in the Darbies*, which appears as the epilogue to his short novel, *Billy Budd*; Billy speaks on the eve of the day when he will be

> Pendant pearl from the yard-arm-end
> Like the ear-drop I gave to Bristol Molly —
> Oh, 'tis me, not the sentence, they'll suspend.

The poem ends:

> I remember Taff the Welshman when he sank.
> And his cheek it was like the budding pink.
> But me, they'll lash me in hammock, drop me deep.
> Fathoms down, fathoms, down, how I'll dream fast
> asleep.
> I feel it stealing now. Sentry, are you there?
> Just ease these darbies at my wrist,
> And roll me over fair.
> I am sleepy, and the oozy weeds about me twist.

EMILY DICKINSON (1830–1886), the daughter of a lawyer in the little town of Amherst, Massachusetts, was the most remarkable of all American poets. Her loneliness and seclusion yielded her an inner emotional life of depth and significance. She wrote hundreds of brief poems entirely unlike anything else in English. The briefest of these, and even single lines, may have the cryptic quality of a spell or a proverb.

> Presentiment is that long shadow on the lawn
> Indicative that suns go down;

or

> There came a wind like a bugle

or

> This quiet dust is gentlemen and ladies

illustrate this gnomic power. At their best, her poems

touch the heights in their expression of pity, awe or wonder.

> Safe in their alabaster chambers,
> Untouched by morning and untouched by noon,
> Sleep the meek members of the resurrection,
> Rafter of satin, and roof of stone.
>
> Light laughs the breeze in her castle above them;
> Babbles the bee in a stolid ear;
> Pipe the sweet birds in ignorant cadence —
> Ah, what sagacity perished here!

Writing like this was so original, so alien to the prevailing spirit of the nineteenth century, that Emily Dickinson's work was virtually unknown during her lifetime; although her reputation has grown steadily during the present century, its full scope is not yet generally recognised.

CHAPTER THIRTEEN

The Later Nineteenth Century

THE lesser poets of the Victorian age have fallen into a disfavour from which they show little sign of recovering. Search where we will in their pages, we find much that is poetic and little that is poetry. In the sonnets, for instance, and the imitation ballads of Dante Gabriel Rossetti we find a chastely sensuous poetic diction, a smooth and lulling rhythm, but little real passion, and little awareness of the world as it is. Indeed Rossetti strove to forget that world and to re-create in the midst of Victorian ugliness an idealised world of medieval Italian art and literature. He was essentially a painter rather than a poet; as the leading figure in the Pre-Raphaelite Brotherhood, he strove to turn men's minds away from the problems of the day, religious, metaphysical and social. The message he embodied in his art was that art has no message. His example and ideas had a considerable influence towards the close of the century.

Christina Rossetti, two years younger than Dante Gabriel, was a better poet than her brother. If there is ever a wholehearted revival of Victorian poetry, her genuine lyric gift and her delicate workmanship will once more receive their due. She was twice engaged to be married, but both times she drew back on account of her scruples as a devout member of the Anglican Church. She was fully alive to the beauty of the natural world and the joys of domestic love, and her religion did not offer a wholly satisfying compensation. In her lyrics, with their clear-cut imagery, their light and buoyant rhythm, their pathos and sincerity, she found her truest form of self-expression. *Goblin Market* (1862) is a long and very strange narrative poem concerned allegorically with her relations with her elder sister. Its rich, sensuous imagery reveals the influence of Keats, and the poem has a magical quality and an intensity of feeling which is at times almost morbid. The volume in which it appears also contains some of her best lyrics, such as *Winter Rain* and *A Birthday*. Most of her other poems, devotional as well as secular, are contained in *The Prince's Progress* (1866). The most characteristic note in her poetry is one of a simple and pathetic stoicism – the note of one with a clear vision of happiness who accepts a life of self-denial. It is to be heard in the well-known *Uphill*, *When I am dead, my dearest* and the bride-song from *The Prince's Progress*.

> Too late for love, too late for joy,
>   Too late, too late!
> You loitered on the road too long,
>   You trifled at the gate:
> The enchanted dove upon her branch
>   Died without a mate;
> The enchanted princess in her tower
>   Slept, died, behind the grate;
> Her heart was starving all this while
>   You made it wait.

Another poet who was profoundly influenced by the ideas of the Pre-Raphaelites was William Morris. His copious and once popular poetry was only one of his multifarious activities. Towards the end of his life he became actively interested in Socialism, which he saw as a means to a new society living in brotherhood amidst beautiful surroundings. He reacted strongly against the ugliness of industrialism and mass-production, believing that happiness is derived from the creative satisfactions of individual craftsmanship. He lived according to his beliefs, and his work as a printer and designer came to have a revolutionary influence on the domestic arts and crafts.

Morris' poetry was partly lyrical but to a much greater extent narrative. In his *Defence of Guenevere* (1858) he attempted a more realistic view of the Arthurian heroes than had Tennyson. In *The Life and Death of Jason* (1867) he offered a new interpretation of the Greek myth. This was followed during the next three years by his most ambitious work, *The Earthly Paradise*, a collection of legends re-told from Greek and medieval sources and designed to be a kind of nineteenth-century *Canterbury Tales*. *Sigurd the Volsung* (1876) is an impressive epic narrative based on the Icelandic sagas, and written in a homespun Saxon diction and a home-made, freely moving six-foot measure which aimed at naturalising the Greek hexameter.

There is about all Morris' poetry the air of a pastiche; his mock-classicism and mock-medievalism are the result of an earnest and sincere exploration into the life and thought of other times. He always wrote with taste and craftsmanship; he never shocks, but often bores. A happy and practical man, he lived without inner conflict or tension, and his passionless verse has a dream-like quality which was perhaps its chief appeal, and of which he was well aware.

> Of Heaven or Hell I have no power to sing,
> I cannot ease the burden of your fears,
> Or make quick-coming death a little thing,
> Or bring again the pleasure of past years,
> Nor for my words shall ye forget your tears,
> Or hope again for aught that I can say,
> The idle singer of an empty day . . .
>
> Dreamer of dreams, born out of my due time,
> Why should I strive to set the crooked straight?
> Let it suffice me that my murmuring rhyme
> Beats with light wing against the ivory gate,
> Telling a tale not too importunate
> To those who in the sleepy region stay,
> Lulled by the singer of an empty day.

So he wrote in the Prologue to *The Earthly Paradise*, as if conscious that his poetry was essentially that of an interior decorator. His conviction of the dignity of personal labour was commendable; but like the other poets of his time, greater and less, he was defeated by the grave problems of his day. As a poet his prescription was a return to some legendary golden age of gods and heroes. To project such a vision in the midst of nineteenth-century commercial barbarism, idle and fruitless though it might seem, was perhaps the most that could be expected of poetry.

Another poet whose reputation can only be appreciated in the context of his period is Algernon Charles Swinburne, whose drama in the Greek manner, *Atalanta in Calydon* (1865), earned him immediate fame. Educated at Eton and Balliol College, Oxford, he had absorbed the spirit of Greece and Rome; and as a young poet of promise, whose work was done in protest against nineteenth-century ugliness and conventionality, he became a friend of Rossetti and his circle. In 1866 his *Poems and Ballads* (First Series) struck the reading public with a shock of horror and fascination, and its first publisher was forced to withdraw it on account of the outcry it caused. These poems, like which nothing had ever before appeared, produced an effect comparable with that of the poems of Byron fifty years earlier. The shock to Victorian susceptibilities was twofold: not only did Swinburne glorify an unashamed pagan sensuality, his outlook was also professedly anti-Christian.

> Wilt thou yet take all, Galilean? But these thou shalt not take,
>   The laurel, the palms and the paean, the breasts of the nymphs in
>   the brake;
> Breasts more soft than a dove's, that tremble with tenderer breath;
> And all the wings of the Loves, and all the joy before death;
> All the feet of the hours that sound as a single lyre,
> Dropped and deep in the flowers, with strings that flicker like fire.
>   (*Hymn to Proserpine*)

When Swinburne was not writing in this vein, however, the public could admire in him the possession of a spontaneous impulse unknown since the death of Shelley. But there is little else in common between the two. Beneath Shelley's lyricism, however vague and ethereal, we are always aware of the existence of a subtle and speculative intelligence. The nebulous garrulity of Swinburne's almost interminable lyrics seems to reveal nothing but a craving for mere sensation, a suppressed relish for violence and cruelty, and a sense of intoxication with the purely musical qualities of language. It is this intoxication above all which his poems convey.

Songs Before Sunrise (1871) expresses Swinburne's hopes for the liberation of Italy; *Poems and Ballads* (Second Series, 1878) shows the poet in a mood of greater restraint; *Tristram of Lyonesse* (1882) is an attempt to recreate the Arthurian legend, and is considered by some to be his masterpiece. Yet for history Swinburne remains the rapturous young iconoclast who shocked the bourgeoisie with the first of the *Poems and Ballads*. In his later life the iconoclast yielded to the conservative, and was saved from the worst effects of alcoholism by the generous care of his friend and admirer, Watts-Dunton. It should also be recalled that Swinburne was an able and perceptive critic, not only of contemporary verse but also of the Elizabethan drama, a region of poetry less fully explored in Swinburne's time than now.

In Swinburne we have Romanticism gone to seed: instead of sincerely felt emotion, there is a whipping-up of spurious passion;

instead of a picturesque but concrete diction enriched by objective personal observation, there is a sort of frothy exuberance of words and rhythm for their own sake, the language encrusted with archaism and alliteration, the rhythm breathless and unremitting.

> In a coign of the cliff between lowland and highland,
>   At the sea-down's edge between windward and lee,
> Walled round with rocks as an inland island,
>   The ghost of a garden fronts the sea.
> A girdle of brushwood and thorn encloses
>   The steep square slope of the blossomless bed
> Where the weeds that grew green from the graves of its roses
>   Now lie dead.
>
> The fields fall southward, abrupt and broken,
>   To the low last edge of the long lone land . . .

– and so on for another nine stanzas. Yet it is impossible to deny that it has a certain immediate, though superficial, appeal. Whenever an interest is shown in the rhetorical resources of the English language, as nearly as possible emptied of all intellectual substance, there may be a revival of Swinburne's popularity.

One of the effects of Swinburne's poetry was to outmode a book which had enjoyed a very wide popularity, *The Angel in the House* (1854) by Coventry Patmore. This was a long series of poems designed to celebrate Christian marriage and domestic love, themes which seemed somewhat tepid after the appearance of *Poems and Ballads*, which had been greeted with an invitation by *Punch* to the author to 'change his name to what is evidently its true form – SWINE-BORN'. It was not until 1877 that Patmore's later book appeared – *The Unknown Eros*, in which he investigates a religious and mystical view of sex. After the death of his first wife, Patmore had been converted to Roman Catholicism, and was later married for a second and a third time. The more pretentious and elaborate of his odes and lyrics have properly been forgotten, but he has a vein of vivid naturalism, combined with simple feeling, which is worth re-discovering.

A more exciting poet is George Meredith, whose *Modern Love* (1862), because of its unorthodox and realistic view of sex, attracted a good deal of comment, much of it unfavourable. *The Spectator*, for instance, wrote: '*Modern Lust* would certainly be

a more accurate title. Mr Meredith evidently thinks mud
picturesque as, indeed, it may be, but all picturesqueness is not
poetry.' Meredith had considerable descriptive power, and the
rhetorical sweep of his verse carries the thought along with an
ease and lightness of touch which almost conceal its occasional
obscurity. His long rhapsodic *Love in the Valley* is notable for fresh
and ardent spontaneity. Even here, however, we are aware of
the psychological interest which turned Meredith away from
poetry towards the novel.

> Heartless she is as the shadow in the meadows
>   Flying to the hills on a blue and breezy noon.
> No, she is athirst and drinking up her wonder:
>   Earth to her is young as the slip of the new moon.
> Deals she an unkindness, 'tis but her rapid measure,
>   Even as in a dance; and her smile can heal no less:
> Like the swinging May-cloud that pelts the flowers with hailstones
>   Of a sunny border, she was made to bruise and bless.

The reputations of all the principal Victorian poets were
established before 1875. The last quarter of the century must be
regarded as a period of decline. True, Tennyson and Browning
continued to write with almost unabated fertility, but their
immense public got little that was new from them. With two
or three important exceptions, who are reserved to the next
chapter, the poets who established their reputations after the
heyday of the Pre-Raphaelite movement cannot be considered,
in historical retrospect, to have added much to the permanent
heritage of poetry. The creative impetus of Romanticism had
run down: the energy of the early and mid-Victorians seemed
to have exhausted the possibilities of poetry in the established
tradition. Talent replaced genius, and metrical experiments
replaced originality.

A significant fact about the period is illustrated by the career
of Meredith, who began as a minor poet and ended as a novelist
of stature. Much of the poetry of the later nineteenth century was
written by men who were equally, if not more, concerned with
prose – literary essays or novels. It would perhaps be an
exaggeration to say that during this century the novel ousted
poetry as the main medium of creative literary expression; but it
appeared as if, by the end of the century, something like this had

occurred. Verse was no longer considered the most appropriate medium for narrative. There are of course later exceptions to this general truth; at the same time, it is broadly true to say that, by the beginning of the present century, fiction had taken, or begun to take, the place of poetry in the esteem and attention of the reading public. Poetry gradually assumed the rôle of a minority interest.

Robert Bridges, however, had no concern with fiction; and apart from some critical prose, and some verse dramas, his whole effort was occupied with lyrical and reflective poetry. He had affinities with the Tudor lyrists, but his carefully controlled feelings seldom betrayed any passion. He was a scrupulous, not to say finicky, metrist, and a love poet of sober playfulness. His carefully modulated verbal melody won him many admirers, and in 1913, at the age of seventy-two, he succeeded the altogether undistinguished Alfred Austin as Laureate. One fact about his writing is symptomatic of his period – the poems which earned him his fame are short. The vogue for the short poem, as distinct from the long narrative or reflective disquisition, has lasted until our own day. True, in 1929 Bridges achieved a philosophical poem of inordinate length called *The Testament of Beauty*, and such was the prestige of the octogenarian prosodist that fourteen editions were sold in the first year. Nobody knows how many copies were read through to the end. A better claim on the attention of posterity derives from Bridges' edition of the poems of his long dead friend and correspondent, Gerard Manley Hopkins, of whom more will be said shortly.

Attempts have been made, and will be made again, to rescue from oblivion the poems of W. E. Henley and his friend R. L. Stevenson, whose principal work was in prose; of Francis Thompson, whose hysterico-mystical *The Hound of Heaven* achieved an exaggerated success on account of its religious subject and the miserable life of its author; of Sir William Watson, of Lionel Johnson, of Ernest Dowson, and even of Austin Dobson – the titles of whose successive volumes of elegant trivialities are enough to show how far poetry had sunk in the last generation of the Victorian age: *Vignettes in Rhyme, Proverbs in Porcelain, Old World Idylls*. A highly serious and partially successful attempt has been made to revive the once popular *Barrack-Room Ballads* (1892) of the novelist Rudyard Kipling. In contrast

to most of the poetry of the nineties, which was either
linguistically flaccid or consciously decadent, these poems are
vigorous, noisy, and consciously robust. They scarcely need
commendation, for to those who can enjoy strongly extrovert
poetry with no subtlety of thought or delicacy of rhythm, their
appeal is obvious and immediate. Other one-time popular poets
who exploited the themes of imperialism and British superiority
were Sir Francis Doyle:

> Let dusky Indians whine and kneel:
> An English lad must die –

and Sir Henry Newbolt:

> For we're all in love with fighting on the fighting Temeraire.

More attractive than most of the minor poetry of the nineteenth century are the verse-parodies contained in Lewis
Carroll's two *Alice* books; and even more acceptable to present
taste are the brilliantly imaginative 'nonsense' poems of Edward
Lear, an 'eccentric' of fastidious technique and strikingly
original vision.

It is easier to recognise than to account for the general poetic
decline of the nineteenth century. One may say that conditions
were unpropitious to the health and vigour of poetry just as
during the late sixteenth century they were propitious. But to
describe the Elizabethan climate as favourable to the production of good poetry is not to account for the existence of such
poetry. Poets are born, not made. It is possible, however, to go a
little further and to say that the health of Elizabethan and the
debility of Victorian poetry have one thing in common: the
attitude of the poets to language. The attitude of the Elizabethans
was experimental, active and conscious; the attitude of the
Victorians was one of acquiescence in an accepted body of
Romantic diction; it was passive and traditionalist. It is true
that some poets explored the possibilities of rural dialect; others
experimented in odd or exotic metres, especially those of the
Greek and Latin poets. But these remained experiments and
hardly affected the general character of English poetry. Tennyson was always attempting metrical innovations, but so far as
the main body of his work is concerned, they taught him nothing.
The diction and imagery of the Victorians remained obstinately
conventional

conventional; their rhythms – which should be a poet's personal handwriting – were accommodated to a general norm of unexciting regularity. On the whole the poets leaned towards either the mellifluous smoothness of Tennyson or the self-consciously roughened raciness of Browning. In either case their language had become divorced from the rhythm and the vocabulary of common speech.

One of the versifiers of the period, T. E. Brown, has gained immortality through a single line – 'A garden is a lovesome thing, God wot!' But he was not the only one to use the expression, 'God wot' – Patmore for one used it. Nor was Brown alone in using words like 'lovesome'. The diction of the Victorians abounds in archaisms like 'Yea', 'perchance', 'lo!', 'yon', ' 'tis', and the ubiquitous 'thee and thou' and all the 'hasts' and '-ests' these necessitate. No doubt this was a legacy from the Romantics, but by the middle of the nineteenth century there was no justification for it. It simply served to elevate poetry artificially to a region entirely detached from common life. It is true that Victorian poetry is full of attempts to grapple with the social problems of the time – religion, science, poverty, the relations between the sexes. But its language turned these realities into unreality. Browning had fewer of the current archaisms than Tennyson, but he introduced oddities and quirks of his own, whose effect was very similar. In reality, the poets of the time were very timid experimenters, more interested in social than in poetic problems, more concerned to be regarded as thinkers than as poets. What was needed to rescue poetry from the debility and acquiescence into which it had fallen was a revolutionary impulse comparable with that of Euphuism three centuries earlier. This impulse appeared in the work of one man, destined to remain unknown until well on in the present century.

Like Emily Dickinson, his contemporary in America, GERARD MANLEY HOPKINS (1844–1889) was a born poet of almost unprecedented originality. Like Emily Dickinson, he was a most improbable revolutionary. Originality in poetry consists in taking the right and obvious course under the appearance of extreme eccentricity; in knowing instinctively, when no one else knows, the only way to write. It requires artistic courage and singleness of mind, a certain gift of good fortune from the Muse, and an inner conviction of rightness which does not require to assure itself of the endorsement of posterity. It is to be the only marcher in step, while all the rest are out of step.

Hopkins was born in Essex and educated at Highgate School. He went to Balliol College, Oxford, where he became a Greek scholar of great promise. A young man of sensitive and artistic temperament, he came under the spell of his tutor, Walter Pater, whose æsthetic doctrines were beginning to affect the work of writers and artists. His early poems show the influence of Keats and of the Pre-Raphaelites. But the influence of the Oxford Movement in religion proved far stronger. While still an undergraduate, Hopkins was converted to Roman Catholicism, and went to teach under Newman at Birmingham. In 1868 he joined the Jesuit order and began a long period of intense intellectual and spiritual discipline in preparation for the priesthood. He destroyed his poems (some of which, however, survive in copies) and gave up all thought of writing more. In taking the Jesuit vows of poverty, chastity and obedience, he surrendered himself, body and mind, to the control of his superiors. In 1877 he was ordained. He spent the remaining twelve years of his life, first as a parish priest in some of the more depressing parts of London, Liverpool and Glasgow, and then as Professor of Greek at Dublin University. Worn out in health and spirits, he died in Dublin of enteric fever in 1889.

The self-suppression of the 'natural man', in Coleridge's phrase, almost, but not quite, involved the suppression of the poet in Hopkins. During his seven years' silence between 1868 and 1875, however, his mind had turned to certain problems connected with the poet's vocation. The period was one of the most barren in the century, and Hopkins's silence coincided with the exhaustion of the Romantic tradition. In 1875, with the encouragement and consent of his superiors, he broke silence with *The Wreck of the Deutschland*, a long narrative and devotional poem occasioned by the drowning of five nuns in a disaster in the mouth of the Thames. The poem represents a complete break with tradition and a new start in diction and prosody. To other readers, if it had had any, it would have appeared as odd as it did to the editor of the Jesuit journal who turned it down. It was written in what Hopkins called 'sprung rhythm', a kind of disciplined free verse, in which the line is based, not on a predetermined metrical foot, but on an irregular arrangement of stressed and unstressed syllables. 'It is the most natural of things,' he wrote. 'It is the rhythm of common speech, of written prose, when rhythm is perceived in them.'

> On Saturday sailed from Bremen,
>   American-outward-bound,
> Take settler and seamen, tell men with women,
>   Two hundred souls in the round –
> O Father, not under thy feathers nor ever as guessing
> The goal was a shoal, of a fourth the doom to be drowned;
>   Yet did the dark side of the bay of thy blessing
> Not vault them, the millions of rounds of thy mercy not reeve even
>   them in?

> Into the snows she sweeps,
>   Hurling the haven behind,
> The Deutschland, on Sunday; and so the sky keeps,
>   For the infinite air is unkind,
> And the sea flint-flake, black-backed in the regular blow,
> Sitting Eastnortheast, in cursed quarter, the wind;
>   Wiry and white-fiery and whirlwind-swivellèd snow
> Spins to the widow-making unchilding unfathering deeps.

Not only is the rhythm something entirely new; the language is highly original, and involves a rejection of accepted poetic diction. Nevertheless, the *Deutschland* remains even now a strange poem; Hopkins is not yet at home in the new medium. About his next attempts there lingers something exploratory, something of the Euphuistic strain. In 1877 he wrote a group of sonnets expressing joy in the beauty of creation, which may be taken as songs of praise to the Creator or as the expression of a rapturous admiration of nature. These include *God's Grandeur*, *The Starlight Night*, *Hurrahing in Harvest*, and the magnificent *Windhover*. In these sonnets we can still feel the surprise, almost the shock of actual observation in all its naked immediacy. This is partly because of their rhythmic subtlety and variety, partly because every phrase has the crisp freshness of a new-minted coin.

It seems to me [Hopkins wrote to Bridges in 1879] that the poetical language of an age should be the current language heightened, to any degree heightened and unlike itself, but not (I mean normally: passing freaks and graces are another thing) an obsolete one. This is Shakespeare's and Milton's practice and the want of it will be fatal to Tennyson's Idylls and plays, to Swinburne, and perhaps to Morris.

Here Hopkins puts his finger on the very centre of the matter. He was right, though neither Bridges nor anyone else would have agreed with him at the time. During that year and the following he wrote a series of poems about man rather than nature – *The Bugler's First Communion*, *Felix Randal* and others – which show his deepening compassion for the frailness of mortality. His diction develops further in the direction of plain and homely speech.

Felix Randal the farrier, O he is dead, then? my duty all ended,
Who would have watched his mould of man, big-boned and hardy-
       handsome
Pining, pining, till time when reason rambled in it and some
Fatal four disorders, fleshed there, all contended?

Sickness broke him. Impatient he cursed at first, but mended
Being anointed and all; though a heavenlier heart began some
Months earlier, since I had our sweet reprieve and ransom
Tendered to him. Ah well, God rest him all road ever he offended!

Hopkins attempted many things in verse which he left un-finished. Whenever he wrote, he was conscious of taking time off from more serious matters. During the early years in Dublin he underwent a prolonged spiritual and nervous crisis, amounting almost to a complete mental breakdown. But later he was able to express his sense of frustration, of failure, of desertion by the God for whom he had sacrificed everything, in a series of sonnets of extraordinary power and compression.

Thou art indeed just, Lord, if I contend
With thee; but, sir, so what I plead is just.
Why do sinners' ways prosper? and why must
Disappointment all I endeavour end?
   Wert thou my enemy, O thou my friend,
How wouldst thou worse, I wonder, than thou dost
Defeat, thwart me? Oh, the sots and thralls of lust
Do in spare hours more thrive than I that spend,
Sir, life upon thy cause. See, banks and brakes
Now, leavèd how thick! lacèd they are again
With fretty chervil, look, and fresh wind shakes
Them; birds build – but not I build; no, but strain,
Time's eunuch, and not breed one work that wakes.
Mine, O thou lord of life, send my roots rain.

So Hopkins wrote in the last year of his life. It is impossible to know if he had any consolation from his achievement as a poet, which was not fully recognised until nearly half a century later.

His influence on the poets of today has been by some exaggerated, by some underestimated. We may discount his direct imitators – those who copy him in form and not in spirit; but we have to recognise that his precision, his use of word-play and puns, his word-combinations, the accuracy of his vision, the compression of his thought, his constant preoccupation with the problem of matching the word to the mood or the object – in all these he appears to be a poet born fifty years before his time. Influence apart, however, his work is to be read for its own sake. The question of the effect of the Jesuit life on the poetry is a hypothetical one: life and work are one. Those who affirm that all was harmony in the inner life of Gerard Hopkins, poet and priest, ignore the evidence of the poems and letters. On the other hand, out of the division came the poetry; out of the assertion or re-assertion of the natural man, destroyed by self-surrender, came the most poignant, original and deeply-felt poetry since the death of Shelley.

CHAPTER FOURTEEN

The Twentieth Century

As we enter our own century, it becomes increasingly difficult to achieve even the degree of objectivity maintained so far in these pages. I shall not attempt to carry the story much beyond the outbreak of the second world war, and it might be supposed that the historical outlines of English poetry up to that time were by now fairly clear. But it is not so. In reading the other day a critical history of English poetry published no longer than fifteen years ago, in which the judgements of poets up to 1900 were balanced and reasonable, I was struck by what seemed to me the author's aberrations and misvaluations when writing of our own century. The fact is that when it comes to discussing recent or contemporary writing, personal factors and the influence of fashion come into operation, and even the events of our time, like our judgement of those events, reveal a continually changing perspective. It is here that we have to own that, thinking historically, the future affects our view of the present. In writing of the Romantics, for example, we unconsciously judge them by our knowledge of all that has happened since. Our own time, however – the actual present – is unique because of our ignorance of the future. One might hope to be able simply to chronicle the literary events of the last half-century without reference to any judgements of value. Logically this would result in a mere list of publications, which alone, apart from being meaningless, would occupy several chapters. To give even an objective chronicle meaning, it is necessary to evaluate and select; yet because of the relativity of history in our own time, such evaluation will be general and can only be provisional. An added difficulty lies in the nature of the period, which has been one of war and turmoil, of rapid social and technological change, of anarchy and eclecticism in the arts.

Two further factors have affected literary judgement during this period: first, the prevalence of anthologies; secondly, the specialisation of criticism. The growth of anthologies after the first decade of the century, while it helped to ensure a wide public for poetry, tended to undermine private judgement and impose a sort of orthodoxy of taste. Anthologies tend to in-breed, and once a poet had acquired an anthology reputation, or no reputation, time was apt to confirm the *status quo*. Partly in reaction against the anthology habit, a caste of professional critics appeared, centred in the universities of England and America and basing their doctrine on the critical utterances of the poets. Thus poetry during the past thirty years has been produced under the arc-lamps of organised professional criticism. It remains to be seen whether it will survive at all in this atmosphere except as an esoteric game for specialists.

Most historians would agree in pointing to a profound change in the climate of literature during the decade immediately following the end of the first world war. We may date this change with precision, if we wish to, by the publication of T. S. Eliot's *The Waste Land* in 1922. This date has been compared in importance with that of *Lyrical Ballads*, 1798. It is true that, after 1922, poetry – that which appears most contemporary in spirit – has a different look from that which preceded it. Pre-1922 poetry continued to be written, but it no longer appeared contemporary. It is true also that the roots of post-1922 poetry are to be found in a much earlier period. But such is the shifting character of historical reality that poems which looked important in the 1930's owing to their contemporaneity already look less important in 1960. What appeared outmoded in the 1920's we may call, for the sake of convenience, Georgianism; what was new we may call Modernism. Adherents of Modernism would once have banished from serious discussion all poets who could be called Georgian, whereas unregenerate Georgians of 1930 would have regarded all Modernism as a temporary aberration, a mere craze or affectation. Both were wrong. Poetry is written by individuals, not movements; and the quality of a poet's work depends, not on conformity to an accepted idiom, but on the authenticity and significance of his experience and his power to give it original and durable expression. These are the factors it is most difficult to assess during or immediately after a poet's life.

Of the three poets who had established reputations before the death of Queen Victoria but who belong rather to the twentieth than to the nineteenth century, only A. E. Housman can be regarded as strictly an ancestor of the Georgians. Of the other two, Yeats has been adopted by the Modernists, while Thomas Hardy spans the present century, aloof from either camp. Yeats and Hardy, however, are regarded as individuals; only in thought, and not at all in technique, are Yeats' poems Modernist – and then only the later poems.

WILLIAM BUTLER YEATS (1865–1939) began as a leader in the Irish national revival of the 1880's, which derived subject-matter from Celtic legend, and a poetic style from the Pre-Raphaelites. Some of Yeats' early poems in this manner now appear precious and somewhat anaemic; others, such as *Down by the Salley Gardens*, have become a part of the lyrical tradition of English poetry. In his middle period, that of *Responsibilities* (1914) and *The Wild Swans at Coole* (1917) he adopted a plainer, more homespun style, and themes of more immediate contemporary interest.

But it was the work of his last period which earned him his posthumous reputation as one of the greatest of modern poets. This later poetry resolves the conflict between the romantic, pseudo-philosophical and mystical side of Yeats' character, and the ambitious politician: the feudal realist. As a young man he had become a disciple of Madame Blavatsky, even after she had been exposed as a fraud, and later he had joined an esoteric order called the Hermetic Students of the Golden Dawn. This almost childish credulity remained with Yeats all his life, and there is no doubt that his own ideas about what even his most widely celebrated later poems mean are startlingly inadequate when measured against the profundities that have been discovered in them by critics. Neither his so-called mysticism nor his aristocratic, counter-revolutionary politics were anything but superficial or self-deluded in themselves. Yet, as has justly been asked, does it really matter that Yeats based his poetry on mumbo jumbo and reactionary ideologies if that poetry itself means something quite different? As we shall see, the same question arises with the later work of Ezra Pound, to whom Yeats, though twenty years older, frequently turned for advice. The question in the case of Yeats is all the more difficult to answer because of his superb artistry. He is certainly, for the time being, established as the greatest poet of this century, with only a few dissenting voices – and even these are unanimous in their praise of his technical achievement. In *The Tower* (1928) and *The Winding Stair* (1929) he assumes the bardic crown and an assured declamatory manner expressing pride in himself and anger at the limitations of old age.

> An aged man is but a paltry thing,
> A tattered coat upon a stick, unless
> Soul clap its hands and sing, and louder sing
> For every tatter in its mortal dress,
> Nor is there singing school but studying
> Monuments of its own magnificence;
> And therefore I have sailed the seas and come
> To the holy city of Byzantium.

So Yeats writes in *Sailing to Byzantium*, one of the doctrinal poems in which he asserts the durability of man-made art as opposed to the transience of nature. For all their oracular assurance, there is about these later poems a certain panache, a hint of posing and of deliberate mystification, which may turn discriminating readers back to the more direct, though less ambitious, poems of the middle years.

The career of THOMAS HARDY (1840–1928) took the opposite course to Meredith's, moving from prose fiction to lyrical, dramatic and narrative poetry. The change took place in the nineties, when Hardy felt that he had exhausted the possibilities of the novel. Looked at retrospectively, he can thus be seen to have been all his life a poet, whose vision was for twenty-five years expressed in fiction. We know that he began writing poetry at an early age; but because most of it was not published until the turn of the century and later, the chronology of his development is obscure. There is, however, about his finest poems a timeless quality which detaches them altogether from the influences which shaped their style.

> Hereto I come to view a voiceless ghost;
>   Whither, O whither will its whim now draw me?
> Up the cliff, down, till I'm lonely, lost,
>   And the unseen waters' ejaculations awe me.
> Where you will next be there's no knowing,
>   Facing round about me everywhere,
>   With your nut-coloured hair,
> And gray eyes, and rose-flush coming and going.

Yes: I have re-entered your olden haunts at last;
    Through the years, through the dead scenes I have tracked you;
What have you now found to say of our past –
    Scanned across the dark space wherein I have lacked you?
Summer gave us sweets, but autumn wrought division?
    Things were not lastly as firstly well
        With us twain, you tell?
But all's closed now, despite Time's derision.

                                                (*After a Journey*)

We may notice a certain linguistic archaism, a certain angularity or awkwardness of movement; we are reminded of the influence of Browning, of Meredith, of Swinburne. Yet the quietness of tone and absence of rhetoric, serving only to emphasise the intensity of the feeling, give such lines as these the very form and stamp of the man – reserved, sardonic, haunted by a profound and irreparable unhappiness. Hardy's great epic drama, *The Dynasts* (1904–1908) is an attempt to render the events of the Napoleonic wars in terms of his view of man as the puppet of huge, indifferent forces. It was not intended for the stage, but the performance of a part of it on sound radio many years after Hardy's death proved that he had considerable command of spoken English. Many of the shorter narrative and ballad poems express the spirit of irony and satire which informs his prose tales. The poems which have raised him to unchallenged eminence are the lyrics of personal emotion which increasingly occupied his attention after the period of *The Dynasts* – such things as *A Broken Appointment*, *I Look into my Glass*, *The Self-Unseeing*, and *Afterwards*.

Because of his tragic stoicism ALFRED EDWARD HOUSMAN (1859–1936) has often been compared to Hardy; and indeed, the lyrics of both men derive much of their force from an unappeasable personal sadness, which was expressed, not with passionate rhetoric, but with dignified reserve and control. Apart from some scattered pieces issued posthumously, Housman's work consists entirely of two volumes of short poems – *A Shropshire Lad* (1896) and *Last Poems* (1922). At the age of seventy-three he embodied in a single lecture his unorthodox and provocative views on *The Name and Nature of Poetry* (1932). The distinguishing marks of his poems are a concrete and economical vocabulary, a rhythm regular but without monotony, a classic brevity and incisiveness of form. These lapidary lyrics, partly because of their technical assurance and partly because of their unmistakable emotional conviction, gained wide and rapid currency; they administered a chilling but salutary shock to Browningesque cheerfulness and optimism, and the strikingly English quality of their background made a strong national appeal. After the full effect of *The Waste Land* had been felt, Housman's reputation suffered; its very qualities of lucidity, simplicity and Englishness counted against it. But Housman, though limited in theme and occasionally facile in expression, was a true poet, and one whose worth will outlast the vagaries of fashion.

Tell me not here, it needs not saying,
    What tune the enchantress plays
In aftermaths of soft September
    Or under blanching mays,
For she and I were long acquainted
    And I knew all her ways.

On russet floors, by waters idle,
    The pine lets fall its cone;
The cuckoo shouts all day at nothing
    In leafy dells alone;
And traveller's joy beguiles in autumn
    Hearts that have lost their own.

On acres of the seeded grasses
    The changing burnish heaves;
Or marshalled under moons of harvest
    Stand still all night the sheaves;
Or beeches strip in storms for winter
    And stain the wind with leaves.

Possess, as I possessed a season,
    The countries I resign,
Where over elmy plains the highway
    Would mount the hills and shine,
And full of shade the pillared forest
    Would murmur and be mine.

For nature, heartless, witless nature,
    Will neither care nor know
What stranger's feet may find the meadow
    And trespass there and go,
Nor ask amid the dews of morning
    If they are mine or no.

It is not at once apparent that so brief a lament as this may be the epitome of as much personal experience as an entirely different poem, Wordsworth's *Intimations Ode*.

In one especial sense Housman was a forerunner of the Georgian movement, which was, during the first world war and for some years after it, the leading force in English poetry. As a movement it was very loosely co-ordinated and had no formal platform or programme. Between 1912 and ·1922 Edward Marsh, a Civil Servant and a friend of many writers, edited five volumes of an anthology called *Georgian Poetry*, which acted as a centre for writers of differing talents and outlook. Partly because of this outlook and partly because of the mediocrity of much magazine and anthology verse published during the twenties, the word 'Georgian' became for a time a critical term of abuse. It became connected with whatever was facile, trivial and over-simple. Now that the word has become, so to speak, neutralised, and has taken on an objective historical significance, it is possible to see more clearly what were the real aims which brought the Georgians together, and who were the poets as distinct from the hangers-on.

Housman had localised his poems in the agricultural county of Shropshire, and like him the Georgians were, first and foremost, consciously *English*, in reaction against the Continental influences which had shaped some of the verse of the nineties. The outbreak of war in 1914 gave the movement a still stronger patriotic impulse, but it never was in any degree jingoistic. Its Englishness consisted rather in an extremely articulate consciousness of the beauty of the English landscape, its ancient villages and declining rural crafts. One of the causes of the later reaction against Georgianism was, indeed, its failure to take note of urban and industrial manifestations, except by way of protest. The Georgians were felt to have been living in an artificial rural paradise.

With certain exceptions the Georgians mostly wrote short poems, free from didactic intention, simple in theme, not strenuously passionate nor intellectually demanding. They accepted traditional lyrical forms and metres, and were conspicuously unexperimental. They appealed to, and reached, a very wide public, and during the period of their ascendancy poetry achieved a popularity it has entirely lacked since their decline. They were, in short, the last heirs of Romanticism, and lived on their inherited capital.

Among the most prominent and prolific of the Georgians was John Masefield, whose *Salt Water Ballads* (1902) celebrated the English seafaring tradition, and made a great many readers think they were more nautically minded than they were. In 1911 *The Everlasting Mercy* inaugurated a new series of realistic narrative poems whose brutality of theme and treatment aroused considerable attention. In 1919 Masefield expressed the Englishman's love of fox-hunting in his long Chaucerian narrative of *Reynard the Fox*, which attained enormous popularity. As a lyric and reflective poet he was somewhat neglected, and his wide appeal was undoubtedly due to his fellow-countrymen's love of action. In 1930 he succeeded Bridges as Poet Laureate.

Walter de la Mare also made his first appearance in 1902 with *Songs of Childhood*. This was followed by further collections of short poems of unusual imaginative quality, notably *The Listeners* (1912) and *Peacock Pie* (1913), one of the most hauntingly beautiful books of poems of its generation.

> Tom sang for joy and Ned sang for joy and old Sam sang for joy;
> All we four boys piped up loud, just like one boy;
> And the ladies that sate with the Squire, their cheeks were all wet,
> For the noise of the voice of us boys, when we sang our Quartette.
> Tom he piped low and Ned he piped low and old Sam he piped low;
> Into a sorrowful fall did our music flow;
> And the ladies that sate with the Squire vowed they'd never forget
> How the eyes of them cried for delight, when we sang our Quartette.

As a writer of poems about, and for, children, de la Mare is almost unsurpassed. In other moods he showed a marked attraction for the uncanny, and revealed a world of suggestion existing somewhere between reality and pure fantasy.

W. H. Davies spent his early years as a tramp in America and England. He remained poor all his life, and preserved a kind of primal innocence, by which his poetry survives. His abundant brief and simple lyrics were for many years his only source of income, and he had a certain knowing instinct for what the public wanted. Nevertheless, he was not as simple as his readers liked to think him, and as the anthologists liked to make him out. This misrepresentation has served his later reputation badly; a discriminating selection could show him for what he was – a genuine poet who combined tender and delicate feeling with a certain realistic humour and wiry homeliness.

James Elroy Flecker was in some ways not a typical Georgian, since he looked back to the æsthetic movement of the previous century and sought the formal perfection of the French Parnassiens. The richness of his imagery recalls Keats, and a certain rhetorical note gives his work the air of greater emotional force than that of many of his contemporaries. He was temperamentally drawn towards the Mediterranean and the East, which are the scene of his best known poems and of the verse drama, *Hassan*. Flecker died of consumption in Switzerland in 1915. It was in this year also that Rupert Brooke died, the poet whose work best illustrates the attitude of the younger men at the outbreak of the 1914 war. His sonnet, *The Soldier*, perfectly expresses the ardent and idealistic patriotism which was so soon to yield to bitterness and disillusion as the catastrophe dragged on through muddle and bloodshed almost to defeat. Siegfried Sassoon best captured the mood of bitterness in his satiric attacks on the higher command; but of all the war poets, Wilfred Owen, whose tragic death in action occurred only a week before the armistice of November 1918, conveyed most movingly the sense of war's futility and the pity aroused by devastation on a scale hitherto inconceivable.

> Move him into the sun –
> Gently its touch awoke him once,
> At home, whispering of fields unsown.
> Always it woke him, even in France,
> Until this morning and this snow.
> If anything might rouse him now
> The kind old sun will know.
> Think how it wakes the seeds, –
> Woke, once, the clays of a cold star.
> Are limbs, so dear-achieved, are sides,
> Full-nerved – still warm – too hard to stir?
> Was it for this the clay grew tall?
> – O what made fatuous sunbeams toil
> To break earth's sleep at all?

Not only does the mood of Owen represent a complete reversal of that of Brooke four years earlier, but his technique foreshadows a revolutionary change. The use of assonance or half-rhyme offered experimental possibilities to the poets of the thirties. Another poet who was killed in action was Edward Thomas, whose best work is distinguished by an acutely objective realisation of the English countryside, combined with intense introspection.

Of the poets on active service who survived the war, the best were Edmund Blunden and Robert Graves. Blunden is a scholar and a lover of the English countryside in the strict Georgian sense. He has a marked preference for the 'quiet' and more retiring of the English poets and essayists; but the war induced a temporary paralysis of sensibility, from which recovery was slow and painful.

> From the dark mood's control
> I free this man; there's light still in the West.
> The most virtuous, chaste, melodious soul
> Never was better blest.
>
> (*The Recovery*)

Blunden was always a technician of scrupulous taste and scholarship; the more emotionally exciting of his poems, however, have to be sought for amidst a large volume of descriptive and reflective work of less urgency. He has survived not only the war, but also the Georgian movement; but the label has remained, and has obscured the contemporary note in his later poetry. Graves, on the other hand, has been far more adaptable in moving with the times, and the times have moved with him. Thus while his work shows nearly half a century's continuous development, its Georgian characteristics – in particular, a tendency to trifle with slight or fanciful themes – have disappeared in favour of a style both traditional and contemporary. This has been achieved only through severe self-discipline. He has consistently pursued the ideal of goodness in poetry, rather than greatness; the rigorous repression of any tendency to self-inflation, and a corresponding respect for the subtleties of language have made him the acknowledged master of a kind of terse, economical lyric, immediately recognisable for its highly personal, yet wholly unaffected, idiom; these lyrics are either explorations of private themes or shrewd comments on whatever is odd or grotesque in the public scene.

Meanwhile, in America, poetry of vitality and significance was being written by men and women born in the seventies and eighties. Of these EDWIN ARLINGTON ROBINSON (1869–1935) was a pioneer, and was one of the first to exploit the satirical possibilities of American speech. Consistently underrated in England, Robinson was as interesting a personality as he was a poet. He determined early in life that he would live by poetry alone, but until he was in his mid-forties he achieved little reputation. He was scarcely able to keep body and soul together until the then President of the United States, Theodore Roosevelt, found him a position in the New York Custom House when he was thirty-six. He lost this job after Roosevelt left the White House, and had again to be rescued from loneliness and heavy drinking. Robinson was most popular in his lifetime for a series of Arthurian legends in blank verse; but he is now remembered for his shorter, sardonic and epigrammatic 'character poems', in which he created a gallery of eccentrics and failures whose individuality and defeat is presented in sharply satirical contrast to the crass commercial values of the society around them. These portraits were in a sense imaginative projections of Robinson himself, unhappy, lonely and defeated:

> Miniver scorned the gold he sought
>   But sore annoyed was he without it;
> Miniver thought, and thought, and thought,
>   And thought about it.

> Miniver Cheevy, born too late,
>   Scratched his head and kept on thinking;
> Miniver coughed, and called it fate,
>   And kept on drinking.

ROBERT FROST (born 1875), who like Robinson was a native of the eastern seaboard, abjured all that was regarded as 'poetic' and based his work firmly on the life and speech of the farming community of that region. To a great many readers he has become the spokesman of all that was most American, so far as rural life is concerned. In our own time, he has become something of an unofficial laureate. His salted and homely phrases, such as 'Good fences make good neighbours', have become the proverbs of modern America. Poems such as *The Death of the Hired Man*, *Mending Wall* and *Stopping By Woods on a Snowy Evening* are known to thousands of readers whose knowledge of modern poetry is otherwise scant. A less well-known but equally characteristic expression of Frost's view of life is revealed in *The Tuft of Flowers*. Here are the opening lines:

> I went to turn the grass once after
>   one
> Who mowed it in the dew before the
>   sun.
>
> The dew was gone that made his blade
>   so keen
> Before I came to view the levelled
>   scene.
>
> I looked for him behind an isle of
>   trees;
> I listened for his whetstone on the
>   breeze.
>
> But he had gone his way, the grass
>   all mown,
> And I must be, as he had been, —
>   alone.

And yet it is interesting to recall that Frost's first two books, *A Boy's Will* and *North of Boston* were published in England, where, between 1912 and 1915 he farmed in Gloucestershire. There is something sad in this, for although Frost himself has always been well represented in England, and although British poetry has on the whole fared well in America, it was not until the fifties that British publishers began to publish American poetry. In the years between 1930 and 1950 there was a serious ignorance of American poetry in England, when the work of such poets as Hart Crane, Wallace Stevens, E. E. Cummings and John Crowe Ransom was either unavailable or to be found only in unsatisfactory early selections or unadvertised pirated editions.

Vachel Lindsay exploited the Negro idiom of the Southern States and the noise and vigour of religious revivalism. By contrast, Wallace Stevens imported into American poetry the alien note of French aestheticism. Stevens was not only a delightful poet, full of curious and wise irony and a highly poetic wit that hovers somewhere between whimsicality and satire, but he was also a fine critic, who said some notable and memorable things about poetry. Like, Stevens, Marianne Moore has always been something of an exotic, standing for minority culture as against democracy. Miss Moore, whose first volume was also published in England – it was in fact 'pirated' by two of her friends – is a poet original in method rather than in content. Her poems, often governed by a syllabic pattern, rely largely on quotations and scraps of encyclopaedic information for their effect. Elegance and feminine perception, rather than warmth, are the main qualities of this modest but highly influential poet.

John Crowe Ransom, a Southerner, is a fastidious technician, drawing some of his themes from local life, and the diction and movement of his verse from a scholarly awareness of the English tradition as a whole. In *Philomela* he wonders whether his native America can ever be the home of lyric verse.

> Not to these shores she came! this other Thrace,
> Environ barbarous to the royal Attic;
> How could her delicate dirge run democratic,
> Delivered in a cloudless boundless public place
> To an inordinate race?

All these poets were strongly individualistic and did not naturally cohere in groups and movements; the one striking exception is the Imagists, whose self-consciously æsthetic aims were for a limited period followed both in America and in England. Indeed, it is probably true to say that with the appearance of Imagism the continued separation of English and American poetry became increasingly artificial. Imagism was a reaction against diffuseness, untidiness and imprecision in verse. A poem was conceived of as a brief, objective expression of the experience of a moment; the form, which was all-important, was dictated by the theme, which was usually of the slightest; rhyme and metre were dispensed with. The prophet of Imagism was the Englishman, T. E. Hulme, not himself a poet but the author of half a dozen Imagist poems. These are hard, precise and anti-romantic. The best known practitioners of Imagism were two

Americans, Hilda Doolittle, who aimed at the gem-like clarity and spareness of the Greek Anthology; and Ezra Pound, too boisterous, eclectic and egotistic a poet to remain an Imagist for long.

EZRA POUND (born 1885) had been influenced by French, Italian and Chinese poetry before he founded the Imagist Movement. His influence on the course of poetry cannot be over-estimated, although this has been due more, perhaps, to his personality and his critical writings than to his own verse. Pound's early imagistic poems were based upon a conviction that the intense economy and condensation of Chinese and Japanese poetry was the perfect antidote to the diffuseness and meaningless traditionalism of the Georgians. It is important, in considering Pound, to remember that his purpose has always been wholly didactic. He set out to influence the course of literature, and if his work is to be judged by this criterion, then he must be said to have succeeded. Yeats, as has already been mentioned, sought and gained advice from him. T. S. Eliot's *The Waste Land* was cut to half its original length at Pound's behest, and was dedicated to him as '*il miglior fabbro*' (the better craftsman). Yet, as Mr. Eliot in writing about Pound's own poetry has implied, his real importance may lie less in what he says than in the way he chooses to say it. *Hugh Selwyn Mauberley*, which Pound published in 1920, is the forerunner of much of the poetry that has been written since. Conversational, ironic and hostile to the values of 'civilisation', in this poem Pound reached the height of his achievement. His later poetry, consisting of a long series of poems, as yet unfinished, *The Cantos*, is as controversial as have been his political beliefs and actions. Being attracted by Colonel Douglas's economic ideas, which were in themselves positive and sensible enough, Pound became increasingly obsessed with anti-Semitic and pro-fascist ideologies. Mussolini, his hero, had – unfortunately for Pound, perhaps – put into practice certain economic theories of which Pound approved. When war was declared between Italy and America, Pound tried to leave Italy; but as he failed, he was persuaded to make a few wild and scarcely coherent pro-fascist speeches on Rome radio; for these, the Allied military authorities were unimaginative enough to charge him with treason. After spending thirteen years in a lunatic asylum, as unfit to plead, Pound was eventually released. He went back to Italy, which he greeted with a Fascist salute.

The Cantos, although they have been hailed by many critics as a work of the first magnitude, ranking with *Paradise Lost* and *The Divine Comedy*, reflect Pound's increasing instability, and it is doubtful whether the later poems in the series maintain the profound pattern upon which the whole project is said to be founded. There are highly poetic and tragic moments in these poems, but for many readers these appear as oases in an arid desert of hysterical abuse and private allusion. Pound is more likely to be genuinely remembered by his early graceful lyrics and by the wry ironic pieces of his *Mauberley* period.

William Carlos Williams, a doctor by profession, began by writing poems in the manner of Pound and the Imagists, but later adopted an *avant-garde* and self-consciously nationalistic style of his own, which has been quite as influential in America as that of Pound. Although he was born in 1883, those poets whose conscious aim is to create an American style still regard Williams as their mentor.

The Englishman, D. H. Lawrence, was associated at different times with both the Imagists and the Georgians. His poetry was, however, too personal and idiosyncratic to belong to any school. At its best it shows delicacy and accuracy in giving the most fleeting moods and impressions permanent form. Lawrence was one of the few poets, either American or English (Whitman, Pound, Williams and Hilda Doolittle were others) to whom free verse was the natural medium of expression. During the twenties there was a considerable vogue for free verse, which was regarded as one of the essentials of modernism. Most poets, however, who discarded rhyme and metre returned to them later in the spirit of the prodigal son. Exceptions are the American poets, E. E. Cummings, whose apparent anarchism in grammar and punctuation has long been recognised as logical and, for him, inevitable; and Laura Riding, a strangely neglected poet in whose best work intellect and imagination are fused and controlled by a fine linguistic resourcefulness and unerring rhythmic instinct.

Cummings' revolt against conventional typography does not mask an essentially lyrical and sometimes, indeed, sentimental poet. This facet of his work will survive less well, perhaps, than that of the authentically poetic comedian and satirist.

Archibald MacLeish, born in 1892, is another influential American poet. His view of literature is unashamedly political, and he may usefully be described as the liberal man of affairs turned poet. He was Librarian of Congress during the Second World War. But the subject matter of his poems has not always been political. *The Hamlet of A. MacLeish* (1928) was a long experimental poem, one of the best of those influenced by *The Waste Land*. His most important poem was *Conquistador* (1933), which dealt with Cortez in Mexico.

Not even a brief account of English poetry between the wars would be complete without mention of the American, HART CRANE (1899–1932). Crane was very much the confused child of his time, and when he could no longer come to terms with the self-destroying element in himself, he committed suicide. He led the wild life of a debauchee and a drunkard, and never seems to have been at peace with himself for more than a few hours in the whole of his short life. His best poems were written early. *The Bridge*, an epic about Brooklyn Bridge, has some superb passages but as a whole fails through over-ambitiousness and confusion of its theme; Crane tried to paper over the cracks in his grandiose scheme with a florid and impressive rhetoric, but the poem is never wholly satisfying. Many of the poems in his first book, *White Buildings*, however, display an originality and a power that put him in the first rank of the poets of his time; as in *Pastorale:*

> No more violets,
> And the year
> Broken into smoky panels.
> What woods remember now
> Her calls, her enthusiasms?
>
> That ritual of sap and leaves
> The sun drew out,
> Ends in this latter muffled
> Bronze and brass. The wind
> Takes rein.
>
> If, dusty, I bear
> An image beyond this
> Already fallen harvest,

> I can only query, "Fool —
> Have you remembered too long;
>
> Or was there too little said
> For ease or resolution —
> Summer scarcely begun
> And violets,
> A few picked, the rest dead?"

But by far the most influential voice in twentieth-century poetry was that of the New Englander, Thomas Stearns Eliot, who came to live in London and became a British citizen shortly after the war. His small volumes of 1917 and 1919, and *The Waste Land* (1922), contain some of his best work and are one of the most arrestingly original contributions ever made to English poetry. By the end of the twenties his reputation was firmly established among the most alert readers as one of the best poets of his time and as the leading critical intelligence. About 1928 his attitude solidified into a somewhat severe traditionalism in both literature and religion. His next series of poems, *Ash Wednesday* (1930) and the *Ariel* poems, record the doubts and uncertainties of the period of his conversion to institutional Christianity. The only other considerable collection of poems, *Four Quartets* (1944), is a religious and philosophical meditation of extreme complexity and obscurity. This is regarded by some readers as his crowning achievement; to others it lacks the vitality and immediacy of his earlier work. The wider and less critical public who were attracted to Eliot in the thirties welcomed in particular two aspects of his work which had scarcely revealed themselves before – the propaganda for Christian resignation, and an interest in verse drama. Eliot's achievement as a dramatist does not concern us here, but it has secured for him wide recognition at a time when interest in poetry in general has narrowed. Eliot has gained a world reputation as the leading writer of the English-speaking nations; the poems he published up to 1922 are not so well regarded as his later writings, but it may well be on these comparatively early poems that his ultimate fame is most securely based. Eliot began as an admirer and imitator of nineteenth-century French poetry – that of Gautier, Mallarmé, Laforgue, Corbière – whose irony, concrete precision of imagery, and above all, artistic detachment he rendered superbly; his highly personal English idiom reflected the tones of the later Elizabethan and Jacobean drama, with which he had an intense imaginative affinity.

> Webster was much possessed by death
> And saw the skull beneath the skin;
> And breastless creatures underground
> Leaned backward with a lipless grin.
>
> Daffodil bulbs instead of balls
> Stared from the sockets of the eyes!
> He knew that thought clings round dead limbs
> Tightening its lusts and luxuries.
>
> Donne, I suppose, was such another
> Who found no substitutes for sense;
> To seize and clutch and penetrate,
> Expert beyond experience
>
> He knew the anguish of the marrow
> The ague of the skeleton;
> No contact possible to flesh
> Allayed the fever of the bone . . .

Poems such as *Whispers of Immortality*, from which these stanzas are quoted, *Prufrock*, *Portrait of a Lady*, *Gerontion* and *The Waste Land*, express the bitterness and disillusion which reflect faithfully certain aspects of the post-war mood. They reveal a hypersensitive and unusually intelligent mind struggling with experiences of guilt, frustration and despair, in which it was deeply and personally involved. What has opened a gulf between Eliot and his first admirers is the gradual depersonalisation of his art, and the institutionalisation of his personality.

One important effect of the revolution in poetic sensibility brought about by Eliot's example was that no poetry which was not intellectually and even emotionally tough had much chance of a serious hearing in the thirties. The kind of vague dream-world which had been associated with the Georgians was no longer acceptable. Eliot's poems, especially the earlier ones, were packed with literary allusions because the very knowledge on which modern consciousness is based was felt to be part of a poet's experience of life. A man's reading, however recondite, is as much a part of him as his sense-perceptions. The thirties saw the appearance of a group of young poets, centred mainly in Oxford around the commanding personality of W. H. Auden. As a technician of extreme dexterity with an uncommon flair for creating a personal idiom from the most diverse elements in traditional and contemporary writing, Auden soon established himself as the leading poet of his generation. Like Eliot, he interested himself in verse drama; but his themes and imagery were drawn, not from institutional Christianity but from psycho-analysis and the exploration of the subconscious. At first, revolutionary politics of a rather nebulous kind played a part in Auden's poetry, and commended it to the rising social conscience of a younger generation shocked by the depression of 1929–1931, and the growth of Fascist movements on the Continent. Auden's æsthetic modernism also influenced his admirers in the direction of a self-conscious interest in the physical features of contemporary industrialism; but it was soon discovered that, while there is nothing intrinsically unpoetic about a pylon or an arterial road, there is nothing intrinsically poetic either. Moreover, a lyric in praise of a steam engine or an aeroplane, though right up-to-date when it is written, rapidly becomes as archaic as the first Victorian poems about the railways. On the whole, it seems likely that the most durable poetry of the years immediately before, during and after the second world war was being written by poets who, amid the distractions of politics, technology and the Anglo-Catholic revival, avoided every form of collectivism and did their best to keep alive their individual sensibility – the private mind and the personal vision without which both civilisation and poetry are meaningless. The Hitler war came as the most powerful and threatening shock to civilisation and the individual life which has ever been experienced. Was it the spirit of the time or the state of poetry in England which was responsible for the comparative dearth of new war poets? The period was not without its poetry, but this had little of the significance of Georgian war poetry. The latter sprang from illusion and disillusion: in the Hitler war there was neither. Its poetry, if there was any, went mainly into prose documentation.

The history of English poetry seems to have come to rest, at any rate for the time being, in a paradox: an immense amount is being written by a large number of poets all over the English-speaking world, and the criticism of poetry is a thriving academic industry – yet never does the status of poetry and the general esteem in which it is held seem to have been more in question. South Africa has produced poets who have made a significant contribution to twentieth-century poetry; Canada has established a native school of considerable vigour; and Australia has an active modern movement whose roots in the local soil are likely to grow stronger as the direct influence of the mother country becomes relatively weaker. An equally encouraging sign is the recent appearance of an indigenous poetic growth among the coloured peoples of Africa. From the point of view of poetry, to be born of English-speaking parents is of infinitely greater importance than to be born in any particular part of the world, with any particular political allegiance. It is to be as indisputably the heir to Shakespeare and Chaucer as if born in Warwickshire or London. But of all the English-speaking communities outside Great Britain only the United States can claim to be no longer a young nation; of the others, scarcely one is entirely beyond the pioneer stage. Poetry must take root, and its roots are slow-growing, even in the century of speed. Chaucer's London was already an older city than the cities of the Commonwealth today.

Some readers may complain of the sketchiness with which the first half of this century has been treated. A partiality for one or other modern poet may be responsible for such a feeling. Students of the turbulent years between the wars may find significance in the rhythmical experiments of Dame Edith Sitwell, the formal traditionalism of Edwin Muir, the Byronic declamation of the South African, Roy Campbell, and the early work of Dylan Thomas. The period was also one in which much foreign poetry, old and new, was translated; Arthur Waley's versions from the Chinese have achieved a permanent place in English poetry, and can justly claim to be regarded as original experiments in free verse. But a roll-call is useless, and a history of literary fashions has only a limited place in a history of poetry. In a record as brief as this a sense of proportion is more than ever necessary; and it is to be hoped that the half-century just ended has not been treated less fairly than any of the preceding eleven periods of equal length.

We live at a time when the *history* of poetry, if not poetry itself, has reached a resting-place. Much good, unexciting, craftsman-like writing is being done, without any compelling sense of direction or any strong impulse to experiment. It is as if all possible experiments had been tried and further attempts were pointless. The young poet of today has the whole of English poetry to learn from: there is no prevailing style, and no taboos. He has *carte blanche* as to form and subject. There is no kind of poem mentioned in these pages, however outmoded it might seem, whose revival, carried out by a writer of originality, might not start a new and fruitful fashion. But the anti-romantic revolution of the twenties is still, more or less, in possession. It has been accepted, and no attempt at a counter-revolution has had more than a temporary success.

Anything may happen – but there is no widespread expectation that anything will. There is, in fact, no widespread concern with poetry at all. Except when a poet dies in a spectacular way or happens to be a television personality, the general public is apathetic. Except among poets, amateur or professional, there is no audience for poetry. This is because it is, by its very nature, unspecialised in a world of increasing specialisation. The moment a person ceases to be a child, he becomes a specialist. Poetry, which is concerned with the basic common interests of all humanity, abhors specialism, and is consequently regarded as childish – something we have grown out of. Only the lunatic, the lover and the poet believe otherwise; so that poetry has become a language known only to these three estates. Poetry will survive, because it is in itself a basic human activity – almost as basic as speech. But whether it will ever again enjoy the prestige it had under the patronage of feudalism, the monarchy, the aristocracy, or even the middle classes – that depends . . .

Index

INDEX